Viceroys and Vicars:

British English for Students

What students need to know to understand and enjoy the confusing bits of English Literature.

Bill Harvey

Sunset Boulevard Press_____ **San Francisco**

ISBN: 979-8-9888182-0-5

Sunset Boulevard Press
775 Post #210
San Francisco, CA 94109

Available at BillHarveyBooks.com

*

INTRODUCTION:

England and America are "two nations divided by a common language."
   Oscar Wilde
   G. B Shaw
   (Take your pick –it's been attributed to both.)

     American, Australian, and Canadian students certainly speak English, but still trip over bits that are perfectly understandable to Brits, but otherwise confuse readers who have not grown up in the U.K. This is a concise British dictionary of some of those bits.

     There are some subjects that are too interesting or too complicated to nail down in a short definition. You will find longer natterings sprinkled throughout listed alphabetically and titled more or less with the words a non-Brit might use to look up a broad or nebulous subject. Some of these longer offerings include:

- Architecture
- The Clergy
- Divisions (Regions, Counties, Parishes etc.)
- Food
- Government
- Henry VIII
- Homes & houses
- Knights & the knighthood
- Military (Army, Navy, regiments, RAF)
- Marriage
- Monarchy
- Money
- Peerage
- Schools
- Servants / Domestics

Do not be frightened of the bits on English History. Some things all but require some historic perspective for the student to really get a grip on. (Some of them are so confusing that not even the Brits really understand them.) There are a few takes on the subject of history, none of which would satisfy a history teacher, but would serve as a nice scaffold or introduction to history studies over and above helping you out in your literature class.

Finally remember that "England' is only one part of the United Kingdom and to dwell just on the "English" is to give short shrift to the Scots, Welsh, and Irish. This being said. I'm still going to call them the "English" or "Brits,"and the place where they all live "England" as I see fit. Deal with it. Then read the bit about *divisions, political.*

There are mentions of movies and TV shows throughout. Watching movies for entertainment is all fine and well, but they are more interesting and enjoyable if you know at least a little of the history. Even more fun is noting the bits where the movie departs from the real history. Pointing this out to friends and family makes you seem very smart.

*Two lions (the king of the beasts) show up on Plantagenet family arms in about 1180. Richard the Lionhearted added another lion in 1198 and about 1340 it started getting complicated with the addition of the French fleurs-de-lis.** Thereafter it was off to the races. Today the royal family's crests all have another lion, a unicorn, and variously the Scottish thistle, the Irish shamrock, the crosses of three different saints, and assorted crowns, coronets, scrolls and whatnot.

**_Lilly flower_ or literally _Flower of the Lilly._ As a symbol, it goes back to before Christ, but in this context, it refers to the French Royalty and their divine right to rule as well as the Catholic Holy Trinity. You can also throw in the symbol for purity as well if you like.

The letter *a* is the third most common letter in English, after *e* & *t*. It comes to us from ancient Egypt where it got its start as an ox's head. The Phoenicians turned it sideways, and the Semites finished turning it upside-down for the Greeks and so it remains. There are a very few words in English that use the double *a* as in aardvark, but other languages are rather more keen on *a*'s -double or otherwise. Spanish, for example, uses the letter fully twice as often as does English. BTW, the two ways to write it are called *single-story* and *double-story*.

A   -the designation for a medium roadway a little smaller than highway or *motorway*. It is typically a paved two-way road but some have as many as three lanes each direction. What Yanks would think of as a freeway, the Brits call a *motorway* abbreviated with an M which are larger and more heavily traveled than an A.

abbey   -either a religious community, or after **Henry VIII** did away with the pope etc., it was a large manorial home that had once been part of an abbey, for example **Westminster Abbey.**

accent, the English   This is an utterly hopeless subject in general, made all the more so by the limitations of the written word. Here are a few thoughts that might help readers understand just a little of what English writers are trying to convey:

- Accents are only about pronunciation. The grammar and vocabulary do not change -unless the author deliberately uses misspelled words and bad grammar to tell the reader something about the speaker -probably that the character is of a lower class.
- Accents may indicate where the speaker is from, as well as his or her social status and education. America certainly has regional accents, probably as many—or even more than the English—but accent does not indicate social or educational level in America as much as it does in England.
- The English can probably tell more about a person from hearing

speak than an American can tell about another American.

Some part of British regional accents might be a consequence of three different Germanic tribes that came to Britannia about 1500 years ago. When this idea taken to America, it has been suggested that America has northern and southern accents because the north was settled by people from eastern England, -the Angles & Jutes, while the south was settled by people from the west side of England, the Saxons.

There are two broad categories of English accents, the MLE -Multicultural London English which is a mix of cockney and other ethnic accents / languages. The other is RP or *Received Pronunciation* or what is commonly called the BBC accent. There are also distinctive accents for Ireland, Scotland, and Wales and even these may be subdivided into northern, southern, eastern, western, urban, rural etc.

According to Hoyle -according to the rules of the game from the highest authority. Edmund Hoyle (1672 – 1769), was a lawyer and big fan of card games. He wrote <u>A Short Treatise on the Game of Whist</u> wherein he listed both the rules of the game along with some how-to.

Admiral In Henry's Navy and onward, an Admiral was the commander of a fleet. Today they come in four flavors; in order of authority they run: Admiral of the Fleet, Admiral, Vice Admiral, and Rear Admiral. see ***military, navy***

Admiralty -much the same as America's old Department of the Navy. It goes back to 1832 and has been under the Department of Defense since 1965.

afters -desert. see ***pudding***

air host / hostess -a flight attendant or what Yanks used to call stewards or stewardess.

alderman -either the head of a ***guild***, or someone appointed by the king for some specific purpose. Now they may be elected like American aldermen or city councilman etc. In smaller boroughs, their role is like a America mayor. see ***divisions***

ale -stronger and sweeter than ordinary beer.

A-levels -voluntary Advanced Level Exams. Much like America's SAT or ACT exams used for college admission, but unlike the general American exams, the A-levels are subject specific, so a student would usually take two or three and the over-achiever might take any number of exams at various levels at various times in his or her school career. Students who have no plans to go on to college also take these tests to include their scores in their resumes. Students are required to stay in school only till age 16.

Alfred the Great (849 – 899) The Saxon king crowned in 871. Alfred beat the Vikings, at least temporarily, and was thought of as an educated and merciful king. He improved the legal system, military, and quality of life for the people. see **monarchy**

alley -a narrow garden path. What Americans think of as an *alley* behind the house, the Brits call a **mews**.

All Saints Day -November 1. This is a somber religious thing to contemplate both the saints and martyrs. The previous day, October 31, is Halloween or *All Hallows Eve* and this is party time. The Brits go in for costumes and parties, but with pagan roots going much back farther even than Christianity. Dead people came back to life on this night so you had to dress up in an equally frightening manner for your own protection if you had to had to go out after dark. This business of going around town begging for candy also has religious roots, but it has a confusing conflation of alms for the poor, apple bobbing, bobbing women to see if they were witches, cracking nuts as treats, thumping doors to scare kids when the living-dead were out and about, and finally carving frightening lanterns out of pumpkins and gourds for protection against the dead. The candy thing is one of those rare instances when something uniquely American had been adopted by the Brits. **All Fool's Day** is much like America's April Fools Day. The origins of either April Fools and All Fools are clearly European and probably comes from the Roman spring-time celebration of *Hilaria*.

AELFREDUS
MAGNUS

American Plan
-a hotel room with meals included. American Hotels no longer follow the American Plan, but it lives on in England.

Anderson Shelter -
a prefabricated bomb shelter, buried in the back yard and used to good effect during the German bombing of England during WW II.

Anderson Shelter

Anglo Catholic -a high church somewhere between Catholicism and the Church of England.

angel delight -a powdered desert which, when mixed with milk makes a mousse-like desert. (Yanks would call it pudding.) It is iconic of all that is horrible about nutrition and instant food.

angels on horseback   -a old fashioned appetizer of grilled oysters wrapped in bacon. *Devils on horseback* are prunes or dates wrapped in bacon and are served at Christmas.

Anglo-Indian   -an English person either born in India or one who has spent a lot of time there. He or she is not an Indian who has immigrated to England.

Anglo-Saxon   -a catch phrase for the ethnic people that replaced the original Celts and finally become the British about a thousand years later.
        The Angles, the Saxons, and the Jutes were a rather warlike crowd

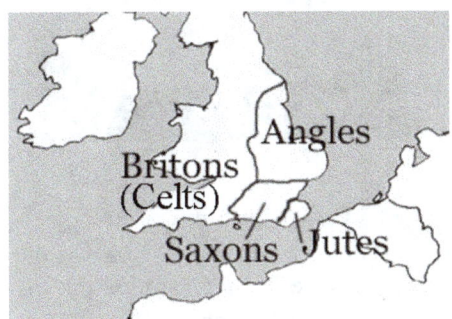 from Germany, Denmark, and the Netherlands -or what would eventually become Germany, Denmark, and the Netherlands. (Add Norway to this list, and you would have also have a pretty good description of where the Vikings would be coming from about 500 years later.) The Angles and Saxons first invaded England in the 3-hundreds, but the Romans kicked them back across the channel. The Romans then left about 450 and the Angles and Saxons came back and stayed. They were joined by the Jutes who settled in Kent and called themselves the 'Kentings.' The Angles settled in East Anglia, and the Saxons in Essex, Sussex, Middlesex, and Wessex. They all blended in with the local Celts.
        In the 1800's, the term Anglo-Saxon became shorthand for self-styled racial superiority, particularly when compared to the locals being colonized in various parts of the world whether they wanted to be colonized or not. It brings to mind the term *Aryan* that was popular in the middle of the 20th century in Germany. Enough said.

Anne Boleyn *(*1507(?) - 1536)   *Henry VIII's* second wife and mother of the future *Queen Elizabeth.* She was born around 1500. (There is some doubt as to exactly when.) She was the daughter of a high-level diplomat and by all accounts a bright, educated, popular girl who served in the various courts in Netherlands, France, and England. Things started going down-hill for her in 1522 when she and her *dowry* were negotiated off to an Irishman who was her cousin. This was to sort out a confusing political difficulty, but *Cardinal Wolsey* decided it wouldn't be quite proper. She was engaged again a year later for similar reasons and to another almost-relative. The good cardinal once again said 'No'.
        Her big sister   Her big sister was a good friend of Henry VIII at the time and she got her a job in Henry's court. The king noticed Anne and wanted to marry her. She resisted till he split with the Pope and had his marriage with his first wife *Catherine of Aragon* annulled. Anne and Henry were married

in 1533, they had a daughter that same year, but by 1536 she had failed to produce a son and heir for Henry so he had her investigated for treason and beheaded about a month later. There is some controversy as to her treason, but it seems she was largely, if not entirely, innocent. The important take-away here is that Catherine's banishment and Anne's execution pretty much put an end to the relation between the English Monarchy and the Catholic Church.

anorak -a rain coat that is usually made from what the English call *American Cloth* and what the Americans call *oil-cloth*.

apartment -originally, the living quarters attached to some other functional building, i.e. the judge's apartment in a law-court building. In the 19th century, it meant a single room rented in a house. What Yanks think of an apartment is a ***flat*** in England. see also ***homes*** and ***bed-setter***.

apothecaries -druggists and/or pharmacists.

apprentices and ***apprenticeships*** -part of the ***guild*** system that was about professional quality control, keeping supply down and prices up, as well as training young men in various crafts. Apprenticeships were common throughout Europe, a good bit of the world, and America too for that matter. Even to this day, many trades and their attached trade unions require some number of years learning the craft and *paying ones dues* as an apprentice.

Craft guilds existed in medieval England and apprenticeships came along shortly thereafter. In 1563 England passed the ***Statute of Artificers*** which set some minimum ground rules for the master. He could have no more than three apprentices at any given time, and had to feed, clothe, and board them. The apprentice was indentured for seven years. It was common for parents to send their 12 to 14-year-old sons off to be an apprentices elsewhere.

approved school -what Americans would call a reform school for juvenile delinquents.

archbishop -the head of the Church of England. There are actually two of them, the Archbishops of Canterbury being the more important.and the Archbushop of York. They rank at about three and a half steps up the ***peerage*** toward the King between dukes and marques.

armourers / armorers The Armourors and Braisers Company made things out of copper and tin like pots and pans

Army Begin with the idea that in the past, England had no army as such; it had a bunch of ***regiments***, and these regiments have not always been the king's regiments. Going way back, a rich nobleman would appoint himself a ***colonel***, gather up his vassals, knights, and what ever peasants

ARMY

could be persuaded to come along, and go off to war. Occasionally, an even richer guy like the king would have need of some fighting men and hire the whole lot at a price sure to make the rich guy even richer.

After the Civil War, Parliament was very leery of having a lot of organized, belligerent, and possibly Catholic men hanging about with weapons so they told everyone to go home and go back to farming. They only authorized and paid for a few of these regiments to act as the king's personnel Guard. Note the capitol G in Guard who were the coolest and meanest most loyal soldiers to be found. Even to this day, being in a Guard regiment means you were better than anyone else.

This worked well enough up until the Napoleonic Wars when England found she needed some serious professional military people to help out the navy. So they organized 109 regiments of infantry, and 31 of cavalry.

Even this didn't work during the ***Crimean War***, which was a dismal failure for the English, so in 1871, Parliament bought up all the ***commissions*** of the colonels and officers that *owned* the regiments. Today THE *army* organizes pay, ranks, duties etc., but it still thinks of itself as a collection of ***regiments***. Enlistment was for life until 1841, but reduced to 21 years for enlisted men, and 22 years for officers, but some of this time could be served in a reserve battalion. There was *conscription* (Yank's *draft*) during both WWI and WWII, but today the army is all-volunteer, all-professional, and among the best in the world. It must be said that they are every bit as good as America's Army today.

America has organized its Army much like the English have but with some subtle differences in vocabulary. These differences are extremely confusing but for the student, the following will help you understand what's what, or at least what's the relative sizes of divisions in England's military.

	Highest / Largest		Smallest	
Infantry	Regiment (2 or more Battalions)	Battalion	Company	Platoon
Cavalry	These three are administered by a general (external) staff.	Regiment	Squadron	Troop
Artillery			Battery	
Engineers			Squadron	

see ***regiment, commissions, navy, ranks, dragoons, lancers, grenadiers*** etc.

Army and Navy -a popular department store in London that originally specialized in selling things to military families. It is iconic for conservative tastes and completely unlike America's Army Surplus stores which mostly sell camping equipment.

Arts Council -much like the American National Endowment for the Arts (NEA). It is publicly funded and supports non-performing, visual, and literary arts.

ascot -an important horse race where formal dress is the norm. It is also a man's necktie or scarf thing worn under the shirt.

ashes, the The trophy for the cricket match between England and Australia is a terra-cotta urn reputed to contain the ashes of a burnt wooden cricket ball. Australia won this important *test* (match) for the first time in 1882. The <u>Sporting Times</u> in England reported this sad event by saying that English cricket died and "...the body will be cremated and the ashes taken to Australia." see ***cricket***

at home -from 1800 to about 1940, being *at home* meant the lady of the house was at home and receiving callers of the proper pedigree.

Australia -discovered by the Dutch in 1606, claimed by the Brits in 1770, and used as a penal colony from 1788. Populated by prisoners or otherwise, things went well and the population grew. In 1901, they federated and became a self-governing ***commonwealth***. Today the Aussies are an important alley to the English. They speak English, their legal and political systems are very similar to the English, and they play cricket, soccer, and rugby all three.

Automobiles The sexy expensive cars like the MG, Lotus, Jaguar, Rolls Royce, and James Bond's Aston Martin etc. are well known in America, but less glamorous ones show up in literature and need a few words. A single picture is sufficient because they all look silly, small, and boxy to the American eye, but in their defense, they are efficient in a place where gasoline (petrol) is expensive, parking is limited, and roads are narrow.

1949 Ford Prefect

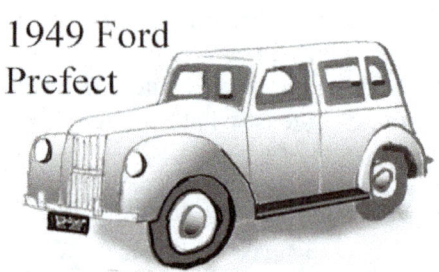

avenue -the driveway to a house or the long tree lined drive up to the manor. In England *avenues* are rarely streets.

Avon -a smallish river that would have had no great importance if Shakespeare had not been named the *Bard of Avon* because he was born in Stratford-upon-Avon. There are actually three or four Rivers Avon and the largest and only navigable one has nothing to do with Shakespeare.

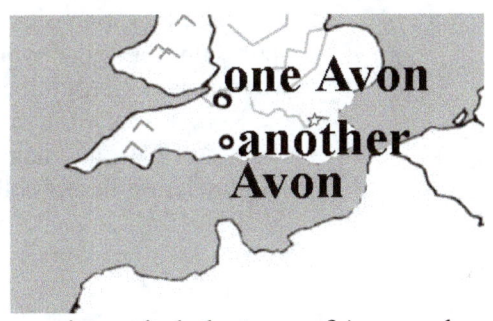

There is also a county of Avon that has as its capitol, the town of Avon and another Avon to the south. Just to confuse things a little more, there is also a Stratford in London.

away with the fairies -crazy, in la-la land. It comes from Irish mythology with the little people -leprechauns and fairies and all.

.

From the Egyptian picture-letter for foot. (?) It shows up in English words like *debt*, and *subtitle* where it is not pronounced because that's the way the Roman spelled it and there was a time when Latin was THE language of the well educated. The pronunciation freaks call *b* a *voiced bilabial stop*.

B `-the designation for paved country roads. see *A* & *M*

back-bench / back bencher   -Parliamentary member of the *Loyal Opposition* party who has little to say about how things go in Her Majesty's Government. They sit on benches behind the *Cabinet* Members, who are located on the *front bench*. They are a little like America's congressional minority but even less influential.

back stairs   -the stairs at the back of the house to be used by the servants. Anything *back stairs*, like gossip, was to be ignored by the family who generally ignored the servants anyway and used the exclusive front stairs. see *below the stairs*

bagman -a traveling salesman

bags   -pants. Debagging in England is like the American *pantsing* a kid. It also means lots and lots of something, i.e. *bags of nerve*.

bailiff   -a sheriff-like officer. They were mostly used in matters of debt, bankruptcy, evictions and other such unpleasant matters. When you encounter a bailiff in your reading, someone probably ends up being homeless or in debtor's prison.

baker's dozen   From the 13th to the 19th century there were various and serious penalties in London if a vendor cheated a customer on the weight of a purchase. In order to protect themselves from this, bakers would toss in a thirteenth bun, loaf, or whatever.

ball   Prior to the 19th century, balls were for courtly rich people who were in the king or queen's *court*. These balls were at least as much about political intrigue as fun and dancing. They didn't get much better during the Victorian era. The Victorian ball was a rather serious thing for daughters of marriageable age to 'come out' and then to sort out who married whom. Balls for fun, dancing, and seduction or mild flirtation were American.

bangers and mash   -sausage & mashed potatoes, classic pub food. During WWII, food was rationed -especially meat. Sausages were made with cheap filling and more water than usual; they fizzled and banged around in the pan more than proper sausage should.

Bank Holiday   -much like America's National Holidays. There are a few more of them than in America and furthermore, England, Wales, Scotland and Northern Ireland have slightly different holidays.

Bank of England   -a private bank founded in 1694 and nationalized 1946. It's role in England is closer to various roles of the Department of the Treasuries and Central Bank in America. In the very earliest times its job was to lend money to the crown.

banking   In England, banking is a far more conservative and time honored business than in America and it also has more history. ***Charles I*** seized all the gold rich people and been storing in the Royal Mint. This was one of the reasons they chopped off his head.. Then the rich people also decided it was better to store their gold with reputable goldsmiths who would then issue negotiable receipts. In 1650, a cloth merchant opened what was almost a commercial bank, with the ancestors of modern-day checks / cheques / bank-notes etc.

In the 1700's the industrial revolution combined with England's growing foreign colonies and the beginnings of ***mercantilism*** prompted the development of merchant banks. By the end of the century two banks dominated this industry, the Rothschilds and Barings.

Early in the 1800's the first joint stock company was formed, various bank collapses and legislation led to a generally improved banking system that by the end of the century would be the best in the world. Barclay became the biggest stock company.

The 20th century was cluttered up with two World Wars bracketing a world-wide depression, so it wasn't until about 1950 that English banking got interesting and then it largely paralleled modern American banking.

Today England's commercial banks are like what Americans would think of as a bank; with deposits, checking accounts and small loans. Mortgages, on the other hand, come from building societies. Nonetheless, the English ***post office*** and its ***Giro*** serve many of the common man's banking needs where he could pay bills, add to his savings (often sent to a bank down the road), and get cash for the pub.

banns   -a Medieval Catholic requirement that the intention to marry had to be announced on three consecutive Sunday services in the home parish of both parties. It was the origin of the "If there be anyone who knows any reason why these two shall not be joined..." part of weddings today.

Baptist   -a Protestant sect founded in 1611. Today the Methodist sub-set of the Baptist sect is mostly a working-class crowd. Their doctrine holds that baptism must be as a matter of mature choice, rather than the Catholic practice of baptizing infants. Like the Protestants, the Baptists do not recognize the strict authority and hierarchy of the Catholic Church or Pope, but rather they would rely on reading scripture on their own and following a pastor who was essentially hired by the local church elders instead of someone assigned by and sent from the church.

barmaid   -a useful character in a lot of 19th and a little early 20th century literature. She tended bar and was therefore around men and alcohol all the time but was never to be thought of as a loose woman but rather she was more of a pretty and out-going little sister to her customers.

barmy -not quite crazy, but eccentric and daft.

barkers   -made tannin from tree bark to tan leather. A carnival *barker* is strictly an American thing.

Baron / Baroness   -the lowest order of British nobility. In England, Barons are addressed as 'My Lord / My Lady". 'Barron Rothenbottom' for example, would be someone from the continent and not English. The word derives from Latin *per baroniam,* meaning tenant in chief (tenant being different from owner). Nonetheless, the barons were the ones who forced King John to sign the ***Magna Carta*** in 1215. Barons are hereditary positions, their oldest son inherits the title. They were an invention of ***William the Conqueror*** and a means to raise money. Today there are about 50 or 60 hereditary Barons in the UK. A *baronet* may inherit the title and sit in the ***House of Lords***. see ***peerage***

barrel   -lots of stuff gets put into barrels in English literature of a certain age. It works out as follows:

pin	4 1/2 gallons	hogshead	54
firkin	9	puncheon	72
kilderkin	18	butt	108
barrel	36	tun	252

BTW -Pork butt is actually from the pig's shoulder. It's called 'butt' because the English Navy provisioned Her Majesty's ships with 108 gallon butts filled with salted pork shoulder and you will find pork butts in the store to this day.

barrister -high level lawyer specializing in courtroom advocacy and not to be confused with a ***solicitor.*** A barrister has been 'called to the bar.' They are often hired by, or consults with solicitors, who deal more directly with the public. Barristers are also the chaps who wear the silly white ***wigs***. Barrister or Barristers-at-law may draft legal proceedings (but not contracts), argue in superior courts, and are considered legal scholars. 'Barrister' may also be an honorific title.

bath -take a bath, often in cold water to build character. To *bathe* is to go swimming.

bathroom -the room with the tub, but not the toilet. The biffy, loo, W.C., toilet, etc., is in a separate room. Back in the day, it was in the back yard.

batman / batsman -An officer's personnel servant was his ***batman*** in the 19th century. In cricket a ***batSman*** was the chap with a flat bat standing in front of the *wicket* and returning the *bowls* which are like an American's pitches.

Battersea Park / Fields -a 200-acre park across the Thames River from Chelsea. In the past, it had what would be called an amusement park in America with roller coasters etc. but today is more like Golden Gate Park or Central Park with museums and art galleries and all, but with a convention center thrown in.

Battle of Agincourt -In 1415 Henry V won a decisive battle in France. The French had a much larger army but the English had better technology -long bows! This battle was so decisive that it failed utterly to end the Hundred Years War which went on for another sixteen years, but it DID occur 100 years after the war started. The French king was back home chewing on the furniture—literally, he was insane. The French forces were poorly lead by a committee of self-serving noble nitwits who didn't actually talk to one another.

Battle of Britain / Battle of England (July 1940-June 1941) Early in WWII Germany bombed England and England defended herself with a small force of young fighter pilots. In all of the history of warfare, this was the first major campaign ever to be fought entirely in the air. The Germans planned to force the English to negotiate a peace. Initially, they bombed ports and shipping in order to blockade food and war materials, later, they bombed factories, and still later, they bombed civilian centers as part of a 'terror bombing' strategy. The Germans lost 1887 of 2550 aircraft (largely bombers) and the English lost 1547 of 1963 working aircraft (entirely fighters). The English won, but it was a very close thing. ***Winston Churchill*** said of the Battle of Britain that "Never in the field of human conflict was so much owed by so many, to so few." see also the ***Blitz***

Battle of the Atlantic (1939-1945)   -unlimited submarine warfare during WWII where-in the Germans tried to prevent England from importing food and war materials and preventing shipments to Russia as well. On the allied side were the Canadians, the English, and the Americans. Another WWII record holder, this time for duration, it ran from 1939 to the end of the war in 1945. It was actually two opposing blockades, Germany attempting to starve the English while the Allies attempted to blockade Germany from importing much of the same. see *food*

It was a close thing. 72,000 sailors and Merchant Marines died on the Allies side, while the German lost 30,000 sailors. The Germans sank 3500 merchant ships and 175 war ships against their loss of 783 submarines. Nonetheless, about 90% of shipping from America to England made it through.

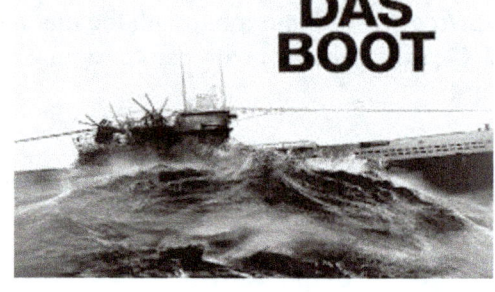

Das Boot is an excellent 1981 movie about this conflict, but does so from the standpoint of a German submarine. There is also a TV series made in 2018. *Das Boot* is German for 'the boat' -what the Germans call submarines.

Battle of Hasings   This was the beginning and decisive victory that kicked off the Norman Invasion. In 1066 **William the Conqueror** defeated -killed actually- King Harold II. It took all of a single day to do it in the fishing village of Hastings in Sussex in the south-east corner of England.

Battle of Trafalgar (1805)

This pretty much put-paid to any plans Napoleon might have had about invading England. This naval battle was fought in 1805 between England's numerically smaller fleet against the larger

combined French and Spanish fleet off the southwest corner of Spain. This is one of the many battles the define England's military pride and their deserved sense of invincibility -or at least their utter security on the island fortress.

The battle was fought between ships-of-the-line, these floating cannon platforms were the largest ships of the day. but tended to be slow and unwieldy Trafalgar is also where **Admiral Horatio Nelson,** one of England's greatest heroes, was killed.

Bayeux Tapestry   -a long (230 feet by 20 inches high) embroidered tapestry depicting the

Norman Invasion. Lots of curious pictures of guys on horses and some guys in boats. It was made in sometime in the 1070's in England, not Bayeux France.

BBC -the British Broadcasting Company. It goes back to 1922 and has been a public monopoly since 1925. It started with radio and began experimenting with TV in 1936 and got serious about it after the war. Each household pays a little under £150 a year for a TV license. This is about $160 year and collected by an unpopular door-to-door functionary. They have the choice of 10 different TV channels, but BBC 1 and BBC 2 does the job about 80% of the time. There are also 15 radio stations, each catering to a specific taste and with even more demographic variety among viewers than among the various TV options.

Yanks think of the BBC as being better than America's vast commercial TV wasteland, but they only ever see the best the Brits have to offer. Some of the best include Agatha Christie's Hercule Poirot and Mrs. Marple mysteries, Black Adder for a funny take on England's history, and Yes Minister for an equally funny take on the operation of government in England.

beadles   From the time of the Norman Conquest till as late as the time of Charles Dickens' writing, they were elected officials in smallish towns who were also the bell-ringer and town-crier with minor and various duties like keeping order, whipping vagrants and looking after the poor. see **police**

Becket, Thomas (1120 – 1170)   - variously *Saint Thomas of Canterbury* or *Thomas of London*. Becket was the *Archbishop of Canterbury* and a Catholic back before the English *Civil War* when it was possible to be both. He got cross-threaded with Henry II over issues that would seem to presage both *Henry VIII*'s and *Thomas Cromwell*'s difficulties about 400 years later.. Becket felt that people in the church like himself were privileged in various ways and should get to keep the taxes extracted from the citizenry. Henry
thought differently. It is not historically clear, but in the excellent 1966 movie *Becket*, Henry he was overheard to say, "Who will rid me of this troublesome priest?" and four knights rode off to assassinate Becket, who the Pope later canonized. Try to find a way to see this movie if only to see Peter O'Toole and Richard Burton acting in opposing roles.

bedsitter   -the most basic urban living quarters. Today a bedsitter is much like an American studio apartment, but in the past, they may have been only a private bedroom with a common bathroom down the hall. There may have been a lounge for sitting about and socializing with the other tenants.

The landlord provided one or two meals, somewhat like the American rooming houses of the late 1800's, but were a little less reputable than in America.

beef   For a nation with Beef-eaters (the nickname for her Majesty's Yeoman Wardens) the Brits don't eat a lot of beef. Per-capita, they eat about three fifths of what Americans eat and it's been trending down sharply. The Danes are the winners when to comes to eating cow, about 12% more per person than even Americans. What Yanks enjoy as steaks, the Brits call a chop and fry it. Otherwise, they roast joints for fancy occasions. Going back to about 1850, the French called the English *les rosbifs* which is almost English for the *roast beef(s)* as a mild insult. see *food*
beefeater -see Yeoman

beer   -the mildly alcoholic beverage not much different from what Americans drink. Before tea came to England and they figured out the need to boil water to make it safe to drink, brewing beer was a common way to kill the bacteria responsible for things like dysentery. English beer is a little stronger than American beer both in terms of flavor and alcohol content.

     As far as per capita beer drinking goes, the countries in central Europe win with between two to three quarts a week for every man, woman, and child. The Irish drink just under two quarts per week, Americans come it at about one and half and England about one and one quarter quarts.

Belfast   -the largest city and capitol of Northern Ireland. Originally it was an unimportant part of the gentle countryside of Ireland. In the late 1650's Protestants came from England to practice a religion different from Catholicism, weave linen, and start all manner of troubles. Tobacco processing, rope making, and finally ship building made Belfast a prosperous city. For example, this is where the Titanic was built.

     In 1888 Victoria granted Belfast *city status* -the only such city in Ireland. Northern Ireland was made a part of the United Kingdom in 1920 and things really started going downhill between the Irish Catholics and Protestant English. *The Troubles* came to a head in 1969 and for the next 25 years the city's economy was all but ruined. Today Belfast is coming back with shipping, film making, aerospace, and education. Now it's home to about 330,000 citizens.

below the stairs   -much like *back stairs*, it refers to matters involving the servants who often did their work and ate their meals in the basement where they were out of sight.

Beowulf   -written sometime between 700 – 1010. It is the oldest English literature. It is a long epic poem about Scandinavians battling the evil monster Grendel. It's author is unknown, but it's likely to have been added to or otherwise edited by poets thru the years.

bespoke   -made to order rather than off the rack -it's clothing that is tailored. *By Appointment to...* refers to products the crown has used for at least three years running.

Bethlehem   -a hospital for lunatics in London from the late middle ages. The corruption of the word -*bedlam*- gives us the term for chaos going back to Shakespeare. As a particularly vivid example of the Victorian 'rectitude,' a visit to Bethlehem was thought to be cracking good fun just to laugh at the poor souls imprisoned there.

bib and tucker   -fanciest dress, tux & tails, or dressed to the nines etc. In the 1700's, a bib was the front of a man's shirt while the same thing on a woman was *tucked* in at her waist.

Big Ben   -it's actually just the bell, but it has come to mean the tower and the clock as well. It's all a part of Westminster and Parliament.

bill   -much like legislative bills in America, but with some differences. In America, a bill is introduced by an individual (or a couple of legislators) from either the majority or minority. In England, a bill is introduced only by the **government**, which **is** the majority party that makes up both the executive (the **Prime Minister**), the cabinet (**Ministers / Secretaries**), and legislative body (the **Parliament**).

billion   There is much linguistic confusion here; it works out as follows.

Number	British	American
1,000,000	million	million
1,000,000,000	thousand million -milliard	billion
1,000,000,000,000	billion	trillion
1,000,000,000,000,000,000	trillion	thousand billion

Birmingham   -England's second largest city. The City (and metropolitan borough) of Birmingham has a population of 1.1 million. Its history is as a market town in the medieval period and an important industrial center as the industrial revolution unfolded in the 18th century. It was a little like America's Detroit, Pittsburgh, and Milwaukee all stirred together. The steam engine, soccer league, and lawn tennis were all invented there. Today Birmingham makes its living with finance, service, retail, transport, and conferences. The people call themselves *Brumies* and have a distinctive accent. The city's nick-name is Brum. Note the <u>U</u>, but the city is spelled B*I*rmingham.
   By 1791, Birmingham was the world's leading manufacturing city and it was from all this designing and building that Birmingham's people, economy,

and perhaps most importantly, its atypical social diversity that made it a hotbed for democracy and the enlightenment with a little *e*.

biscuits   -cookies to Americans. Yank's cookies are *sweet biscuits* or a *tea biscuit* in England.

biscuit tin -cookie jar in America, but in England they are actual tins and are used to hold odds and ends (*odds & sods*) when the biscuits are gone.

water biscuit -cracker.

ship's biscuit -hard tack. It was hard as a rock, but it lasted forever.

take the biscuit -Americans might say *take the cake*.

bishop   To understand the importance of bishops in English history and literature, readers need to consider medieval feudalism wherein the two biggest things were the lord's castle and the bishop's cathedral. If you look closely at feudalism, it becomes clear that religion and the whole nobility system were both effective ways to keep the peasantry in its place with threats of excommunication and eternity in the fires of hell and all.

While kings dealt with want we might think of as foreign affairs, the church tended not only to matters of the soul, but also local government and education. Indeed, up thru **Henry VIII**'s time (1491 - 1547), the monarch's best and most educated advisers were from the church.

Another reality that is little hard for Americans to get a hold of is that bishops were already rich when they were appointed by the king for political reasons; their religious devotion had little or nothing to do with it.

The industrial revolution in the late 1700's and the need for educated workers (together with the Reformation) lead to increased literacy among the common man. This in turn diminished the advantage the bishops had enjoyed by virtue of their monopoly on literacy and education.

Even so, they remained politically important. A bishop was automatically a member of the **House of Lords**-at least until the **Reform Bill** of 1832 which redistricted the various boroughs to better represent people. It was not until 1872 that the number of bishops who were given an automatic admission to the House of Lords was limited to 25.

By the 20th century, bishops were mostly still wealthy, but expected to act with some pious restraint and look after the members of his (or her, but only quite recently) diocese. Today there are two Arch-Bishops (the big one for Canterbury and a back-up one for York). There are also another three for London, Durham, and Winchester. The third-string runs at about 60 more bishops of here and there, and some have additional duties like health, education, prisons, urban life, etc.

Despite huge wealth and power, a bishopric was not a hereditary position. Whatever of the diocese's wealth the bishop was not able to tuck away as gold for his children went back to the crown when he died.

bitters   In the 18th and 19th centuries, *bitters* was patent medicine for bad tummies, i.e., *digestifs*. The stuff is made from herbs and spices steeped in a strong alcohol solution and like any good medicine, it tasted awful. It was bitter, sour, or bitter-sweet. Eventually bitters evolved into something to add a little zing to cocktails.

Black Death (1346 – 1353) Rats and their fleas brought a fatal pestilential fever to Turkey and by 1349 to Europe, and finally to southern England by 1353. It killed as many as half the people in certain places. There are historians who say that fewer people sharing resources, horrible as it must have been, was one of the things that kicked off the *Renaissance*.

blackguard   -rhymes with *placard* -an utter louse. It goes back to Shakespeare when a *black guard* was the lowest form of laborer and often black with filth.

black pudding   -breakfast sausage. It's not pudding, but sausage with the usual meat ingredients, but with oatmeal and sometimes corn grits or barley. Its color comes from blood and it might be thought of as a toned-down version of *haggis*.

Black Watch   -the 42nd Royal Highland Regiment and a very tough bunch they are. They are sometimes called the *Black Jocks* (Jock being a common Scots nickname), or the *Ladies from Hell* because of the kilts. The Black Watch first saw action in Egypt in 1882, and every war England has been in right up to 2009 in Afghanistan.

blimey   -a cockney expletive for *Gorblimey* pronounced *Gor, blimey.* which in turn is from the medieval oath *God blind me*.

Blitz, the   The German bombing offensive that led to the **Battle of Britain.** It's a less an academic term but a more historic one and more along the lines of what the people who lived thru it call it. The bombing of London and other industrialized cities was so intense that they sent all the children off to foster homes in the country out of range of the Germans. The *Blitz Spirit* is mentioned with some pride in response to terror attacks even today.

Bloodless Revolution see the *Glorious Revolution*

bloody   -simply means *very* or even *very very*, but it has an interesting history of varying vulgarity. From Shakespeare to the middle of the 1700's it was respectable, but vulgar during the Victorian era. After WWI it starts showing up again, but often written as "b____". After WWII, it was sometimes replaced with *bleeding* or *blooming*. It is increasingly acceptable today, particularly in Australia.

Bloody Mary (1516-1568)   -*Henry VIII's* daughter Mary I, by his first wife *Catherine of Aragon*. She was a devout Catholic like her Spanish mother. During her reign from 1553 to 1558 about 300 Protestants were burned at the stake.

board school   -not to be confused with *boarding schools* but rather a primary school administered by the local board like an American Board of Education in a given town. They go back to the late 1800's. see *education*

boarding houses   Renting out a room was a very common way to bolster the family income, but if it was rarely more than one or two rooms. These rooms were also the least expensive 'homes' for working people. see *inns & taverns*

boarding schools   These show up in a lot of English writing and by all accounts, were & are as bizarre and horrible as described. The Harry Potter stories got some things right; many boarding schools are very old (as far back as 12th century medieval monastic schools). Bullying etc. has not been exaggerated (it was thought to be character building) and boarding schools were expensive and admission often depended on who your daddy was, and finally, blazers and school ties were required. Like Hogwarts, there are co-ed schools, but the oldest and most conservative are still strictly for young men.   Like Hogwarts, which specializes in which-craft and magic, today there are boarding schools specializing in preparing students for further education and careers in the military, performing arts, and religion, as well as schools for students with what is politely referred to as having b*ehavior challenges* and/or other learning difficulties. Today about 1% of English kids attend boarding schools.

In defense of the whole thing, in the 1700 and 1800's, England was spreading itself all over the globe and people were sent off to look after England's interests, be they diplomatic, mercantile, or military. They understandably wanted their kids to get a proper English education so they packed their kids off to boarding school before they left England's shore.

Other than a curious insistence that people be able to speak and read Latin, these schools arguably did a good job of teaching children what society thought was important, at least until well into the 20th century when the need for scientists and engineers became more important than the need for rhetoricians and linguists. see *schools* and *mercantilism*

bob   -slang for one shilling. It depends on the era, but it is about $5.00 see *money*

Boudica, Queen (circa 25 – 60 AD)   -a Celtic queen and right pain to the Romans. Boudica's husband was a king (a tribal chief actually) and more or less a Roman ally. However, after his death they flogged the widow Boudica, raped his daughters, ignored his will, and took all his land. Big mistake ! Boudica lead a revolt against the Romans, killed a bunch of them, and very nearly beat them. She did succeed in burning down London (Londiniun -a Roman fortress and market-town at the time) before she either was captured and killed, or almost captured and killed herself first –no one is quite sure. She was supposed to have flaming red hair, been a beautiful woman, and an utter hell-cat. As such, she makes for great legends.

bobbins -rotten or rubbish

Bob's your uncle   -something that is dead easy. For example, "Two right turns and the first left, and *Bob's your uncle,* you're there". It also has a hint of sarcasm implying it's not what you know, it's who you know.

bog   -a wet muddy area common in Ireland and north-east England. Or the bathroom.

Boers   -Dutch farmers who resented England's rule in South Africa. They fought two guerrilla wars against them in 1880 and 1899-1902. It's also sometimes spelled *boor;* but it's not a *bore* is which is a tedious person.

bollix / bollicks / bollox etc.   -to confuse something (verb), or a confused mess (noun), or an annoying difficult person (insult).

Bond, James Bond   Before he was a mainstay of the movies, Bond, James Bond was a character in a series of 12 novels and short stories by Ian Fleming published between 1953 and 1964. Bond was a Commander in the Royal Navy working for ***MI-6***, the Foreign Office's Secrete Intelligence Service during the cold war. Ian Fleming, on the other hand, was an officer in the Royal Navy's Intelligence Office.

Bond Street   -a shopping district in London for tailors and handmade suits for the very rich and the very conservative. see ***Carnaby Street***

Bonnie Prince Charles (1720-1788)   -one of England's colorful *pretenders* to the throne. Born in 1720, he was the grandson of James VII and leader of an unsuccessful Catholic insurrection in 1745. He then was a playboy around the (European) continent till his death.

Book of Common Prayer   -more than a prayer book, this is the liturgy the ***Church of England*** used to oppose Catholicism. Its importance to the English language is second only to ***Shakespeare*** and the ***King James Bible***.

boot -a car's trunk. The *bonnet* is the hood.

Borough   (Important but confusing history.) -originally a town with the right to make its own laws, but through history the meaning has changed. As Parliament unfolded as a real legislative force, a borough was a town that had its own ***MP***. By ***Henry VIII***'s time a borough probably had a cathedral, and a cathedral had to have a bishop. The Industrial Revolution made some boroughs the largest towns in the land and they were granted city status by the crown. (This had no special benefit other than status.) Some other quite large towns were neither boroughs nor cities, but were technically mere *parishes* with no MP. Throughout all of this, boroughs were Parliamentary divisions, but divisions based on old Reformation demographics going back to the middle of the 1500's. As the Industrial Revolution grew, there were some large populated industrial areas that had no representation at all. At the other extreme, some -the *rotten boroughs*- may have had a rich MP representing little more than himself, his family, and his servants.

In 1832 they sorted it all out with the ***Reform Bill*** and in 1835, they standardized the municipal laws and procedures across the land. In 1965 London did away with all its boroughs, and in 1972 all boroughs in England were changed to either metropolitan counties or districts. Except some were allowed to remain ceremonial for tradition.

An *open borough* is one wherein neither party has a majority and therefore is what Yanks would think of as a swing district. A *pocket borough* is the opposite -the landlord had all the votes in his pocket. see ***divisions, political***

bosun　　　-a sailor in charge of a ship's sails and rigging. He is the highest enlisted man and equivalent to the army's sergeant. The bosun's whistle was a call to work.

bound over　　　-a little like probation in America. It is not so much a sentence as a promise that arrest and sentencing will quickly follow any further bad acts.

bounder -not merely a cad, but a cad who has bounded above his proper state.

bowler　　　-a derby hat. Originally a bowler was worn to protect a rider's head from low branches. Take away the horse, add a rolled umbrella and you have the iconic conservative English gentleman. The verb to *bowler-hat* meant to retire from the military and put on such a hat. In cricket, the *bowler* is the pitcher and has nothing to do with hats.

Boxing Day　　　-the day after Christmas. It has nothing to do with pugilism. Boxing Day is when servants and trades-people are given their *Christmas Box* from their masters or employers. Think of it as an American Christmas bonus, but going way back. Today, Boxing Day is also a huge shopping opportunity when stores mark down everything that wasn't sold during the Christmas rush.

braces　　　-suspenders for the trousers. English suspenders hold up a man's socks or a woman's stockings. (BTW -*pants* are underwaer in England.) A *garter* was the belt to carry a sword -as in the ***Knights of the Garter***.

brass   -slang for money. To *brass-up* is to pay off a debt. *Brassy* is impudent, but in America is takes on more of the sense of loud and vulgar. A *brass hat* is a high ranking military officer with lots of brass fiddly-bits on his hat or is simply the boss.

Breach-of-promise   Getting cold feet after the proposal but before the wedding is a big deal to the English, particularly after the middle of the 1700's. For the reader to understand this, it is important to understand that for the *middle class*, marriage was hugely important not only to the bride and groom, but the whole family. Huge amounts of effort and cost went into *balls*, negotiations, and intrigues. When a proposal was accepted, it was game-over and if a better or richer suitor happened along, well, that was just too bad.   The money awarded in breach-of-promise cases was considered a form of alimony awarded to a woman of now doubtful virtue for what presumably would be a life of spinsterhood.
   The whole thing got out of hand at the end of the 1800's when there were a number of sensational cases wherein chorus girls brought such suits for huge amounts of money. It all wound down with changing attitudes and laws that allowed women to own property in their own names.

bread   -much the same as American bread, except white bread made from wheat was for the wealthy up until about 1800. Before that the common folk ate rye or barley bread and the Scots ate oat bread. The English do bread pretty much the same way Americans do, with one or two exceptions. At the beginning of the 20th century, they fried thick slices in lard and ate it with a fork. More Brits like to slice their own bread than do the Yanks.

breakfast   Back in the day, breakfast was bread and butter or cheese and beer. The iconic English breakfast at the manor was served as a buffet for the convenience of family and guests who arose at various times. The continental breakfast of tea and bread was a pitiful thing compared to the manor's spread of fried egg, *kipper*s, sausage, bacon, fish with rice, tomatoes, toast, and fried bread. The poor ate porridge or gruel. Coffee was not a large part of it all. The sugary stuff Americans eat cold out of a box with milk has only recently began to make some appearances on the English breakfast table. see *food*

breeches   -what Yanks think of as knickers which are worn by (American) football players and cross-country skiers.

Brigade-a military unit temporarilymade of two regiments and commanded by a *brigadier* -not a *Brigadier General* like in America, just a Brigadeir.

Brighton   -an unimportant fishing village until George IV (1762 – 1830), got in the habit of going there for various pleasures. It then followed a common trajectory; first the royals made it a play-ground then the *middle class* came for a season or two. Then, because it was a pleasant 50-mile train ride from London, the working class came and Brighton came to be seen as tasteless and tawdry, at least by those with real taste. It's still a popular weekend get-away for the younger set who enjoy the quirky glitz.

Bristol   -an important port city from the middle-ages that exported wool and imported fish, wine, grain, and dairy. It lies at the confluence of the Rivers Avon and Frome and was among the most important cities in England up until the Industrial Revolution when cities like Manchester and Liverpool surpassed it. Today its population is around 440,000 people. It is a little like San Francisco which was an important port until its land, particularly water-front land, became too valuable for cranes and docks, so shipping moved across the bay to Oakland. Bristol's waterfront is now a Center of Heritage and Culture and this business of loading and unloading ships has moved to Avon Mouth in the distant suburbs.

British Invasion   In the early 1960's, American R & B music crossed the Atlantic, became rock music, and crossed back to America where it became hugely popular. Bands include: the Beatles, the Dave Clark Five, the Kinks, the Rolling Stones, Herman's Hermits, the Animals, and The Who.

Britain/ British   -a slippery word with lots of curious and often contradictory meanings. It goes back to the Romans who called the island *Britannia*. This was news to the Celts who lived there and thought it was part of Gaul, or what the Romans called Normandy, which would eventually become France. By comparison, *England* is simple. It's Old English for the Germanic for *Angul-land* -land of the Angles of Anglo Saxon fame. The words *Brit* and *Brits* are mildly vulgar. It's better to say someone is a Briton.

Britannia   She is thought to be the national personification of England. Originally, she was a minor Roman goddess in charge of war and water -note her trident. She was largely forgotten by the second century. In the 16th century the English resurrected her as their cultural icon. see ***John Bull***

British Airways   -England's premiere airline founded in 1974. In 2011 British Airways and a number of other airlines were squired by International Airlines Group which is a confusing conglomeration British and Spanish concerns headquartered in Berkeley California. Its largest shareholder is Qatar Airlines from the fabulously wealthy oil country Qater.

British justice - isn't just and often violates common sense.

British luck - is an ironic comment on good luck that goes to no good end.

British Isles – a bunch of islands in the North Atlantic that may **or may not** be a part of England. They include Great Britain (England, Scotland and Wales), Ireland (the Republic of Ireland), The Orkney and Shetland Islands, the Isle of Man, Hebrides (including the Inner Hebrides, Outer Hebrides and Small Isles) and the Isle of Wight. See *divisions, political, of England*

British Museum -a huge museum containing artifacts more or less politely looted from Greece, Rome, and Egypt by English archaeologists before anyone else knew what archaeology was. It also has a library that has every book or magazine ever published and the central reading room under a dome bigger than that of *St. Paul's Cathedral* about a mile down the street. It is most famous for being home to the Rosetta Stone. It was found by Napoleon's soldiers in 1799 outside of Alexandria as they conquered Egypt. The English and allies eventually defeated Napoleon and all manner of this and other keen things made their way to England.

British Telecom / BT -was originally part of the post office, then it was independent but still nationalized, and finally privatized in 1984. see *BBC*

British Rail -was a national asset until it was privatized between 1994 and 1997. By all accounts, it is well run and probably better than America's Amtrak.

broderers / broiderers - men, and most were men, who did embroidery. Women made lace. Rich women sitting about in drawing rooms doing fancy things with needle and thread would become popular in the late 1800's.

brogue -a thick Irish shoe originally worn by Irish laborers who were thought to speak with a thick Irish brogue.

broom -an interesting example of word's meanings being a moving target. Broom is a wild bush whose twigs could be gathered and tied around the end of a stick to make a *besom* for either sweeping out the barn or for witches to ride. It was not at all suited to the drawing room, so about the same time *besoms* became *brooms*, the material of choice became broom-corn -which is not corn at all, but rather a kind of grass.

bubble and squeak   -left-over vegetables and potatoes fried up till they bubbled and squeaked.

Buckingham Palace   -the official London residence and

administrative center of the Monarch. They hold lots of receptions and official doings, but parts of it are open to the public from time to time. It has 775 rooms, 19 state rooms, 52 royal guest bedrooms, 188 staff bedrooms, and 92 offices, but only 78 bathrooms. see **Windsor Castle**

buffer / old buffer -an old foggy or an old duffer in America.

bugger   -a friendly reference to a silly person. **I'm buggered** means I'm confounded. **Bugger-up** is to screw up. **Bugger off** means to go away and stay away. **Bugger about** is to fiddle about, **Bugger-all** is none at all, and **play silly buggers** is act stupidly.

burberry   -raincoat, but unlike a **Mackintosh** which is made from rubberized cotton, a Burberry is made of more expensive waterproof wool. The name comes from Thomas Burberry who started the company in 1856.

burgess   -originally, a full citizen of a borough, later a mid-level gentry, and in the 20th century, a middle-class businessman similar to and derived from the same root as *bourgeois*. **Burgesses** are either a **MP** for a smallish area, or a freeman of a borough.

Burke's Peerage and Burke's Landed Gentry   The definitive lists of who's who and how important they are. It was first published in 1826. The 2003 version is 4700 pages long and costs about $500..

burser -either the corporate treasure or a *bursary* -a scholarship student.

Bus, double decker   -from the days of the horse drawn stage-coaches, These were the economy means of getting around, so much so that passengers were sometimes stuck up on the roof. This gave way to London's iconic double-decked buses with the top enclosed only in 1940 see **coach**

butler   Originally, this was the chap in charge of the master's wine cellar. By about 1850 the butler came to be the supervisor of all the servants, but only in the very largest households. In most literature (and in other than all but the very richest households) the butler was more apt to fulfill the role of valet and /or steward. see ***servants***

by-election   The equivalent of the American *special election* when a MP dies or otherwise leaves office before his term is up and a new one is elected.

**The lion is just one
of the symbols of England.**

The letters *c* & *g* started out as the same letter, but by the time the Irish got a hold of Latin and taught the English how to read and write, the Old English *c* got tangled up with *k*, and so it remains today. Words with a hard *k*-like *broken,* were originally spelled *brocan*. The soft *c* in words like *spice* are probably from the French speaking Normans. To make it even more complicated, words with a *qu* in English today were spelled with a *c* in Old French.

Cabinet   It's like the American cabinet, but made out of English **Members of Parliament** or simopley **MP's.** In America, the cabinet is made from—we hope— non-partisan experts in the various subjects whose advice the president needs from time to time. The English Cabinet is more political because the cabinet *ministers* are selected from the current party in *government*. The English get their professional expertise from non-partisan **Permanent Undersecretaries**. There may also be a small number appointed by the **Prime Minister** from the **House of Lords**. They are all variously referred to as *Ministers* of This or *Secretaries* of That. Check out the BBC show YES MINISTER for a hilarious take on how it works in England.

cake   -nothing at all like the American two or three layer things covered with frosting. English cakes are smaller and they are often closer to what Yanks might think of as sweet-roll, with some varieties are made with fruit like raisins or currants. The expression for the good life, *'cakes and ale'* goes back to Shakespeare who stole it from the ancient Greek story teller Aesop who said *"Better beans and bacon in peace, than cakes and ale in fear."*

call -to visit, not to make a phone call as it is in America,

Cambria   -the Latin word for Wales. 'Cambria' is important to the paleontologists (fossil guys) because Wales was where Adam Sedgwick, an English priest and amateur geologist, first noted many large and varied fossils that would give raise to the notion of the 'Cambrian Explosion'

Cambridge   A city of 123,000 people about 50 miles north of London and named after a bridge over the minor River Cam. Cambridge University goes back to around 1200 and today about one-fifth of its population are students. Over 40% of its workforce has a college degree or about twice the rate in the rest of England. see *education*

Camelot-no such place, but it is the center of King Author's legendary kingdom. Author Pendragon was a powerful warrior-king who fought the Saxons in the 5th or 6th century. He also didn't exist.

canon   -a clergyman involved with a cathedral or large church. Usually one of a staff of similar clergy and similar to the priest(s) of a Catholic *parish.* Canon Law are the rules of behavior. (A *canNon* is a piece of artillery.)

cap   -the proper headgear for a tradesman etc. Going *cap-in-hand* was for a working stiff to go ask something of a swell.

capital punishment   -hanging, or if the rope was too short and there was not enough of a drop, capitol punishment was actually slow strangulation. This was for commoners; the nobility got to be decapitated -quicker that way. Crimes and dates work out as follows; in 1783, it was taken from the town square and brought inside of the prison. This spoiled the fun for the townspeople who before then would take the day off to go enjoy a nice hanging. Up until 1838 any felony was sufficient cause for hanging, but thereafter capital punishment was limited to murder, treason, arson, or piracy, and after 1965, murder was also taken off the list. Now capital punishment is still available for treason or piracy, but it hasn't been used since 1964 when two men who murdered a robbery victim were hanged. see *hangmen*

caravan   -a camping trailer, usually towed by the family car on *holiday.*

card   -what American's might call a *calling card*, but much more complicated. Back when servants were all the norm among the middle class, the card with just the caller's name engraved was carried by the butler to the master or the mistress of the house who would than decide it the caller was to be admitted or sent away. The complexity dealt with folding down one corner or the other to indicate the caller would come back or would not come back etc.

Business cards now are used in England much as they are in America.

Playing cards were for gambling until early in the 20th century when the Brits and Yanks both went crazy for bridge and proper women could only then play cards.

Cardiff   The capitol and largest city in Wales and a popular tourist destination. Its history involves some impressive engineering done to the harbor and canals to move that coal and iron ore -both of which were very import6ant to the industrial revolution in the late 17 hundreds. Today it has a population of about 350,000 *Cardiffians.*

Cardinal Thomas Wolsey (sometimes Woolsey) -see ***Wolsey, Thomas***

carmen, carters, carriers   Delivery men, but their license strictly prescribed what they might carry. At varying times and in varying places, one could carry only agricultural products, another only passengers, and still another, only cargo.

Carnaby Street   -a small street off ***Soho*** synonymous with 1960's fashion.

carriage   -almost any type of horse-drawn rolling thing, but there needed to be a horse, and place to store both the horse and carriage, and a servant to care for it and drive the carriage. This was all very expensive, so the *carriage trade* refers to a wealthy clientele.

cassock -   the long black garment worn by clergy. Until comparatively recently it might be thought of as business wear for such people. Only when it was worn with a white linen ***surplice***, was it for services or sacred ceremonies.

castle   -a fortified administrative center, home, and sometimes granary. Rich people lived in medieval castles and in theory allowed the common folks to take shelter if the area was under attack. They were for defensive warfare -withstanding siege. This gives castles their most iconic architectural

Battlement or Crenelation

merlon

embrasure

features, the battlements or crenels from which arrows or crossbow bolts could be fired or even rocks and boiling oil could be heaved. (Moats and drawbridges were not universal.) From the 12th to the 16th century, a castle needed a *License to Crenelate* from the king to fortify. Insofar as doing so could make it harder for the king and his knights to come along and take over again, such a license meant the king trusted the Lord of the manor. Palaces came along later but their battlements etc, these were a decorative architectural feature as they were built more for comfort and status rather than defense. see ***royal residences***

cathedral -the seat of a bishop. From the Latin *cathedra* meaning *seat*. A cathedral is probably a huge imposing church, but not necessarily so. It can, in theory at least, be a small unimpressive church, but it must have a bishop and his diocese. If the bishop and / or the surrounding countryside was poor, the cathedral might be small. For example, *Westminster Abbey* is not a cathedral. It is big and impressive, but it is the seat of an abbot, not a bishop, therefore not a cathedral.

Catherine of Aragon (1485–1536) *Henry VIII's* first wife and mother of *Queen Mary.* She was one of his wives who was *not* executed. Her parents were Queen Isabella and King Ferdinand of Spain (the same Isabella who financed Christopher Columbus) and in 1501 she married England's Prince Arthur who died six months later. She was the ambassador for Spain to the England and the first woman to serve as ambassador in all of European history. In 1513 she served as Henry's *regent* for six months while he was in France. At about this time, she was instrumental in one of England's victories over Scotland. In 1516 she gave birth to her only child Mary I (later known as *Bloody Mary*) but no sons. By 1525 Henry was infatuated with *Anne Boleyn* so he used the lack of a son and heir as an excuse to try to get their marriage annulled. *Pope Clement VII* refused, so Henry assumed the supreme power over the church. (This was not quite the start of English Protestantism, but it was an important first step toward the coming *English Civil War.*) Henry then was able to annul his own marriage and send her off to live out her life in the country. She died in 1536.

One tends to think of Catherine of Aragon as one of history's most hapless victims if not quite to the extent as some of Henry's other wives, friends, and advisers who were beheaded, but she was an impressive and accomplished woman by her own rights. Her banishment was widely resented and her death was mourned by the English public. She was a proponent of educating women, spokesman for the poor, and an important intellectual part of Renaissance Humanism. If nothing else, she lived in the center of very interesting times for England and for Europe.

Notice the poor woman's chin. The Spanish Hapsburg Dynasty was so inbred that the recessive genetic deformity–the Hapsburg Jaw–ran thru generations of this family. Catherine didn't have to too badly, but one of her younger cousins was so deformed he couldn't chew, could barley talk, drooled constantly, and died at age 30 looking like a very old man. Over a period of about 200 years, there were nine marriages between Hapsburg cousins and two between uncles and nieces.

Catholics It was a dicey thing to be a Catholic in England, but it wasn't always so. For the time between Christ and the Romans leaving about

450, it was OK to be a Christian. When the Romans left, they took Jupiter, Neptune, Venus and all the other planets / Gods with them. Things went back to the old Celtic pagan gods. In 597 the pope sent what we might think of as a *Catholic* missionary effort to England. The old-fashioned pagan gods (Roman and Celtic Gods stirred together) and the trending Catholics got along fine, at least until *Henry VIII* wanted a divorce. It was about then that things started going downhill for the Catholics. There was some back and forth between the Protestants and the Catholics, but under *Queen Elizabeth I* (1558–1603) and again under *Oliver Cromwell*'s *Commonwealth* (1649–1660) it was a decidedly bad time to be a Catholic. Catholic priests were regularly executed if caught, and only after the restoration in about 1700 could you even be a Catholic, but you were not allowed to hold office until 1791. In 1829, Catholics could be in Parliament, and by 1853, they could even go to Oxford.

Today England is comparatively non-religious but even so, Catholics were viewed a little dubiously. Things are changing, but to the English mind, being Catholic implies being Irish, poor, and uneducated -if only a little.

caution   -the warming given to someone being arrested along the lines of *Anything you say may be taken as evidence*. As a verb -*to be cautioned*, it is like being *Mirandized* in America.

cavalry   This is a generic term for soldiers mounted on expensive horses, or later, driving various machines. From the times of the mounted and armored *knights*, they were distinct from infantry, but some cavalry got there quickly and then climbed down to do a little actual fighting. The Calvary was for gentlemen who could afford *commissions* and horses. Living, fighting, and getting killed in the mud was strictly for the infantry which was largely made from commoners.*

The cavalrymen were THE coolest soldiers up until WW I when it was discovered riding a horse did not keep you alive against machine guns. Even so, England keeps a few of them and their horses around in the *Household Cavalry* for parades and whatnot. see *dragoons, hussars, lancers, regiments,* and the *army.*

*An interesting bit of American History attains. During the American Revolution, the colonists had very accurate hunting rifles that could not be reloaded quickly and furthermore, needed to be taken apart and cleaned every few shots. So they used what we might think of today as guerrilla tactics. They would shoot from a long ways off and do so from behind a rock or tree. They would then have to run off and reload etc. They also liked to shoot the guy on a horse -an officer. The English thought this was deucedly uncivilized. The foot soldiers were supposed to line up a short distance from the enemy, who was also lined up all neat and proper. Then they would each bang away at one another with short range muskets that could be reloaded quickly. Whichever side ran out of common soldiers first lost, and the officers on both sides were able to ride their horses back to camp in time for dinner.

Celts -Iron age people from central Europe that flourished and spread all over the continent and the British Isles between 500 and 100 BC. Then the Romans came along. In Britannia, the Romans didn't bother with Wales, Scotland, or Ireland so versions of the ancient language are still spoken in these places.

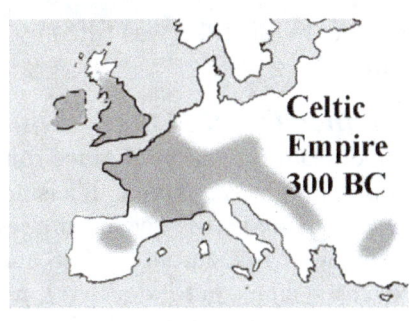

Celtic Empire 300 BC

CH Order of the Companions of Honor. It started in 1917 for civilians who contributed to art, literature, music, science, politics, industry and religion. The rules are that there will never be more that 65 of them plus the monarch.

Chad -England's equivalent to America's *Kilroy*. Both are military and both are WW II era. While Kilroy was satisfied to simply state he was here (there?). Chad was a little more inclined to complain "Wot, no beer / sugar / internet etc.?"

chair / sedan chair -all the rage form about1600 to the early 1800's when streets and roads got good enough for horses and carriages. King *Henry VIII* was a big fan, but by the end of his life he was so fat and crippled that it took four big guys to do the job.

chalk & cheese As similar as chalk and cheese which are not at all alike. An American might say *apples and oranges.*

Chancellor -originally the king's secretary and therefore the primary administrator. Now there are various chancellors including the Chancellor of the Exchequer (treasury) and Lord Chancellor overseeing judicial matters. see *government, cabinet, Prime Minister*

Chancellor of the Exchequer This office is the equivalent of America's Secretary of the Treasury and the second most powerful office in *Her Majesty's Government* behind only the *Prime Minister*. (Numbers three and four are the *Foreign Secretary* and the *Home Secretary*.) He or she is appointed by the Queen on advice of the Prime Minister. This is a very old office and until 1923 was filled by the same chap who was also the Prime Minister.

Channel Tunnel / the 'Chunnel'   -31 miles of high speed railroad tunnel from England to France running under the English Channel for people, freight, and autos. It's is not the longest tunnel in the world, but it is the longest under the ocean. It goes as deep as 250 feet and runs at 99 miles per hour. Work started in 1988 and finished in 1994. It is said to go from Dover to Calais, but it doesn't; it really goes to the suburbs -Folkstone in England to Pas-de-Calais in France. It carries north of 50,000 car passengers per day, 85% of whom are English, often on holiday.

chapmen   Chaps or chapbooks were small often religious books. The door- to-door peddlers who sold them from the back of a donkey or horse were called *chapmen*. They also sold cloth, looking glasses, toys, combs, knives, and all manner of knick-knacks. By1696, they needed to be licensed.

char /char woman / charlady   -an old fashioned term for a cleaning lady or a servant who does not live in the house. Today she (or he) would be called a *daily*.

charcoal burners   -nothing to do with BBQ, but rather they made the smokeless hot-burning charcoal from wood that was used in steel making, black-smithing and making gun-powder. They were also called *wood colliers*.

Charing Cross   An intersection in London by Trafalgar Square. It is considered the center of this city and the location of a main rail-road station. Its name is a combination of the Old English word for a bend in a river, 'cierring,' and Elanor's Cross erected by Edward I in 1291 as a memorial to his wife.

Chartered Accountant -like an American CPA.

Chaucer (1343 – 1400)   Geoffrey Chaucer, was an author (fiction, nonfiction, and a little mild pornography), poet, philosopher, bureaucrat, and diplomat. The most popular of his many works is The Canterbury Tales. This was the first book written in the Middle English vernacular rather than the usual Latin used by the intellectual swells of the day. (This is not to say it's easy reading to those who speak American. It's not even easy for the people who speak British.)

chav / chavs   -a 20th century juvenile delinquent snot. These are from the lower class and wear what they think of as designer clothes to go about being "brash and loutish". The origin of the word is unclear, but it apparently does not derive from "Council Housed And Violent," but this is thought to be as good an explanation as any. (*Council Houses* are like America's *housing projects*.)

Cheapside   -a street in London and the financial center of the realm. Think of it as England's equivalent to America's Wall Street. It comes from the Old English *ceapan* to *buy* or *shop*. Other towns have Cheapside Streets or market streets. It has nothing to do with the inexpensive meaning of *cheap*.

cheddar cheese   The most popular cheese in England and second most popular in America (behind mozzarella) and the most popular in the world. It goes back to at least AD 100 and it is possible the Romans brought the recipe to England. During WW II and for many years after, 'government cheddar' was pretty much all there was to eat cheese-wise. *Mack and cheese* was a popular meal on both sides of the Atlantic during WWII because it could be gotten with fewer ration stamps than other foods, particularly meat and dairy. see *food*

Chelsea   -an extremely expensive and largely residential neighborhood in London. Chelsea is bordered by Sloane Street. This gives rise to a number of deprecating terms for what American might call spoiled yuppies and hipsters. For example, 'Sloan Rangers' are women who ride horses. Chelsea also has more Americans living there than anywhere else in England. No one knows why this is.

chemists   Pharmacists made drugs in apothecaries, but chemists made industrial chemicals, often nasty ones. Druggists etc. became *chemists* only in the 20th century.

cheque   -a check from a bank. Working Brits received a pay packet with cash because few of them had bank accounts as late as the 1990's.

chimney sweeps   Yes -like the guy in the movie who was as lucky as lucky could be. But if you were a young orphan, the smaller the better, you were hired / adopted / bought to crawl up and down a chimney scraping off tar and soot. It was a tossup to see if you died of lung problems before you got to be too big for the job. It got worse when England went from burning wood to burning coal. The round brush on the end of a long flexible handle was only invented in the early 1800's.

chin wag   -chat, as in "Have a nice cup of tea and a bit of a *chin wag*."

chips   -American French fries ("Freedom fries"?) Witness English *Fish and Chips. Crisps* are potato chips.

Christmas   England's idea of Christmas is increasingly as commercial as it is in America, it has not always been so. The Celts did a mid-winter's festival of lights with yule logs, naughty frolics, and lots of wassail. The Catholics kept much of the fun of it all, but stirred just a little solemnity surrounding the birth of Christ. During Shakespeare's time, **Twelfth Night** was the big thing. Then the Protestants decided it was entirely too much fun and sinful so they went back to work right after church service on Christmas morning and that was about it for Christmas until Charles Dickens came along. He got a little help from Queen Victoria's husband Prince Albert who was from Germany where they still liked a little fun. Prince Al insisted on a proper Prussian Christmas tree and such became popular among the swells. Even so, it was a gradual thing that had involved little more than Christmas cards and the **Christmas goose**. December 25 was far less important than **Hogmanay**, January 1, in Scotland and **Boxing Day,** December 26, when gifts were given to the **servants.** Even now, the Brits only go shopping crazy for about two weeks before the holiday, rather than beginning right after Halloween like the Yanks do.

Christmas Goose -the traditional Christmas dinner. English Christmas dinner is very much like America's Christmas dinner, except the English have *pudding* for desert rather than pie. The history of the main course shuttles back and forth between turkey (**Henry VIII**'s favorite) and goose, with a little boar tossed in and even swan and peacock for the rich. But goose was the thing for dinner during the Victorian Era; *Goose Clubs* which were sort of a poultry lay-away plan that allowed the common folk to save up all year for a nice fat goose. BTW -the Christmas dinner from Dickens's <u>A Christmas Carol</u> was turkey.

Chunnel -see **Channel Tunnel**

Church of England   As far as doctrine is concerned, the church straddles Catholicism and Protestantism. It is the *official* church of England and therefore it had be a compromise. From its earliest history, the Church of England was as much a political thing as a religious thing. The **Restoration** (1660) gave some of the Catholic bishops back their property and made them rich and powerful once again. It was only during the 1700's that the Church began to take on what we think of today as charitable Christian functions with things like parish **schools**, poor relief, and concern for widows & orphans. As far as people's mortal souls and their fear of hell, this was arguably more about keeping the peasantry in line and profitable for the bishop than anything else.

This compromise lead to war both among **Thomas Cromwell**'s Protestant crowd, as well as more strife between Protestants and Catholics. Some of the most devout Protestants like the Puritans, Pilgrims, and Calvinists emigrated to the colonies for more religious freedom & tolerance.

Today, most of the English identify themselves as Church of England, but the number who actually attend church is small and getting smaller. This is, however, the case with most Christian religions in most of the world.

Churchill, Winston (1872 – 1965)   Ask ten Englishmen who the most important Englishmen (or women), were thru history and Winston Churchill would be near the top on every list. He was the middle son of a politician from an illustrious old English family, but not a terribly rich one. His mother was an American socialite and a famous beauty. Without the prospects of his eldest brother (and even these were limited) he went off to fight in -and write about- the Cuban War in 1895, India in 1896, the Greco-Turkish War in 1897, and the Sudan in 1898. He was recognized both as a great writer and heroic soldier throughout. In 1899, he returned to England, ran for Parliament, but lost, so he went to South Africa to write about the Second Boer War where he was taken prisoner, escaped, saved a bunch of other people. He was considered for the Victorian Cross, until someone noticed he did all this as a civilian and was therefore was not eligible.

Between 1900 and 1915 he took something of a breather by going into politics. In the summer of 1914 Austrian Archduke Franz Ferdinand was assassinated and it was off to the races with WW I. Churchill resigned from government and went into the Army -first as a Major and then as a Lieutenant Colonel. Along the way, he was also a Lord of the Admiralty at the same time Franklin Delano Roosevelt was the Secretary of the Navy in America.

Between the world wars, Churchill was out of politics or *in the wilderness* because he was in favor of India's Independence, warned against Nazi Germany, and finally, was vehemently opposed socialism. All of these views were contrary to popular notions of the times, and all would later come to be proven to be spot on. In 1940 he was once again the First Lord of the Admiralty, and as WWII began, Churchill became the Prime Minister.

Churchill probably did more to win WWII than anyone else in the world, but the English were astonishingly ungrateful so he was out on his ear again between 1945 and 1951 when he was back in until 1955. He died in 1965 at 91 years of age.

There is much to be said about and learned from Churchill and his life. He was an extraordinary man by all accounts. Perhaps the biggest take-away for the American reader is that he was half American, 1/64 American Indian, and loved Americans. One writer suggested he was more comfortable among Yanks than any other Englishman has been before or since. The Darkest Hour (2017) is an excellent movie about Churchill at the beginning of WW II

circus from the Latin for 'circle' and a roundabout or traffic-circle see ***Piccadilly Circus***

civil parish   -the smallest or lowest political division involving local administration. While it is an oversimplification, Americans might think of a civil parish simply as a town that concerns itself with elementary education, local roads, fire protection, libraries, and some planning. It is smaller than *civil* districts and counties, but some of then are as large as 80,000 citizens, but some are villages with as few as a hundred inhabitants.

A *civil* parish is not to be confused with an *ecclesiastical* parish which divides up parishioners from one church to another and goes back to the time before Cromwell.

Civil Service

Her Majesty's Civil Service is the permanent professional bureaucracy or secretariat of the Crown. They are employees of the crown rather than elected members of **Her Majesty's Government. Cabinet Ministers** are chosen from elected **MP'**s, of the majority party and liable to be replaced every 5 years, but the Civil Service is perpetual. In America, the civil servants may be a local politician / bureaucrat, but in England, they are considered Crown employees (England's "*the Crown*" equals America's "*Federal.*") At the highest levels, permanent *under-secretaries* being the

very top, they are presumed to be above mere politics and very wise and skillful in their fields. The Humphry character in the excellent BBC sit-com <u>Yes, Minister</u> is a civil servant.

Civil War, English   Three wars actually, between 1642 and 1651 between various factions of Protestants vs. Catholics and Parliamentarians vs. Royalists. It worked out roughly as follows: Catholics were generally loyal to King Charles but the Protestants were in favor of the Parliament being in charge. Charles was beheaded in 1649 and things went badly for the Catholics under **Oliver Cromwell**. Cromwell was something of dictator and things weren't all that great for the Protestants either particularly if they opposed Cromwell.

The final brief war between 1649 and 1651 saw **Charles II** return to the throne with Parliament giving its consent, but Parliament kept hold of the purse strings, not unlike what congress does today in America.

The 1970 movie <u>Cromwell</u> does a pretty good job of doing the history, but buckle up, it's a very intense two and half hours long. It also has a phenomenal cast. see **Oliver Cromwell, Commonwealth, the Protestant Restoration, Charles I**

clergy   Members of the clergy have long shown up in English literature. They are either pious and poor, or rich and rapacious. There seems to be no middle ground and there are a lot of them.

As is often the case, a historic perspective is the best way to sort it all out for the reader. When the Romans left, things were increasingly owned by a king or by the Catholic church. A little later it was owned by the Normans and the church and later still, rich English guys and the church. The church was the constant and the church also had a monopoly on literacy. This brings us to one of the church's first responsibilities; they kept track of births, marriages, and deaths in a given parish until at least the middle 1800's. (Looking after people's souls was only incidental.) From the earliest days of the organized church, it also served an educational role, but originally it was just to educate more clergy. English priests were not expected to have a degree, but were expected to have at least a little college. It was only after WW II that the Catholic church required a theological degree. Even so, history, science, archaeology, and literature all benefited from work done by the clergy. Later science and exploration would also be done by *gentleman* like Charles Darwin and others.

The following roles may be Catholic, Protestant, or both in one form or another.

Position	Job / Responsibility
Archbishop	The top bishop in the Church of England. There have usually been only two of them, the Archbishops of Canterbury and of York.
Bishop	Supervised a large area and had their own cathedrals. Bishops and Archbishops are the highest level of cleric administration and automatically became members of the *House of Lords*.
Priest	A mid level clergy. Priests usually had their own church and Church of England priests were usually married.
Deacon	The lowest level of the church's hierarchy. Deacons in England were priests-in-training, not *church elders* like deacons in America.
Archdeacon	Not so much a supervisor for deacons as an assistant to the bishop.
Dean	Supervises a cathedral's Canons.
Canon	A member of a cathedral's staff of priests and one who conducts service
Rural Dean	Supervises several churches in a *see.*
Rector	The head priest out in a parish and entitled to that parish's tithe.
Curate	An assistant to a rector.
Vicar	If the rector didn't want to be bothered looking after his parish, he could hire a vicar for some minor portion of the income he derived from that parish. Vicars in literature were usually devout, if poor.
Chaplain	A priest without a church. He might serve at a nobleman's private chapel or serve a military function.
Warden	Supervised the church's charitable undertakings.
Beadle	Back when the church oversaw local law enforcement, beadles were the village policeman. In the more modern Church of England, their role was to keep order during service.

Sacristan	Looked after the church or cathedral's holy vessels etc.
Precentor	The church's choirmaster.
Sexton	Maintains the church grounds.
Verger	Maintains the church building.

There is one final role in the clergy that shows up in literature, that being the Vicor's wife. (Catholic priests etc., did not marry, but Protestant and Church of England clergy could.) The Vicar's wife was usually the center of all matters involving the women of the parish, notably charities & appurtenant fund raising, local morality and culture, and she often did a little common-sense matchmaking.

clerk   -pronounced *clark* -an office worker or an agent for a ***barrister.*** American sales clerks are referred to as *shop assistants* in England.

climate   England's is a *temperate maritime* climate. England is cooler than the rest of Europe in the summer, but warmer in winter, rarely below freezing or above 90° F. Rainfall averages about 30 inches per year, but with great variation from west (wet, windy and mild) to east (dryer and cooler). There is no rainy season —it rains all year round, with January and October being the wettest. It does snow in England, but rarely and it melts quickly. None the less, the Scottish Highlands have five or six ski areas and there are even a couple in northern England, but none are as large, high, popular, or having seasons as long as those in the Alps or Rocky Mountains.

The sun shines thru clouds etc, for about one third of the time and June is the sunniest month. Fog is also a year-round phenomenon, but is heaviest in the winter. Incidentally, should climate change bring about a raise in sea levels, England will suffer greatly because much of the River Thames is essentially a tidal basin. Even without global warming, there has long been a problem with tidal storm surges. So much so that in 1984 they finished the Themes Barrier, which are massive gates that can be rotated into place and close the river.

clothing   To understand clothing in England, it is important to remember two things, First, England is wet and chilly -never seriously cold, but never toasty warm either. Second, until the industrial revolution, fabric was hugely labor intensive to make and therefor very expensive. The old portraits and historic moves show people wearing astonishing amounts of fabric back in the day. This is because it was only rich people who could afford lots of clothes and had their portraits painted. The common man probably wore a knee-length wool tunic and his wife wore one a little longer.

Consider scratchy wool as underwear. Two ways to go back in the day. You would simply go without, or wear linen if you were a little richer, or you did so until about 1666 when the English discovered cotton from India. In 1721 when Parliament passed the Calico Act because English hand weavers were facing too much competition from cotton. The solution came from the *Industrial Revolution* and vast improvements in spinning and weaving that allowed England to import raw cotton. India became both a source of the raw product and a market for the much more valuable finished fabric etc. The Calico Act was repealed in 1774. Note the date; the Crown insisted that the American Colonists would also buy finished products–for example tea–from England. (The Boston Tea Party was in 1773.) But returning to cotton and clothing, England would also import cotton from the American South and was, in fact, on the side of the Confederates during the Civil War a little later.

clotted cream   -somewhere between butter and cream cheese. It's spread on scones or crumpets and a necessary part of a proper *cream tea*. In America, it would be classified as butter because of the fat content.

club   Before the days of hotels in London, the rich men who came to town on business or to do their parliamentary duty needed a respectable place to stay that was more comfortable than a rooming-house or an inn. Furthermore, it needed to be a place that was respectable if only from the outside. Some clubs were a refuge for the gentry to indulge in things that were frowned upon—but enjoyed by—the gentry, gambling being but one of the more innocent possibilities.

After WWII, the relaxing of the idea of respectability, as well as the increase in restaurants, hotels, as well as the ability to drive -or be driven- in from the country in your own car, changed London clubs back to exclusive refuges for *gentlemen*. Today, what Americans think of night-clubs were never quite as popular in England as they were in America, particularly during prohibition. Only after the mod era of the *British Invasion*, and later, *disco*, gave a new éclat to England' night-clubs.

The excellent BBC TV series <u>Jeeves and Wooster</u> offer s delightful peek at an idle nitwit of an English Gentleman spending time in clubs. The Jeeves character is his valet or gentleman's gentleman. It was set sometime between WWI and WWII.

coach   Back when, it was an enclosed house-drawn vehicle and bigger than a carriage. Later it was not unlike an American stagecoach that traveled, literally, in stages and on a schedule. In the 19th century, it came to mean the passenger part of a train. Now a carriage is a bus traveling between cities.

coalition government   When the largest party political party in Parliament does not have a majority, a coalition may be negotiated between two smaller parties. The alternative is a *vote of no confidence* and that is disruptive for everyone, especially the politicians. Such a coalition is sometimes called a *national unity government* or a *grand coalition*. There were coalitions during both World Wars and they are now more the rule than the exception.

cockle -a small shellfish sold from push carts in times past. (Sweet Molly Malone sold cockles and mussels, calling 'Alive, alive-o.') A cockle is also a small purple flower. A cockleshell is a small rowboat.

Cockney An insult going back to Chaucer when it referred to a pampered city dweller. It has variously meant a *swell* or (ironically) the opposite, a working class individual. It has always meant a Londoner and probably one from the *East End*. Finally, tradition holds it is someone born within earshot of the bells of St. Mary-de-Bowls or the *Bow Bells*.

Cockney rhyming slang This was all the rage in 1840. What we would think of as trendy young in the *East End* and the criminal underworld in the 20th century. They would take a common phrase of two or three words wherein the last word rhymes with the word the speakers really wants to use. Then he or she says only part of the second expression. For example, *'wife'* becomes *'trouble'* because *wife* rhymes with *trouble and strife* rhyme, but the *...and strife'* part is dropped. *'Apples'* becomes *'stairs'* because it rhymes with *apples-and-pears*. It's very confusing and that is the point; to confuse the uninitiated. Here are some more examples:

Meaning	Original Phrase	Slang word
feet	plates of meat	plates
road	frogs and toads	frog
laugh	Turkish bath	Turkish

coddiwomple -to travel quickly to an unknown destination. It's old English slang. *Cattywompus* means the same thing in Ireland, but in parts of America it means uneven, crooked, or even *skew-humple*.

codswallop -nonsense

coiners Copper coins go back to about 100 BC in England, and AD 150 first saw (Roman) machinery being used to make coins. Coinage, silver & gold bullion, money, banking, National Treasuries, indebted kings, and various forms of fraud and debasing the currency complicated the issue, but the Royal Mint has overseen English coinage since 886.

cold dish / cold plate -a cold meal usually consisting of cold meat and bread, but with history. Single, young, rich. *middle class* people of the 1800's were not expected to cook, so a servant would leave a cold meal out for them following an evening's carousal.

Cold Stream Guards   -England's oldest standing regiment. It got started in 1661 from odds and ends of Cromwell's army to guard **Charles II** and still does so for the monarch. A subset of the this crowd are the ones who wear the tall bearskin hats and old fashioned red uniforms while standing un-moving outside **Buckingham Palace**. The rest of them also wear the elaborate old uniform when on parade, but when they put on combat dress, they are very good at doing lethal things and have done so all over the world.

college   As in America, colleges are the bits and pieces that make up a university, but as is always the case in England, colleges have lots more history. Originally and theoretically, colleges had more to do with research than teaching. Lectures, reading, and exams were pretty relaxed. Schools with regular classes, schedules, grades and what Yanks might think of as college were called *academies* up to the middle of the 19th century and even then, they were more like what Americans would think of as a high-school.   Note the spelling of the word *colleagues* and *colleges*. Going way back, a college was a company of colleagues, perhaps even more or less a **guild**. see **education, schools** etc.

collier   -may have been a coal miner, a cargo ship which carried coal, or a **charcoal maker**. Dirty jobs all.

Colonel   -the commander of a **regiment** or the owner of a regiment until about 1871 when the crown bought out their **commissions**. This lead to a lot of surplus colonels who were loath to give up the status of their rank so they insisted on being address as 'Colonel' even though they were retired. They show up in literature of the late 19th and early 20the century as well as on the side of buckets of fried chicken in both America and England to this very day. The word *colonel* comes from the Latin *columna* who was the leader of a column of soldiers.

Colonial   -someone from the colonies, but of European descent. They are from places like Australia, Canada, or New Zealand, but never Hong-Kong, Africa, or Jamaica. Caucasians born in India or America may or may not be considered Colonials.

colonies, the   In no particular order and at various times, the colonies were Ireland, America, Canada, India, Australia, Hong Kong, Bermuda, parts of the West Indies, lots of Africa, and parts of the Middle East.

Americans tend to think of the thirteen original colonies, but English possessions were far more extensive. The first one was Ireland and called an 'over-seas settlement' or a *colony*. This is to say Englishmen went there to live, like in America, but with an important difference; the people who came to America did so to farm and work and get rich, whereas the people who left England to go to Ireland were already rich, and exploited the Irish to get even richer, and then returned to England for parties and fox hunts, or so the Americans and Irish remember it. Bermuda and the West Indies were also over-seas settlements on this side of the Atlantic, and both are still more English than American today.

The English also established trading posts, or *factories*, in the East Indies and coastal India, and picked up Bombay and Tangier in West Africa as the dowry of a Portuguese princess whom Charles II married in 1661. To round out the list of possessions / colonies / settlements etc. consider Gibraltar, Hong Kong, Nova Scotia, and the Falkland Islands.

Hong Kong is an interesting example. After the First Opium War (1839–1842) it became a colonial cession, but England transferred sovereignty to a special administrative region of China in 1997.

To understand English history, one must understand the English Empire at least as much as one understands the monarchy. Both are huge complicated subjects, but for the reader, it is perhaps sufficient to understand that a LOT of their best stories, particularly those set from about the beginning of the 18th century and extending to WW II, take place in exotic places. America has the Wild West, and the Brits have the Colonies. But here again, there is an important difference between the Brits and the Americans; America has held on to its legendary wild west and it is where they keep many of its mines, ski-areas, casinos, and Californians. England has lost most of its exotic possessions.

Today the English are ambivalent about the loss of their possessions. Arguably self-government is a better thing than economic exploitation for the people involved, and the English are nothing if not civilized at least for the last so many years, but England is still nostalgic for her colonies; at least the older folks are. As one reads English stories, one is struck at what wonderful travelers the English are. They seem to be able to effortlessly appear at dinner in full **bib and tucker** after having spent all day traveling on the back of an elephant.

A final word on the subject; as some of England's possessions were breaking away from the crown, some others sent delegations off to **Whitehall** to say –in effect- "Thank you very much, but we would much rather keep things just the way they are." and they drink a toast to the queen at every cricket match to this very day. see **Commonwealth**

combinations   -warm long underwear for men, or a warm top and bottom combination for women.

come out   Originally, it was when a young woman was presented at court. Later, from about 1700 to 1900, it referred to a young woman coming out of her house for parties and balls for the *season* in order find a suitable husband.

comforter -either a baby's pacifier or a nice woolly neck scarf.

commissions, purchasing Army   To get a grip on this confounding practice, it's helpful to compare the English Army to the Royal Navy. The navy needed some few people who could do clever things -things like doing math and trigonometry in order to navigate, or people who understood enough physics to shoot cannons and later, to tend to steam engines. Therefore, the navy adopted what was at that time the wildly radical policy of promoting people based on their ability rather than who their daddy was. The army, on the other hand, needed people who looked good riding around on horses while wearing uniforms.* Lest this seem too strong a statement, consider the English view of the barbaric American colonists who persisted in shooting and killing officers rather than foot-soldiers. Foot soldiers couldn't afford houses after all, and so killing them was only the civilized way to fight a war.

There is some small logic to the English practice. The commission served as sort of a deposit. If the officer deserted, or was a coward, or was found to be incompetent (and the bar was set pretty low) he was cashiered or kicked out of the army and the crown kept his commission. On the other hand, if he lasted, and most of them did, he could sell his commission to a young hopeful and retire as sort of an 18th & 19th century retirement plan.

Over and above this apparent logic, there were some more compelling, if less obvious, reasons for buying and selling commissions among rich people. Mostly, it kept power where it belonged, among the rich, who would preserve the status quo. There was to be none of this pesky revolutionary notion that all men were created more or less equally. If the officers were already rich it kept looting down to a minimum and there was less of a tendency to cheat the real soldiers. Mostly however, it gave rich daddies a convenient way to keep their younger sons out of the casinos.

The Napoleonic Wars killed more than a few officers and so sometimes someone would get promoted based on need and presumably, ability, but such people were looked down upon by those officers who bought their commissions all proper like. Clearly, this lead to some incompetent leadership. This sad incompetence reached its highest (lowest ?) level during the Crimean War between 1853 and 1856. One chap -Lord Cardigan of sweater fame paid a record $5,200,000 (in 2016 dollars) for a Colonelcy. He led and was one of the few survivors of the reality that inspired Alfred, Lord Tennyson's famous *Charge of the Light Brigade*. There is some debate if Cardigan was more incompetent than his boss, Lord Raglan, who invented sweaters with raglan sleeve. (You can't make this stuff up.)

To attach some fiscal perspective to the whole thing, in 1837 Queen Victoria was just beginning her reign, the telegraph was patented, and Lee and Perrin began making Worcestershire sauce. There were no wars to speak of. Nonetheless, prices of commissions in the army ran roughly as follows:

Rank	Branch	Cost then	Cost now
Cornet / Ensign	Infantry	£450	$58,500
Lieutenant	Life Guards	£1785	$232,050
Captain	Cavalry	£3225	$ 419,250
Major	Life Guards	£5350	$695,500
Lt. Cornel	Foot Guards	£9000	$1,170,000

As to why the Foot Guards were the most expensive club to join, understand that the foot officers rode horses, and had the prettiest uniforms. As silly as this sounds, the prices of commissions varied with rank but also with whatever branch was most fashionable at the time. It all started unraveling in 1855 when Parliament tried to figure out why the Crimean War was such a dismal failure. They did the *Commission on Purchase* (of Commissions!?) and found unfavorably. It ended completely in 1871 when the crown bought its army back from the officers for some £40,000,000, which was a lot of money at the time.

*There were two exceptions to this practice and once again, education, particularly math, was the issue. The Royal Engineers and the Royal Artillery both needed people who could build things or shoot things. These officers had to graduate from a military school, and were promoted based on seniority. They didn't go quite as far as the Navy who promoted on ability, but it was a start.

common   -pejorative for ordinary or lower class.

commons, the   -from the old legal term of common land meaning resources in the environment owned, or at least used, by everyone. In medieval times, the commons were part of the manor and therefore owned by the lord of the manor, but everyone could at least walk on the commons. Today *commons* refers to air, water, and land.

Commonwealth

At the end of the Second *English Civil War* in 1649, England considered itself a republic. Technically, it became a Commonwealth rather than a Monarchy, but the Commonwealth also refers to the period between the execution of *Charles I* and the restoration of the monarchy in 1660.

In contemporary use, the word refers to former British Colonies with various ties to England, either political or ceremonial. Typically, these are places where they either play cricket or call soccer 'football'. America does neither and is therefore not considered part of the Commonwealth.

Etymologically, a *commonwealth* is a voluntary association of political entities for the common good. Kentucky, Massachusetts, Pennsylvania, and Virginia are not technically states; they are commonwealths.

Comprehensives England reorganized what Americans would think of as its public school system between 1965 and 1972. These secondary schools are tax-supported and any student between the ages of eleven and eighteen could attend, much like America's middle and high-schools. This is to say there are no admission requirements. And much like American schools, they struggle with various problems, some of their own making, and some thrust upon them with changing times. Integration is one such problem. Race is not the issue, but rather class. see ***schools***

confectioners Once the English were able to get their hands on cheap sugar from the Caribbean about 1750, candy making got to be big business. see ***food***

conscription -the draft, not that the Brits did much of it, despite a long history of pretty successful wars. They did the draft for a short time during WWI, but only two years after it started. Again in 1939 but then only 20 and 21-year-old men. Between 1940 and 1942, conscription was expanded to men from age 19 to 40, and single women. From 1947 to 1962 all fit men had to do two years of national service.

There is one notable but extra-legal exception practiced by the Royal Navy during the Napoleonic Wars. They pressed / kidnapped / Shanghaied, anyone the could find on the waterfront and a lot American sailors they happened across on the high seas. This was one of the causes of the War of 1812.

Conservative Party -similar to America's conservative party but with lots more history. They derived from the older ***Tory*** party in 1832. The Tories supported the monarchy and rich people. The later Conservatives pretty much stuck to this script. Consider Winston Churchill, Margaret Thatcher, free enterprise, monetarism, and privatization as all part of the conservative party. see ***political parties, Tories, Whigs, liberal*** and ***labor***

continentals Historically, these were the American colonists. To the English mind, the continentals were rather ungrateful for all the mother country had done for them and not without some justification. These days, it means anyone who lives on the continent of Europe and is therefore someone of somewhat suspect manner and up-bringing.

coopers -a barrel maker but not quite that simple. There were white coopers who made household barrels, bowls, buckets, etc. Dry coopers made barrels for apples, butter, fish, gunpowder, and soap. Wet coopers made barrels for jam, sauce, and most importantly, wine and liquor. see *barrels*

Cornwall -a vacation spot in the far southwest corner of England. It calls itself England's Rivera, but it is not the only place making this claim. During the middle ages, the Cornish mined tin & copper to make bronze, but mining there goes back as far as the actual Bronze Age. Metal mining petered out and they started mining china clay for porcelain. At the very western end of Cornwall is Land's End, which shows up in literature as the first sight of England for east-bound ships.

corn -America's wheat or any grain like oats. America's *corn* is *maize* in England. The oldest meaning of *corn* implied something grain shaped -like corns of salt -as in *corned beef.*

Corn Laws Between 1816 and 1848 steep tariffs were imposed on imported grain to protect the price of corn (wheat) and thereby, the wealth of the rich land-owners. It was repealed only when it sort of bumped into the Irish *potato famine* of 1846 to 1852. About a million people in Ireland starved before they did so.

costermongers A street vendor with a permanent stall -think farmer's market, flea marker, and craft fair all mixed together, but open every day of the week except Sunday.

Cotswold -very pretty rolling hills west of London. *Cotswold* means *sheep enclosure* in the Saxon language. There are lots of sheep to this day and lots of fossils as well as Cotswold stone which are used to build lovely yellow stone houses.

Count -not English at all; Counts were from the continent from Germany and whatnot. They show up in English literature often involved in political intrigues.

county There are three varieties of counties in England. Some are not counties but districts, and sometimes a given piece of land may be in two overlapping counties of two different varieties at one time. It's confusing but it works out as follows:
 -39 traditional counties (shires) going way back to the Anglo-Saxon times.
 -33 non-metropolitan counties. Six have set aside their district functions and are now unitary authorities. They are supervised by councils that are called *county councils*, but they are really *district councils*.
 -48 Ceremonial counties that may take on several unitary authorities.
see *divisions, England's political*

County Council To simplify, it's the local government, but *county* is not a single entity in England. Think of them as smallish states by American standards. Nonetheless, they fulfill equivalent functions taken on by America's states, counties, and cities. These include education, social services, fire & rescue, libraries, planning and some local roads & highways.

Covent Garden   --a suburb just west of the *City* of London. It used to be the place to go to buy fruit and vegetables, but now is a touristy shopping area including the world's largest Apple Store. Covent Garden Square and Covent Garden Market and The Royal Opera House all go by the name of Covent Garden.

cream tea a light afternoon meal of ***tea, crumpets, clotted cream***, and jam.

Cricket   Take a baseball diamond and throw out all the bases, add more outfielders, and put an extra home plate behind the pitcher's mound and you would almost be ready for a rousing game of cricket. A mention of something like cricket showed up in court records as far back as 1597. By 1660 at least a few people got paid to play cricket, and by the mid 1700's, it was a huge spectator sport. Cricket's 'golden age' was the 20 or so years before WWI, which was about the same time football (soccer) was becoming more popular.

　　　　　International matches (*tests*) are played between England, India, Australia, Pakistan, Sri Lanka, the West Indies, Zimbabwe, Bermuda, and Bangladesh; in short, pretty much everywhere England colonized except America, where the game morphed into baseball. One of the most popular tests is between England and Australia and the trophy is referred to as "The *Ashes*." To compare it to American baseball…

Issue	Cricket
The field of play	Only the pitch, the flat path between the bowler and batsman, is defined as 66 feet. The pitch sits in the middle of a big field of whatever size it happens to be.
Hits	The batter may hit the ball which ever direction he wants to – even backward if he is that good.
Runs	The batsman keeps running back and forth between the wickets as many times as he can while the other team chases down the ball, and then he gets another chance to bat. 20 to 40 runs is the about average for test level at-bats. One guy averaged just under 100 runs. If his hit clears the boundary, he automatically gets six runs without even needing to run.
Outs	The wicket is broken (the bail gets knocked off the wickets), his hit is caught on the fly, he puts his leg in front of the wicket to protect it (he cheats), or he is run out -the wicket is broken when an outfielder throws the ball at the wicket while the hitter is off running between the wickets.

crisps   -potato chips -not to be confused with *chips* which are what Yanks call French (or Freedom) fries

Cromwell, Oliver (1599–1658)

Cromwell, Oliver (1599–1658)   He was related to **Thomas Cromwell**. Oliver's great-something grandmother was Thomas Cromwell's sister and she kept her name for confusing reasons having to do with title and inheritance. Oliver was born in 1599 and didn't show up much in history till he became a Member of Parliament in 1628-9, but was still a comparative nobody. He was, however, a devout Puritan, and a tolerant Puritan, at least initially. He did another stint in Parliament starting in 1646 and was one of the signers of Charles's death warrant in 1649.

He surfaced as a military leader during the English *Civil War,* and killed a lot of Catholics, particularly the Irish and Scottish ones. He appointed himself the **Lord Protectorate** of the Republican **Commonwealth** from 1653 to 1658 when he died. Historians disagree, but no one less that **Winston Churchill** thought he was a genocidal dictator. *See* **Civil War, English**

In 1970 the movie Cromwell was released with an astonishing cast and a fair degree of historic accuracy. It wan an Oscar -for costume design of all things. It's worth running down and watching.

With two Cromwells, Henry executing people all willy-nilly, and the Catholics & Protestants burning one another at the stake, it's all a little confusing. There's nothing like a time line - even a crude one- to clarify things.

1480	1490	1500	1510	1520	1530	1540	1550	1560	1570	1580	1590	1600	1610	1620	1630	1640	1650	1660
Columbus (born 1451)																		
Sir Thomas More																		
	Sir Thomas Cromwell																	
		King Henry VIII																
					Queen Elizabeth 1													
							William Shakespeare											
											Oliver Cromwell							
																	Civil War	

Cromwell, Thomas (1485–1540)

Cromwell, Thomas (1485–1540)   He was an ancestor of **Oliver Cromwell**. Tom was a lawyer and chief minister to **Henry VIII**. You may take your pick, he was either a political hack who betrayed all and sundry (including his one-time friend **Anne Boleyn)**, or the chief architect of England's Reformation and Parliament's ascension over the monarchy. The monarch in question, **Henry VIII**, was one monarch who probably needed some Parliamentary supervision.

Cromwell was the 1st Earl of Essex and the king's right-hand-man from 1532 to his execution eight years later. He engineered Henry's annulment to **Catherine of Aragon** but failed to get the pope's blessing, so Henry dispensed with the pope and made himself the head of the **Church of England**. Cromwell set up the rules of how the church would work and Henry made him the Vicar General as well as the Vice Regent. This was new; one guy who was second only to the king in both matters political as well as religious, but politics and religion were much more intertwined then.

Things went well for Cromwell as he saw Henry thru three more wives (one died in childbirth, one was divorced, and one was executed) until Cromwell engineered Henry's sixth marriage to a German princess. He had hoped to stir some German rectitude into the English Reformation, but it turned out Katherine Parr was not attractive enough to suit Henry so he had Cromwell tried for treason and promptly executed. Years later, Henry would admit he felt badly about how things turned out for his old friend and adviser.

crown -five shillings or one forth of as pound. Today it would be about a nickle, but in the Jane Austen's time for example, a shilling would buy you a modest meal. see ***money***

crumpets -a biscuit-like thing, but cooked in a frying pan. It's classic English breakfast and accompaniment to tea. They are a little like 'English muffins' which are actually an American invention. Just for the fun of it and some extra credit, here is a recipe to make your own.

	CRUMPETS
2 C Flour ½ t Salt 1 t Sugar- 2 C Milk 2 t Yeast ½ t Baking Soda 1 t Vegetable Oil	1. Mix everything EXCEPT the baking soda thoroughly. You should end up with a thickish batter but not as thick as bread dough. 2. Cover and let it do its yeasty foamy thing in a warm place for about an hour. 3. Stir in the baking soda and knock down the fluffiness. Let it ferment for another 20 or 30 minutes. 4. Preheat the pan, (ideally a heavy cast-iron job), and rings over low heat. Add enough oil to your pan to get to a non-stick state. 5. Pour about ½ inch of the batter into the rings Cook about 5 to 8 minutes for the first side. The first side is done when the top is full of little holes and looks dry. 6. Remove the rings and flip them over to cook for another minute or two. Start another crumpet in the ring. Serve with jam or jelly and entirely too much butter.

If you can't find crumpet rings, use the biggest round cookie-cutter you can find or cut the top and bottom off of a large (tuna fish) tin can about 3 to 3 ½ inches in diameter.

Crusades, the There were seven (or eight -it depends on whom you ask) wars off and on from 1095 to 1456. The Crusades were in the Mid-east and England was far enough away not to get too wrapped up in this hot mess. The Normans (French) were in charge during the crusades and the Norman kings viewed England as a questionable source for only barely reliable soldiers, but these kings rarely actually cleared their own calendars enough to schlep off to that hot, dusty, dry, poor, miserable corner of the world

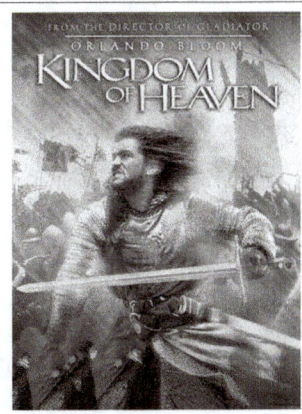

to kill and be killed. One important exception involves the legend of **Robin Hood** and the evil Sheriff of Nottingham filling in for King Richard who might–or might not–have been off in the Holy Lands.

The 2005 movie <u>Kingdon of Heaven</u> is an excellent movie about the Crusades. There are also a number of movies about the legend of Robin Hood, who may -or may not- have been a part of the Crusades in one way or the other. Nice movies to be sure, but based more on legend than history.

currants   -either regular raisins, white raisins, or a little dried gooseberry.

curry   Chicken *tikka masala* has been called England's 'true national dish' with good reason. This version of curry comes on potatoes, rice, chips, and sometimes even pizza. Furthermore, it is served everywhere.

To understand the English love of curry, you need to begin with the notion that while it comes from India, Indian curries and English curries are not necessarily the same thing. For starters, Indian curry has a lot of hot chilies. More confusion comes from England's first cook book <u>The Forme of Cury</u> published circa 1390. The word 'cury' (one R) is from the French 'cuire' *to cook*. It appears to have no connection to the Tamil (Indian) word for sauce, *kari*. And for that matter, 'curry' in India means sauce or gravy rather than a whole dish. "You want a nice dish of curry?" in India would be a little like asking "Do you want a nice bowl of gravy?" in England or America.

In England, curry–the English version of curry–goes back to 1747 and used only black pepper and coriander for spice. Later it would also include turmeric and ginger, and later still, the hot spices. "Curry powder" is entirely an English invention with a long list of spices. Any good cook in India would have his or her own recipe to make a curry sauce.

Between 1858 and 1947, the English were big in India with civil servants and soldiers running back and forth between the sub-continent and home, all the while fetching home a fondness for curry. After WWII, there were also a lot of immigrants from India and curry became even more popular. Today in England, curry means meat (any meat or fish, but most often chicken or lamb) with a thick mild curry sauce often served over rice.

custard   -not to be confused with *pudding* in England. Pudding is (almost) any desert. What Americas think of *pudding* is called custard in England. English custard is thick, sweet, with cooked milk or cream, eggs, sugar, vanilla, and various other things like chocolate, butterscotch, or maybe raspberry, lemon etc.

citaway   -a man's tuxedo coat going back to 1840. The front is cut away and the back or tails are left long. By 1900 it was only worn for very formal occasions.

cutlers   -made cutlery as well as scissors, skates, razors, swords etc. or basically anything with a sharp edge. see *Sheffield*

Scapa Flow

North Sea

North Atlantic

Scotland

Northern
Ireland

Edinburgh

Glasgow

Belfast

Isle of
Man

Pennine Hills

Dublin

L:iverpool

Ireland

Birmingham

England

Cambridge

Wales

London

Cardiff

Thames River

Dover

Southhampton

Brighton

Calais

Portsmouth

Cornwall

Isle of
Wight

English Channel

Gernsey
Jersey

France

Dee comes from Semitic picture-letter for door or fish. Later it came to be Delta -Δ- in Greek and a handy letter for algebra and such. In Old Scottish and Gaelic, D is pronounced as an *unvoiced aspirated apical alveolar stop*. This is to say it's pronounced like a T.

Danelaw   As the Vikings settled in England and came to be farmers more than pillagers and raiders, they hashed out some rules for peaceful coexistence among themselves. This code held sway up the northeast side of the *Angle's Land* (England) and ran from the 9th to 12th century. Now the term refers to the territory under Danelaw as much or more than the law itself.

dawn chorus, the -birds singing in the morning.

degree   English students enroll in colleges, but only universities hand out degrees after exams. Degrees are far less common in England than in America, and by far the greatest part of higher education is done in their polytechnics, which are what Yanks would think of a cross between junior colleges and vocational technical schools. see ***schools***

Department of State see ***Secretary of State***

Devon   -a ceremonial county to the south west. DevonSHIRE is the old name. Exeter is the county's *administrative center.* (American's might say it was the 'county seat', but 'state capitol' would be more accurate.) A mild climate leads to a lot of farming and the coast attracts tourists.

Devonshire Cream -see ***clotted cream***

different from / to / than   Grammar teachers in England insist that it is *different to,* but American teacher say it's properly *different from.* Neither crowd approves of *different than*.

digestive -a small bland cracker like a soda cracker in America.

dinner   -the largest meal of the day. It has shifted around thru history and among the classes. Among the wealthy, dinner would be eaten late in the evening. Among the common folks, dinner might be eaten mid-day, but this is possible only if work and home were very close together. The Elizabethans all had dinner at noon, and 18th century swells had it around 3:PM as did all the classes for Sunday dinner. With the coming of railroads and autos, work and home moved farther apart and going home for a midday meal became the exception. Dinner was pushed to later in the evening. see ***supper***

dinner jacket   -a tuxedo suitable for a formal dinner, but not the one with tails. James Bond often shows up wearing a diner jacket.

Diocese   To Catholics, a diocese is a division of England under the supervision of a Bishop. There are 22 of them in England and they are gathered into Ecclesiastic Provinces supervised by one of two Archbishops.

   Dioceses in the Church of England are called bishoprics. There are 41 dioceses but only two provinces, These are supervised by boards and councils that are more democratic than ecclesiastical.

divisions, political, of England

For starters, *England* is probably not what Americans think it is. It is just part of *Great Britain* along with Wales and Scotland. Add Northern Ireland and you have the *United Kingdom* or the *UK*. The **Republic of Ireland** is NOT a part of it all -not since 1922 when the Irish War of Independence undid a previous war in 1801 when the English more or less invaded and occupied the entire island. Northern Ireland is still part of the UK. The Republic of Ireland to the south is an independent sovereign nation that was actually neutral during WWII.   There are also three small islands, Mann, Guernsey, and Jersey that add to the confusion, but the last two are much closer to France than to England.

Overall, England is divided up into somewhere between 8 or 9 regions. (It depends on what you do with London.) They go way back to the Anguls, Saxons, and Jutes. London is an important exception with historic, but very confusing and overlapping authorities.

Smaller than the regions are the unitary authorities, and the counties. Counties are further subdivided into metropolitan and non-metropolitan counties. Think of English counties as bigger than American counties, but smaller that American States. For the reader, they are somewhat like big American cities wherein the political duties of both the city and county are combined, but in England, they are more like a combination of state and county. History attains throughout. Originally, counties were the possessions of dukes -the top of the peerage heap. Sometimes mere earls could run things, but dukes and earls both appointed a **Lord Lieutenant** to make sure the income kept coming in. With the coming of the **Industrial Revolution,** populations moved around so eventually they had to reshuffle and re-sort just to keep Parliament more or less Parliamentary with the **Reform Bill of 1832.**

Below counties etc., are districts that may also be called cities, boroughs, royal boroughs, or metro-boroughs or metro-districts. These were sometimes further divided into civil parishes. These last are rare, small, and when they exist, they are important historically because they are what remains of the Catholic church's local authority from before the Protestant Reformation.

If a student were to spend the time to understand the modern-day layout of it all (and it would be a thankless effort) then he or she would have to start all over again to figure it out for Scotland, Wales, and Northern Ireland.

Takeaways for the Reader:

- All of England -the UK -England, Scotland, and Wales- would fit comfortably into California.
- The modern Brit feels about *the council* in much the same way a Yank would feel about *city-hall.*
- The local church ran things in town until about the time of the **Protestant Reformation.**
- The Lord of the Manor ran things on his manor but occasionally the reader will find a rapacious Lord who also ran things in town to greater or lesser degree.
- The English tried to sort it all out legislatively in 1956, 1972, and once again in 1995. Progress has been made, but it's still confusing
- One possible reason for the UK voting to withdraw from the European Union was the possibility that the whole thing would have to be adjusted yet once more to comply with the Union's thoughts on how it was to be done.

The following table might be of some use if the reader really wants to understand it all -if only a little.

	Regions	County	District	Parish
All of England	1. North West 2. North East 3. Yorkshire & Humber 4. East Midlands 5. West Midland 6. East of England 7. South East 8. South West	6 Metropolitan Counties	36 Metropolitan Districts	(many) Civil Parishes
		27 Non-Metropolitan Counties	201 Non-Metropolitan Districts	
		56 Unitary Authorities		
		Greater London	32 London Boroughs	
			City of London	

Scotland, Wales, and Northern Ireland all use a completely different set of rules and organization.

divorce Divorce thru history in England illustrates the roles of marriage and ***women,*** and it's not a pretty picture in some ways. For starters, it was difficult to get divorce thru most of England's history, particularly for the rich. This is because marriages were all about combining two estates and lots of wealth. Marriage often began not so much with love and affection, as much an involved business negotiation. Divorce would have been an impossibly complicated thing to unravel.

On the other hand, marriage was expensive and difficult for the common couple, so they often didn't bother. Divorce might have been marginally easier for the common man, but death at a young age and especially during childbirth sadly made divorce a little redundant. Barrenness and adultery were grounds for divorce, but only if the wife was the adulterer. Up until about the time of Shakespeare, a divorce could only be granted by ***Parliament. Henry VIII's*** invented the ***Church of England*** so he could set aside ***Catherin of Aragon***, but this did not make divorce easier for anyone but Henry.

Some American trivia: Benjamin Franklin never married Debora Read, the mother of his two children and whom he loved and with whom he lived happily for 44 years till her death in 1774. She had been married before, but her husband disappeared. It was rumored he had run off to be a pirate, but it could not be proved, so there could be no legal marriage to Ben..

dock -where the accused sits during his or her trial. It is not clear how it might relate to the word *docket* if it all; the later being an official list of cases to be tried.

dog collar -slang for the cleric's collar.

Dole, the -originally money paid out from the parish to various people and for various ends. It applied to unemployment benefits only after 1919 and was a derisive term. *On the dole* is not charity, but more like America's unemployment insurance.

donkey's years   -a very long time -think of it as America's *a coon's age.*

doolally / go dolally   -gone crazy or insane. It probably refers to a soldier and is considered a consequence of battle fatigue.

Doomsday Book   William the Conqueror sent out what we would think of today as county assessors to determine every man's holdings and what they were worth for purposes of taxation. Because the decision by these assessors was absolute and could not be appealed, it came to be called The *Book of Judgment* and later, the Doomsday Book.

dormitory   -what American's might think of a bunk house or barracks with many beds in a large room, particularly in a **public school**. A *dormitory suburb* or *dorm town* is like what Americans think of a *bedroom community.*

Dorset   -both a county and a region on England's south coast. Dorset is a **ceremonial county**, a **non-metropolitan county**, and has its own **County Council**. Despite all the confusion as to its political and governmental status, it is a nice place to vacation because of the scenery. see **divisions**

double cream -whipping cream.

Dover   A town of 33,000 people on the south-east corner of England. It is the closest point to France, and was an important ferry harbor before the **Chunnel** and airplanes. It was also within range of German long range cannons. Over 10,000 houses were destroyed during WWII and it was nick-named *Hell Fire Corner.*

Dover, White cliffs of
-a geological formation of chalk (calcium carbonate or fossilized algae) that sticks up out of the ocean as much as 350 feet.   They are hugely popular to the Brits as a natural wonder and even more so as a symbol of protection against the rest of Europe, i.e. Napoleon and Hitler. If you read about WWII pilots, you will surely come across the relief they felt when they nursed a damaged plane over the English Channel and at long last spotted the White Cliffs of Dover.

dowager   -initially a widow who got to keep her husband's title and / or property after his death. This was often because she was the mother of the inheriting peer. Now it likely means any woman of wealth, a certain age and deserving respect

dower and curtsy   Dower was the property a woman could retain when her husband died -hence the word *dowager.* Curtsy is what a surviving

husband got to keep. A *dower house* was a small house on a corner of th
e estate for the inheriting son's mother. see *women* and *marriage*

dowry   This is the seemingly archaic system of buying and selling
daughters, but for two things: It lasted well into the 20th century, and it had
more to do with making sure that daughters could continue to live in the
manner to which she had grown accustomed while living with her parents.
Back in the day, the money was given to the father of the husband who
guaranteed things for the daughter if the son and husband ran off or died.
None the less, a rich young woman's dowry made some cracking good stories
of contemptible young men, often in pretty uniforms, and sad brides who
often took ingenious revenge on the swine. While the aristocratic practice of
dowry may have gone somewhat underground, it really took a hit in 1882
when women were permitted to own property in their own names. see *dower
and curtsey*

Downs, the   A sheltered area at the south-east corner of England off
the coast of Kent County. It wasn't quite a harbor, but more of a staging area
for fleets during the age of sail. It has shallow water with good anchorage.

Do you hear there?   In the Royal Navy "Do you hear there?"
proceeds a ship-wide announcement. It's like America's "Now hear this."

dragoon   -a mounted
soldier going back to the early
1700's. They fought as a light
to medium cavalrymen with
both a saber and a large
handgun called a dragon.

They would get there quickly, and then get off their horses to fight with a
musket like infantrymen.. As you might have guessed, the word comes from
dragon because their guns breathed fire. see *Army, English*

dram   -a very little of something. In very old cookbooks, it is more or
less a teaspoon. If a reader runs into the word in another context, it probably
means some small but non-specific measure of liquor.

drapers / linen drapers   These were the only people licensed to buy
cloth from manufacturers or to import it from the continent. Today's system
of going into a store and buying something off the rack that was ready-to-
wear simply didn't happen until early in the 20th century. A customer would
buy his fabric from a draper and take it to a tailor who would then make the
garment.

drawers   -underwear or a swimming suit. In the old days, they were
men's stockings and later, long underwear. see *combinations*

drawing room   -originally, the room where women were presented at
court. Later, is was the room where women withdrew after a formal

Victorian dinner while the men were having a cigar. In a public house, it was where the family could withdraw to enjoy some privacy. see **houses**

drovers   English cowboys that drove cattle from Scotland to the rich grassy midlands to be fattened and then drove them on to market. Drovers were, however, much more civilized than America's cowpokes, and probably rich, at least until the railroads took over because it was cheaper and faster to put cows on trains to get them to the big city. Drovers had to be licensed as early as 1552, had to be landowners, and had to be married. Set aside the image of the American cowboy and his horse. A better picture of an English drover would be a rich guy brokering deals involving lots of cows that he may never have seen.

duel   The English were sensible in this matter, or at least after the days of mounted knights bashing the stuffing out of one another in medieval jousts. Dueling never gained the faddish popularity in England that it did on the Continent, particularly among the French. It is estimated that 10,000 French twits got themselves killed during a dueling fad late in the 16th century and about 4,000 more during a similar fad about a hundred years later. Even so, one historian suggests the only about 20% of these *single combatants* actually got killed. Consider America's Andrew Jackson who claimed to have fought 14 duels. Later, western cowboy gunfights (exceedingly rare though they actually were outside of the movies) were uniquely American *affairs of honor* but with considerably less ceremony than was thought to be the proper form involving rules, seconds, and witnesses as it was the case in Europe.

Duke / Duchess   Just under the Monarch, Dukes are the highest of the English peers. The oldest son of the king is always the Duke of Cornwall, and other sons are always the Duke of Somewhere Else, but there are other non-royal dukes. There are only about a dozen of them these days.

dustman   -a garbage collector in the old days, but to use a more current and accurate word, a *recycler.* There was value in rags, metal bits, bones, wood scraps, etc. in an economy where everything was made by hand. Today the English dustman, like the American garbage man, simply tosses it all in a truck and hauls it away to the ***tip.***

dyers   Here is an example of a seemingly simple thing by today's standards that was complicated back in the day. ***Elizabeth I*** was concerned about the amount of money being sent overseas to buy dyes, so tariffs were erected as a matter of course. To her government's credit however, they did some 16th century research & development and came up with local sources of blue, black, purple, orange, red, maroon, brown and yellow dyes. Cochineal (beetles) for bright red, and indigo (a flower) for blue-purple still had to come from somewhere else.

E is THE single most popular letter in English and a lot of other languages as well. It descended pretty much unchanged from Greek (epsilon) to modern usage. **E** sits smack in the middle of the *Great Vowel Shift*.

Earl / Countess   -the third level of the peerage, below the Marquess, but above Viscounts. There are no official titles for Earl's wives because there are no female earls -only men may inherit earldoms. *Countess* is the best we can do for the wife of an earl, but there are no English Counts. There are not a lot of female peers who are not married and none at all before the 17th century. There are now about 25 to 30 earls and some of them are also Marques. This is another area wherein you would have to be English to even begin to understand this. It has to do with one guy owning land over here where he is an Earl and owning some other land over there where he is a Marques.

East Anglia   -the eastern most part of central England. It is named for the Angles and is very flat and marshy -at least until the Romans built sea barriers. More land was turned to farmland in the 17th century with drains and diversions. At about this time, it was also where England kept its Puritans until they went off to America. During WWII it was where the Brits and Americans kept their bombers. Now it's where they keep the counties of Norfolk (*northern folks*) and Suffolk (*southern folks*).

East End   -the poor part of London to the east of the city, but with fuzzy and contentious boundaries. Back when London was a small walled village, there was a separate area of docks, warehouses, and what we would call slums today. Crime, prostitution, dive-bars etc. were all part of it. In the 19th century it became a center of small manufacture and sweatshops. Throughout and to this day, it is where new poor immigrants first make their way in England. It is also the center and origin of *cockney*.

East India Company In 1600, a private stock company was set up to trade in India. First, they set up trading posts, then they had to oust the French. This was done with a private army. Next, they had to corrupt the local leaders and nobility. They did this with admirable British efficiency by making the Brahmins richer than they were before. Things started going downhill in 1857 with the Sepoy / Indian Mutiny. A lot of people died and the crown dissolved the company and took over things in India in 1873. see ***colonies, commonwealth,*** and the ***English Empire***

Edinburgh -the capitol of Scotland and its second largest city. Edinburgh is on the Firth of Forth and was the trading center for eastern Scotland and a center for brewing and medicine. During the 18th century, it was also an intellectual and cultural center -often called the *Athens of the North.* (Edinburgh was more philosophical but Glasgow leaned more toward science and engineering).

Edward VIII *(1894 – 1972)* Edward was the king in 1936 for about ten months when he abdicated the throne to marry Wallis Simpson. He was a fan of the Nazis, didn't like court fussiness, and perhaps worst of all in the eyes of the powers that were, the object of his affection, Mrs. Simpson, was an American who had had two previous husbands. Both Ed and Wallis had to go. Edward was given the governorship of the Bahamas as much for the allowance it paid as it was to get him out of the public eye. The couple spent the rest of their lives in France. Edward was a rather sad character.

egg It is strange that something as ordinary as a hen's egg can be telling in England, but it is so. Rich people boiled eggs and served them in little porcelain egg cups or had the cook gently poach them. Working people on the other hand liked their eggs fried and often put them in sandwiches. English *egg mayonnaise* is what Americans could call egg salad. English *eggnog* is powerfully alcoholic and while it may have an egg, it does not have cream.

Egypt -an English possession / colony / protectorate from about 1800 when they took it away from the Ottomans and the French. They kept it till 1936. What is interesting about this is that this explains why they write books and make movies about Victorian Egyptologists being pestered by re-animated mummies. It's also why some of the best collections of ancient Egyptian artifacts are in England's museums. see ***Suez***

elections National elections in England are for Members of ***Parliament***. The members of the majority party then select the executive part of the ***government*** made from the ***Prime Minister*** and his ***Ministers / Secretaries.*** The elections are scheduled every five years, but if the ***majority party*** is not actually major, they have to either form a ***coalition government***, or start all over with more elections. Local elections might be held more often, but usually every two years.

eleven -a cricket or football team

first eleven -to be on the varsity cricket or football team at school

eleven plus -an exam given to children at about age 11. It was discontinued as schools converted to the *comprehensives.* see *schools*

elevenses -morning snack at 11:AM

Elizabeth I (16th century)   Born 1533, crowned 1558 at age 25, died 1603 at age 70. Elizabeth was the daughter of Henry VIII and *Anne Boleyn* -his second wife. She was born a year after Anne and Henry were married, but there is some confusion as to when they were married publicly rather than secretly. When Elizabeth was three years old, her mother was executed.

    She was crowned eleven years after her father's death and a confusing royal family squabble. Edward the Sixth was the king after Henry. He was

Jane Seymour's son -his third wife, and the only one to give him a male heir. The boy was about ten years old when he was crowned and died at sixteen. Next up was *Mary 1*, the daughter of Henry and his first wife, *Catherine of Aragon*. Catherine and Mary were both devout Catholics and Mary won the title of "Bloody Mary" because she executed many Protestants. She died five years later and finally Elizabeth got to be queen at age 25.

    She was a pretty good queen and never married, hence the nickname the 'Virgin Queen.' She was Protestant, but not rabidly so. She also followed the advice of some reasonably honest councilors. She fought some inconclusive wars against the French, Dutch, and Irish. The most important war was with the Spanish, but she got some help from the weather which sunk the Spanish Armada in 1588.

    During her 46 year reign the English did some pretty important things. William Shakespeare and Christopher Marlowe were writing. Francis Drake sailed around the world, and the Catholics and Protestants more or less got along. All of this was not so much her doing, as it was the consequence of her being a long-term survivor, skillful in foreign policy, and predictable in her policies. There are more than a dozen movies about her. Perhaps the best one is the 1998 movie Elizabeth with Cate Blanchett, but Elizabeth R with Glenda Jackson is also very good.

Elizabeth II (1926 - 2022)   Born in 1926, crowned in 1952 at age 26 when her father George VI died, who became king when *Edward VIII* hung it up and ran off with an American divorcee.

    She was thirteen years old when England entered WWII and this became her entree to public duties. Other than some discussion among the Brits of Republicanism and the abolition of the monarchy, she was a popular queen, who has traveled all over the world to visit England's *possessions* in ceremonial or PR roles.

England has gone thru some significant changes during her long reign, and like Elizabeth 1, the changes were not so much her doing as her having lived thru a lot of history. She has reigned longer (70 years) than her great-great-grandmother Queen Victoria at 64 years. She was also the longest lived British monarch ever at 96 when she died in 2022. Elizabeth has four children, her oldest son Charles was married to Dianne, and fathered her grandchildren William and Henry. In his turn, William had two further great-grandchildren, George (born 2013) and Charlotte (born 2015).

For a very deep dive (50 episodes !) into England from WWII to the 21ˢᵗ century, there is Netflix's The Crown (2016–2023).

Elizabethan Era   When you come across this expression, think of William Shakespeare. Or if you read about the Shakespearean Era, think of Elizabeth. She was born in 1558 and Bill was born 6 years later. She died in 1603 and he shuffled off in 1616. They knew each other. She was a patron and he wrote some beautiful poetry about her in A Midsummer-Night's Dream.

While art and literature flowered in Tudor England, there was more to it than that. Elizabeth saw the beginnings of colonial expansion (Virginia and Canada), significant economic growth, and even the little guy was doing better, or at least eating better.

Any movie made from a Shakespeare play will give you an insight to this era, but carefully note where the play is set. The Merchant of Venice, for example, happen in Venice, not England and Hamlet takes place in Denmark.

Empire   -almost, but not quite, the colonies. Go back far enough in history and northern France might have been a part of the English Empire, but they gave it back to the French about 1550. Then there were the American Colonies, but that also proved to be temporary. The real English Empire upon which *the sun never set,* involved parts of the Caribbean, Africa, & China, and the jewel in the crown of empire, all of ***India***. see ***colonies***

Enclosure Acts (old spelling ***Inclosure Acts***)   Up until the industrial revolution, farming was so primitive and inefficient that land was not a limiting factor -labor was more important. There was plenty of land–the common land or simply the *commons*–to go around. If one plot of land was depleted and no longer good for growing oats, the farmer would simply plow up the next patch of land. Starting around 1500 farming and land husbandry was beginning to be understood and practiced and so farmers began to take better care of the land. They used fertilizer etc. which was expensive and so this effort only made economic sense if the farmer owned the land or had a very long lease. One popular proverb of the time ran...

Lime and dung for yourself. Marl for your son and grandson
...and another one ran...
Manure for yourself, sand for your son, marl for your grandson

Sanding is just that, hauling sand into the field to break up heavy soil and marling is to treat the acidic soil with lime or calcium carbonate. Both are expensive and difficult, but over the long term, these practices made for more profitable farms.

The Inclosure / Enclosure Acts then were all about taking land from the commons, and putting it under the care of long-term investor-farmers. Presumably this was a good thing as far as feeding people was concerned. Not so much if you were one of the guys who had been farming in the commons. Between 1604 and 1914, some 5,200 individual acts took 6.8 million acres of the commons and enclosed it so rich people would recover their investments in soil improvement and conservation.

engineers   This occupation has evolved alongside science and technology. The first mention of engineering functions in England goes back to the early 1600's and dealt with draining fens or swamps. They built bridges and roads a bit later and were surveyors in the 18th century. They only started doing things with actual engines after James Watt invented – perfected actually– the steam engine about 1781. But the guys who built these engines and railroad locomotives, as well as power looms and such, were called ***machinists***.

English Civil War   Several wars actually, two big ones, one from 1642 to 1646, another from 1648 to 1649, and several smaller ones in Scotland and Ireland. There were some distinctions between these wars, but it all came down to the Catholics against the Protestants.

The importance of these wars comes down to two things; the ***Protestant Reformation*** that split off from the Catholic church, and the ascendancy of ***Parliament.*** This was not yet our modern notion of democracy, but getting closer.

Catholics	Protestants
Loyal to the king	Supported the ***Parliament***
"Cavaliers" because they were big on the flamboyant fashions of the day.	"Roundheads" because they didn't go in for fashion and cut their hair short.
Didn't actually execute anyone, but killed a lot of Protestants anyway.	Executed ***Charles I*** and exiled his son Charles II.
Loyal to the pope.	Called Catholics "papists."
Felt the king's authority was absolute.	Were pretty sure the king could govern only with Parliament's

	consent.
Would eventually crown **Charles II** and see some of the church's property be restored.	Lead by **Oliver Cromwell.** Allowed **Charles II** to be crowned, but kept him well under Parliament's control.

The best movie about the Civil Was probably is <u>Cromwell</u> released in 1970. See *Cromwell*.

English Commonwealth see *Commonwealth*

English Muffins   -not even English. They are an American invention.

English Peerage   -basically, rich people. The Peerage of England was replaced by the Peerage of Great Britain in 1707 with the Act of Union with Scotland. (Ireland and Wales were still out in the cold.) Up until the House of Lords Act of 1999, all peers could sit in the House of Lords. In order of status, it works out as follows:

1. Duke / Duchess
2. Marquess / Marquesses
3. Earl
4. Viscount
5. Baron / Baroness

These positions are hereditary; the oldest kid gets the title. Baronets are hereditary, but not peers. **Knights**, Dames, and **Ladies** etc. don't rate as peers.

Enlightenment   After the Renaissance (roughly 1400 – 1600) spread from Italy to the north, the Enlightenment spread south from France, Germany, and in no small measure, from Scotland. The French philosopher Descartes, Englishmen John Locke, Francis Bacon, & Isaac Newton, and the Dutch Baruch Spinoza, are all responsible for the notion that *reason* might be more useful in sorting out things than Catholic dogma.

To oversimplify to a huge degree, French Enlightenment concerned itself with the proper role of government, the Germans pondered the proper role of everyman, and the English, the Scots actually, either ignored it or found a way to make a buck out of it.   Benjamin Franklin visited Europe and brought some of this thinking home to Thomas Jefferson, who used it in some of his writing.

Ensign -either a military unit's flag, or the young officer-in-training who carried it. Ensigns were replaced by sub-lieutenants in 1880. The US Navy still has ensigns as its lowest ranking officer.

entail   -this legal idea means that property may be entailed to several people successively. Consider knights and their non-hereditary estates that could not be given to their children. This means that someone could live off the income of the property, but when he died, it went back to the king and then on to the next guy. Entail could also be used to assure that the property went to the oldest son and explains why finding the correct husband for many

of Jane Austin's characters was such an important issue.

Essex   -the county just north-east of London on the North Sea. There is industry to the south, very high unemployment to the west, and wealthy bedroom communities to the east. In the 1990's *Essex Man* came to be the stereotype for people a bit like Americans would label as rednecks.
Essex Girls Think of them as America's Dumb Blond. The expression got started in 1980, but now applies to such women all over the country.

Eton   -a small town known for an old (1440) and prestigious ***public school***. The *Eton crop* is a woman's short hairstyle a little like what American flappers wore at about the same time (the 1920's). An *Eton jacket* was originally a short jacket for children, but occasionally coming into and going out of style for women.

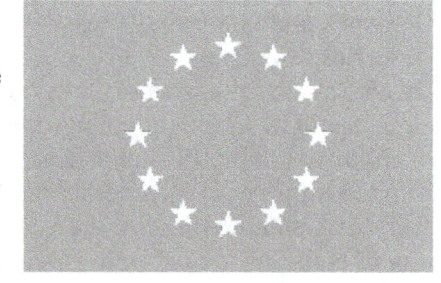

European Economic Community   - founded in 1957, it is an organization to simplify certain matters regarding the movement of goods and money between its members including Belgium, France, Italy, Luxembourg, Netherlands and West Germany. It may be called *European Common Market* of just the *Common Market*. Initially it concerned itself with customs & tariffs, coal & steel, atomic energy, and materials. In the 1990's it gathered up most of western Europe into the *European Free Trade Association* and by 1994 the *European Economic Area* consisted of 15 countries. It culminated with the ***European Union***.

European Union (the *EU*)   -The *EU* is now a country about half the size of America, but it has about half again more people. When WWII ended in 1945, ***European Economic Community*** got its start. In 1957 they went on to have themselves various associations, treaties, & conferences. It's hard to say when it was finally unified, but 2002 is as good a date as any because this was when they unified their currency. Today it has 28 member countries, a population of 510 million, and a nominal GDP of $19 trillion -$37,900.00 per capital. (America's GDP is $16.8 trillion and $53,000.00 per capita.) This is all well and good, but in June of 2016 England voted to exit the EU.

Exchange, The Royal   -dates back to the 16th century and was where merchandise could be bought and sold in London. In fact, many towns had similar but smaller markets. As the economy grew, commodities like grain, metal, and even money were exchanged.

Exchequer -not quite the equivalent of the American Treasury, but close. Originally, it was little more than the nation's book-keeper, but about 1620, HM's Treasury took over this function. Now the Chancellor of the Exchequer is very much like America's Secretary of the Treasury.

Exeter -a town in the far south west corner of England famous for its cathedral -the Church of Saint Peter. It may also be a college at Oxford that had J. R. R. Tolkien as a student.

Express -a daily paper, but over time, and in various iterations, the word has taken on shades of what Americans might call tabloid journalism.

F is tricky. In old Greek it was a vowel, but in Latin, it is the ancestor to U, V, and W. 300 years ago, it showed up in printing in place of *s* -but not really. The italic looking *f* is actually a double **ss**. In German (the ancestor of the English language) they use an *eszett -ß-* for the double **s**. In modern English, **f** can be pronounced as f as in *off*, like a *v* as in *of*, but in German, *f, v,* and *w* are all mixed up—at least to the minds of English speakers.

F

Factory Act   A rather grim bit of history, or an attempt to correct a grim situation, but one that illustrates how difficult life was for Dicken's poorer characters like Oliver Twist. In 1819, the first act forbade children under the age of nine from factory work and limited sixteen-year-olds to a mere twelve hours a day. In 1833, a second crack at the situation limited those less than thirteen years of age to no more than a forty-eight-hour workweek, and those under eighteen to only sixty-eight hours. In 1844 women could only work twelve hours a day, and children under thirteen could only work six and one half hours a day. In 1855, all textile workers were limited to twelve-hour days. see *work* and *apprenticeships*

fair   There are lots of fairs in English literature. In medieval times, a fair was a big and more or less an annual *market* gathering while a market was smaller and happened more often. Fairs were often for a specific commodity like wool, sheep, geese, etc. These annual fairs often attracted sin and vice of every description, sometimes to such an extent that the original commercial purpose of the fair was eclipsed. *Pleasure fairs* or *fun fairs* came to be like American traveling circuses or the smaller and deicer carnivals. *Trade fairs*, however, still happen but these are now more like conventions in America held for assorted professions and /or industries.

farriers - looked after horse's feet.

FC   When you see the name of a city followed by F. C. or just FC, it refers to a football (soccer) club. i.e. *Chelsea FC* or *Manchester United FC*.

Father Christmas   England's Santa Clause. He brings gifts and has a white beard like in America, but in England he wears a long white robe and doesn't do the reindeer or chimney thing.

feast   Up until the early 1700's a feast most likely referred to a given saint's day and only after that it was a big meal and / or celebration.

fellers   -were more than just tree chopper-downers. This they did, but they did so in fall and winter when the sap was down. They dried the wood very carefully, and shaped trunk & limbs into curved knees to make ships etc. Trees were important things and nothing was wasted. see *barkers* and *charcoal burners*

fiddle   -to cheat or avoid the tax-man.
fiddling -of trifling importance but not necessarily dishonest.
Fiddler's Green   -heaven for sailors full of rum and tobacco.

fiefdom
-basically, the estate or domain of a feudal lord. A fief or fiefdom was inheritable and given to a vassal in exchange for 'fealty,' (*in fee*), by the king or other over-lord.   A fief did not have to be land. It could also be a governmental office, a monopoly, or taxing authority.

fire   -a fireplace, furnace, or space heater of any sort burning wood, fuel oil, propane, natural gas, or even coal, at least up until 1956 when the Clean Air Act was passed, coal was banned, and replaced with natural gas.
Fire see **Great Fire**

flannel -washcloth
flannels -flannel trousers, casual wear usually, and just the thing for hunting.

flashers -turn indicators on a car. (*Hooter* is old fashioned word for horn.)

flat   -an apartment. A self-contained apartment on one floor of a building large enough to have several flats on that floor. Originally it meant all the rooms on a given floor.

Fleet Street   -alongside the Fleet River which is a tributary to the Thames in London. It is now synonymous with printing and publishing. Fleet Street was also the location of a debtor's prison that shows up occasionally in literature, but it was torn down in 1846.

floors, building   -a bit confusing but important. In England, the bottom floor is the Ground Floor and the next one up in the first floor. The American third floor is the English second floor, and so on up.

fog   Yes, London has a lot of fog, but in 1952 it turned out it was actually smog. A combination of peculiar weather patterns and coal burning *fires* made it so bad it killed between 4000 and 6000 people and made another 100,000 sick.

food   Any large group of people going back centuries will evolve a cuisine based on what the environment might provide that could be eaten; no great surprise there. From the viewpoint of the 21st century, it is vital to remember that thru-out most of human history, getting enough to eat from that environment was no small thing. While starvation still exists and is not to be made light of, we live in a time of wonderfully plentiful, healthy, and cheap food. As recently as the 60's, a middle-class family might spend as much as a quarter of its income on food. Today it's a little over 10% and now it involves lots more meat and far less home-grown vegetables. As we look at the history and evolution of English cooking, it is important to keep the specter of starvation in mind.

For starters, England is an island and fish have been an important part of the diet for millennia. Fish are easily dried and dried fish can be tucked away for a rainy day. They are easily transported and therefore good for trade. They are a good source of protein and protein is ever the tricky and expensive part of any diet. During much of the Middle Ages, cod and herring were northern Europe's single most important source of protean. Dried fish are naturally salty and salt is also important.

Consider this: cows provide beef, deer give us venison, pigs are made out of pork, but the stuff we eat that comes from fish is called 'fish' and when we dispatch a chicken, we eat 'chicken.' Why the disconnect between big animals and little ones? Remember the Norman (French) Conquest of 1066. The victors and anyone who wanted to hang out with them spoke French (or Latin) and ate beef, venison, or pork. The little guy, who shoveled up after the big animals, still spoke the common language that would become English, and he ate fish or chicken if he was lucky.

Consider also the knight in shining armor. He is an expensive fraud and far more likely to be a soldier for hire than he was a rescuer of damsels in distress. Take his horse; a little horse weighs about 850 pounds and a big one that was big enough to carry around an armored knight might weigh north of 2000 pounds. People were smaller back then (but not as small as you might have heard) and a man weighed in at 160 pounds on average. Now a horse can eat hay, but the people who had horses were more likely to feed them about 10 to 20 pounds of oats every day. Anyway you do the math, you could feed an entire family or one horse.

Porridge (oat, pea, or wheat with maybe a nibble of meat or fish) was what kept the Medieval common-man alive, at least till the next harvest. In today's terms, think of life for the little guy back then as having hot oatmeal three times a day up until about 1589.

This was then that Sir Walter Raleigh came back from the new world with these astounding new things called *potatoes*. Much to be said for potatoes and a lot of what was to be said was that potatoes weren't porridge. The Irish were so keen on the potato and the Irish environment so potato-friendly that an entire Irish family could be fed on as little as a quarter acre. At least up until 1845 when the potato famine killed all the potatoes. About a million Irish starved and another million left, most of them for America.

The stereotypical English gentleman with his glass of claret was a long way off. Not a lot of grapes grew in England, particularly during the mini ice age from 1645 to 1710, so what to drink? Cider and beer. Drinking water was apt to kill you, but let apple juice ferment and you get mildly alcoholic cider, or toss a handful of grain in water and then let it ferment, and you get beer. Both were safe to drink. Make you a little tipsy, but you didn't die of cholera. If all you were doing was plowing the oat field, being tipsy was not a big deal. And everyone was tipsy pretty much all the time -men, women, *and children*.

Louis Pasteur figured out how germs caused diseases about 1857, but old wives knew that boiling water made it safe to drink long before that. Taste some boiled water (after it cools) and you will find it tastes filthy. But if you steep some leaves in it, it gets tasty. Or make coffee and it becomes not only tasty, it keeps you awake. Actually coffee got to England a little before tea did.[1] Coffee came from places like West Africa but tea came from China and India, and the colony of India was an important English Colony. Some Englishmen in another colony liked tea as well as the ones back in England, but got into a twist about the price of tea so they threw a bunch onto the Boston Bay and decided they weren't going to be English anymore, but rather 'Americans.'

But tea is only half the story. Sugar is the real economic engine. Several big trends start trending about 1750 and sugar sits in the middle of a lot of them. First, the English little guy has began to leave the farm and comes into the city to work in factories around whirring buzzing dangerous machines. Being tipsy is no longer a good option. As the industrial revolution unfolded, the English developed a taste for sugar. Follow this trend: in 1700 the English ate 4 pounds of sugar per head per year, in 1800 it was 18 pounds, 36 pounds in 1850, and 100 pounds by 1900. (BTW, in the US in 2012, the figure was 130 pounds of sugar and high-fructose corn-syrup per person per year.)

Sugar was a luxury product, but it was getting cheaper throughout the 18th and 19th centuries, and a lot of it went into tea. It also went into jams

---

1 Lloyds of London -the famous old insurance exchange got its start as a waterfront coffee shop. Lloyd found a clever way to bring the customers in. He hired guys to go out and gather gossip about the ships which he would post on a chalk board in his shop, sort of a 17th century gossip web-site. This information was useful to rich guys who were willing to write their names under a posted insurance solicitation (to *underwrite* a risk) as well as the ship owners who wanted insurance on their ships and posted these contracts, also in Lloyd's London coffee shop. The rest -as they say- is history.

and jellies like never before, and candy became common and affordable. (Chocolate would come along later.) But a nice sweet cup of hot tea was just the thing to keep workers productive. England's sugar came from the West Indies with the help of slave labor. A byproduct of cane sugar manufacture was and still is, molasses and molasses makes rum. Furthermore, while England was starting to make things out of iron like railroads and steam engines, they were also making a lot of big rollers, gears, and levers to use to crush sugar-cane, drive sugar mills, and run distilleries in the West Indies. By 1750, all of England's Navy was paid for with sugar revenue. All manner of history lies at the feet of sugar, slavery, the Industrial Revolution, and the English Navy, but let's stick to food.

As England got good at making things, it got wealthy and the population grew -in number, size, and health.[2] Agriculture, however, didn't keep up. England simply imported food as well as cotton, lumber, and certain metals. Cotton came from India (when it wasn't coming from the American South, like during the American Civil War) and India was also the source of the most English of all food. It's not roast beef. It's curry. **Curry** is not so much an Indian food as it is a complete Anglicization of something vaguely Indian and of minor importance in real Indian cuisine. No less a personage than Queen Victoria was mad for curry and now almost 180 years after her coronation, the English are still eating more chicken *tikka masala* than any other dish. According to their Food Standards Agency, today two-thirds of eating out in England is Indian food, or perhaps more accurately, what the English think of as Indian food. Real Indian food is so spicy that it would likely melt the faces of most Englishmen.

England was still an Empire when Queen Victoria died in 1901 and Edward VII became king. The Victorian Era was thought to be very proper and straight laced if not prudish. Those of a psychological bent say that the Victorians were repressed and given that their new and popular king was a big eater and an even bigger philanderer, the Edwardians really cut loose and had themselves a Dionysian Ball. The 14 years between Edward's coronation and the start of WWI were a good time to be a super-star chef. Dinner parties were competition to see who could spend the most money. Eight courses and as many as 50 pieces of cutlery and china for twenty guests. Meals often ran to five hours.

It all ended with the start of WW I. One of the many causes of this war was England's terror of a naval blockade and starvation on a biblical scale. Throughout most of the 19th Century (and all of the 20th century) England was a big importer of food. The importance of her navy is very clear. Things didn't improve much after Armistice. The Depression hit England nearly as hard as it did America.

German submarine warfare nearly fulfilled the English concern about

---

2 Despite legend to the contrary, Napoleon was actually about average in height for the French of his day, it's just that the English were taller than the French, about two inches on average and better nutrition was probably the reason.

starvation during WWII, but things weren't any better in Germany. During this war, the German pilots who were shot down over England were interrogated by a very smart and crafty Brit. All very polite and proper, it was more of a conversation than an interrogation that started the afternoon the pilot was brought in. The English officer would begin by apologizing for the fact that there were no beds available in the POW camp for officers. They would sort it all out in a day or so, but in the meantime, the pilot could bunk with the enlisted POW's. This was an intolerable affront to a German officer, particularly old-family Prussian officers.

But there was another option. If the German would give his parole as an officer and a gentleman, this is to say, a promise not to try to escape for the next day or so, he could come home with the English officer and have a nice bath, eat a meal with his family, and sleep in his own room, just until they sorted out the POW officer's quarters. Usually the pilot would choose this option and give his parole. They would drive off together in the Brit's car. On the way home, the English officer would mention that his wife had asked him to do a little shopping and they would stop in at a little neighborhood grocery store to buy beef, butter, cheese, eggs, sugar and maybe even a little bacon for breakfast the next morning.

The next day, they headed back to the POW administration building to process the pilot and have a nice chat about the war and how things were going back in the father-land. Now it is important to remember that for a good bit of the war, Germans were eating rye bread and little else. The meal he had so casually been given the night before may have been best food he had enjoyed in a long time. The pilot had to conclude that the war was going very poorly for the Germans while the English were only slightly inconvenienced by it all. The following chin-wag often produced more useful information from a sadly deflated and discouraged enemy than beatings and torture ever would.

Now the reality was that the officer did not have his own car. Nobody did except maybe some generals and they had drivers. The grocery store was a scam and only opened when this English intelligence officer was coming by with a German pilot.   The other shoppers were actors and once they had 'bought' their food, they went around to the back door and returned it.

While the Germans were eating rye bread, the Brits were mostly eating oatmeal. Again. This reality would only become clear to the POW pilot when he was processed into the actual officer's camp and found himself eating oatmeal as well. To put food in perspective in England during WWII just a little bit more, in the eyes of the English, American pilots and soldiers stationed in England were said to be "Over fed, over sexed, and over here."

When WWII and rationing ended, the Brits discovered Italian food but having just finished a war wherein the Italians were the enemy, they called it Mediterranean Food. They loved it, but not as much as curry. (Wiener schnitzel and sauerkraut don't show up on the English dinner table very often even to this day.)

The English language shamelessly borrows words from all over the place and no less do the English absorb food from everywhere. Besides

India, they enjoy dishes from China, Thailand, Ethiopia, Greece, and France. The influence of French food goes way back, but it is ever at the high-cost end of the spectrum. What have the Americans contributed to the English table? Sadly, not much except the Colonel's Chicken, the fast-food hamburger, and the American version of pizza which is nothing like Italian pizza. Curiously, one hears from Yanks that it is nearly impossible to get a taco or burrito anywhere in England, but that may be changing.

All cuisines have sauces. The French, for example, have five mother-sauces which are used to make dozens if not hundreds of daughter sauces. The Brits have simplified this. They have three. First is a bland form of mayo called salad-cream for cold vegetables (**salads**), a sweet custard sauce to pour over deserts like **bread pudding**, and finally, there is HP Sauce (for House of Parliament) for everything else, usually meat and potatoes; a little like a mild American steak sauce.

A final word on food in England. It isn't just the Americans who are getting fat. In Europe, England is #5 for percent of the population that is merely overweight (49%) and #4 for obesity at 10%. This according to the World Health Organization. France finished in a slim 10th place. The fattest? Turkey and Andorra are tied. (Andorra is the tiny country in the mountains between Spain and France.) See **crumpets** and make yourself a batch.

Football / Association Football (soccer)   Americans do not quite reach the level insanity and rabid *football hooliganism* the Brits do, but Yanks do know enough about football / soccer. Even so, some history and statistics might be interesting.
- 250 million people play it in 200 countries.
- It is the most popular sport in the world.
- In 1863 the first game was played per written rules in England.
- The International Football Association Board was founded in 1886.
- It became an Olympic event in 1900.
- The Canadians actually call it 'soccer' like Americans.
- The Chinese played a ball-kicking game circa 200 BC.
- The Greeks played a kicking game in 100 BC
- The Romans were playing a similar game by 200 AD

football hooligans   Rabid soccer fans who were often drunk and prone to beating on the other guys. They show up as far back as the 1970's and England's fans are so bad that the rest of Europe is getting very tired of them. see *chavs*

Foreign Office   Up until 1968, this ministry stood alone when it was merged with the *Commonwealth Office*. Its job was to look after England's interests overseas. After '68, it became the Foreign and Commonwealth Office (FCO) headed by the *Secretary of State* for Foreign and Commonwealth Affairs who might be thought of as like America's Secretary of State. The *PM, Foreign Secretary, Chancellor of the Exchequer*, and *Home Secretary* are the four Great Offices of State. Like other ministries, this office has a professional un-elected Permanent Under-Secretary of State for Foreign Affairs.

Characters in the Foreign Office often show up in English literature in the 19th century and early 20th. It is a matter of faith (or bias) that the best and brightest *civil servants* in the Foreign Office were sent off to India. The second string went off to various possessions and colonies, and the least capable civil servants were kept safely in England. For example, *James Bond* worked for *MI-6* (Military Intelligence, Section 6) as a part of *SIS* (Secrete Intelligence Service) and therefore worked under the auspices of the Foreign Office.

fortnight   -two weeks. It may used after the day of the week meaning two weeks later, i.e., 'I'll be back from holiday Monday fortnight.'

French Fancy   -a small pastry similar to -but much fancier than- the American cupcake.
French leave -desertion

frigate   The smallest *ships** in the Royal Navy; it was not a *ship of the line*. Frigates were typically 140 feet long and as long as bigger ships that had more decks and carried more canons, but frigates were fast, nimble, needed moderate crews, and had *long legs*. They could go longer distances without replenishing. They carried respectable firepower of between 20 and 40 guns and were the work horses of the Napoleonic Wars. (The USS Constitution is a frigate.)
*The navy had big *ships*, medium *sloops*, and small *boats*. Most or all of which would look like ships to the modern eye, at least until put one along side a modern ship.

frock   A useful word, 'frock.' In the medieval, a frock was a monk's habit and 'defrocked' meant he was no longer ecclesiastic. Later it came to mean a man's long coat, but by the Elizabethan era, it moved over to women's wardrobes, and even later, it was for children.

full stop   -a period, but in speech it means 'This argument is over. Full stop." This sentence does <u>not</u> have a full stop   This sentence ends in some *inverted commas* for no good reason""""""

funerals   Much can be learned about a society from its burial ceremonies whether primitive tribes in some remote jungle or the historic English. Medieval cemeteries were sort of bone processing plants. When a small parish cemetery got too crowded, they dug up the old bones and piled them all together in a single grave. They also thought best place to be buried was to the south-east corner of the graveyard and facing that direction because the bodies closest to Jerusalem were the first to be resurrected.

This is a comparatively modern letter. It showed up about 230 BC, much later than the Egyptians and Phoenicians dreamed up most of the other letters about two-thousand years earlier. The Romans decided *K* wasn't getting the job done so they invented *G* for the softer sounding *g* -words like *bridge* and *gaol*. *BTW, t*his is the way the Brits spell *jail* but they pronounce it the way Yanks do.

game pie   -a meat pie made with game. In time past, they were made with partridge, pheasant, or venison. Now they usually are rabbit.

Gaelic   -the ancient Scots and Irish languages, but now it usually refers just to the Irish.

gammon   -either ham or nonsense.

gaol -jail. Sound it out -soft G, long A, followed by 'ol'

garden   -another useful word with lots of meanings. Americans have front yards and back yards, the Brits have only the garden. They might have a wee kitchen garden way out back by the muse -the alley. The English garden is for flowers and other pretty things, with one important exception; during WW II when food was scarce and every possible scrap of dirt was used to grow food. Before that, however, gardens were a set-aside on a large manor for formal fussy geometry, topiary, and even an occasional maze on the very wealthiest manors. In the 19th century, gardens became more casual and natural. Other meanings of the word include:
   garden variety -ordinary
   everything in the garden -everything but the kitchen sink
   lead up the garden path -sweet murmurings to influence or seduce

gas   -natural gas is used for lighting in the 19th century, and heating & cooking now. Brits put petrol in their cars and use paraffin where Yanks might use kerosene.

Gatwick   -a back-up airport to the south of London. It is mostly for charter flights and minor league airlines and as such, it implies something just a bit second rate. On the other hand, ***Heathrow***, the larger of London's two airports, is symbolic to the Brits of all that is hateful about modern life.

general   In general, a general was part of a general staff doing thing in a general way far from the action and not as exciting as colonels, majors, or even the occasional captain who make for exciting literature. In times past, anyone high enough to be a general was also a duke or earl and so adding *general* to his title would be a bit much. see ***regiment, army, military***

General Strike   In 1926, the lingering austerity brought on by WW I lead to labor problems. Coal miners went on strike, followed by dockyard, railroad, and utility workers who also went on strike in sympathy. It lasted all of about ten days, and tends to show up in literature as something of a turning point in the English class struggle

genteel   -a word with various meanings. Perhaps it can best be understood when followed with the word *poverty*. (In Gothic literature, governesses were the very model of *genteel poverty*.) The merely *poor* could work and maybe improve their state. But to work was to cease to be genteel or of good birth. *Genteel* characters of the 20th century might have a little latitude in this direction because the word evolved to mean people who lived quiet, respectable, reserved and the altogether stereo-typically dull English life.   see ***gentry*** and ***middle-class***

gentleman   This is yet one more slippery term that tends to mean what the speaker or writer wants it to mean, and furthermore, one that changes with history. Before Shakespeare, it meant a man of good birth, but one who was not fortunate enough to have been the first born. After this, it came to mean any man who didn't have to work for a living, but rather spent his time hunting and riding horses and whatnot. He may have been in the army, but that wasn't really work. Gentlemen show up in government, the church, and the brightest of them sometimes became lawyers.

By the 19th century, some gentlemen were doing science; they researched rocks, plants & animals, physics, history, and often went off to pester primitive tribes in various jungles. For example, Charles Darwin was a gentleman and went off to study finches in the Galapagos Islands. There were contributions made in all the other fields by England's educated but otherwise unoccupied gentlemen. A businessman, even a successful one, was NOT a gentleman. His grandchildren might become gentleman if they went to the right schools and waited until late in the 19th century to do it.

After WW II, anyone with good manners and at least one suit, could claim to be a gentleman. See ***schools, middle class,*** and ***aristocracy.***

Gentry   -yet one more of the many words the English use to separate themselves into *our kind of people* and *everyone else*. In the broadest terms, the gentry fit between the nobility and *middle class* -but England's middle class was very well off compared to what Americans think of as middle class. The gentry owned land in the country, but didn't have titles, and they had to have inherited their wealth. They looked down upon the business of actually making your own money. see *middle class*

George III   -king from 1760 to 1820. He was the third monarch from the House of Hanover but of greater importance, he was the king during the American Revolution as well as the Napoleonic Wars. He was also thought to be mad toward the end of his life but it may have been he was severely depressed. His son, George IV filled in for him as Prince Regent during the *Regency Era.*

Gibraltar, the Rock of   -at the very southern end of Spain, it is a huge rock mountain that forms a perfect fortress to guard the entry to the Mediterranean from the Atlantic Ocean. The distance between Europe and Africa is only eight miles at this point. In 1704 the Dutch and English took it away from Spain. In 1957 and again inn 2002, there were votes as to returning to Spanish rule. The 30,000 people of the city of Gibraltar voted to remain self governing, but the UK still handles its defense and foreign relations. The Rock of Gibraltar and the *White Cliffs of Dover* are both very important symbols of England's invincibility.

gig   -a small coach with one axle, one seat, and one horse, or it's a long narrow rowboat (sometimes with sails) used to get important people between ships and shore.

gin   William of Orange brought a taste for gin to England about 1672 from Holland where it had been a medicine made from juniper berries going back to the middle-ages. It tasted filthy, but medicine was supposed to taste bad. Gin and tonic actually was a medicine after the early 1800's but not because of the juniper berries. It had more to do with the quinine in tonic that was a treatment for malaria in the tropics.

ginger   -a redhead.
ginger up   -to give a little encouragement, as in "Ginger yourself up"
ginger beer   -ginger-ale, but with alcohol.
ginger nut   -a ginger-snap cookie

Giro   -an English *post office* that also operates as an almost-bank for the common folk who don't have checking accounts. Bills can be paid and deposits receipted to be delivered to ordinary banks. Social security payments are mailed to recipients as Giro money orders and cashed there.
Glasgow   The largest city in Scotland and forth largest in the UK,

behind **London,** and **Birmingham,** and **Manchester.** The University of Glasgow was founded there in 1451 and by the 1700's, it was a center of both the Scottish Enlightenment and shipping.

Glorious Revolution Even after all the excitement of the English Civil War, beheading Charles I, Protestants killing Catholics and vice-versa, and finally restoring Charles II to his dead father's throne etc, things were not as quite as settled as things might have been. James II was tolerant of the Catholics and this did not set well with the Protestants, so Parliament went to William III and Mary (James II's daughter) and asked them to be king and queen as co-monarchs in 1688. Bad news for Catholics, but they did sign a Bill of Rights that still serves to limit the monarchy to this day. This revolution was sometimes called the **Bloodless Revolution.**

GMT -Greenwich Mean Time -THE most important time in the world -at least for people on ships who need to know what time it is in England in order to navigate anywhere in the world. see **Greenwich**

go   -get, as is *go sick* in England is *get sick* in America
go-by   -pass.
go begging   -extra or left-over. It often refers to food.
go up   -enroll in school
go down   -leave school
go west   -die
go off   -spoil (as in food)
have a go   -try
go to the country   -throw a general election

going native   Given the Brit's adherence to always doing the right thing, and given their fascination with the exotic east, going native is the ultimate rejection of all things dull and proper. This theme shows up vividly in a lot of the writing of Somerset Maugham, for example **The Moon and Sixpence** about a stock broker who chucks it all to be a painter in Tahiti. It's loosly based on the painter Paul Gauguin. Consider also Joseph Conrad's **Lord Jim** about a sailor who ends up a leader in South East Asia.

Goodman / Goodwife   -a medieval address of respect for an independent householder and his wife. He was probably a master craftsman with **apprentices,** and his wife probably supervised some number of **servants**.

Government, English   Much of England's history has been a long and admirable march to democracy or something very much like democracy. They arguably lead the world in this direction with a little input from the

Monarchy

America	England
None. This is rather the whole point of what made some English colonists into Americans back in 1776.	While the monarch King Charles is largely a ceremonial figurehead. Even so, the Brits are not quite sure what to do with royalty, so the Government is formally referred to as *His Majesty's Government* and the ***Prime Minister*** trots back and forth from ***10 Downing Street*** (like America's White House) to Buckingham Palace (where the king lives) to advise him and get his (ceremonial) blessing on the government's goings-on.

Executive

America	England
The President -elected every four years from one of two parties by an electoral college.	***Prime Minister*** -selected by which ever party in Parliament has the majority. Lately, there has been no single party with a majority, so a ***coalition government*** is formed and they pick someone.

Cabinet:
The English has a cabinet like America to advise the PM and tend to matters divided up much like America's various departments and administrations. The English cabinet, however, is made out of ***MP***'s (Members of Parliament), and therefore political. They are advised by non-political experts in their fields, the ***Permanent Under-Secretaries***.

Legislative

America	England
Two houses: the Senate -fewer of them serving for longer terms, and the House of Representatives -more of them and serving shorter terms. The Senate is presumed to be the wiser and more conservative crowd and the House of Representatives are the more rambunctious and more beholding to the people.	The ***House of Lords*** and the ***House of Commons***, but do not confuse these two bodies with America's division. The House of Lords is now largely ceremonial being as it was made up entirely of rich people back in the day. The House of Commons, on the other hand, is where it's at. The majority party in Parliament IS the government. The word *Commons* as in the *House of...*, does not mean it concerned itself with the common man, but rather that these legislators served everyone in a given district *in common*. As for the House of Lords (more correctly the *House of Peers* -as in *Peers of the Realm*) being largely

	ceremonial now like the monarch. There is, however, one important job for the House of Lords / Peers. They are the source of the Law Lords / Supreme Court Justices.

Judicial

America	England
FEDERAL: Supreme Court -9 justices appointed by the president w/ the consent of Congress. -hears cases at its own discretion. US Courts of Appeal -Justices are appointed like the Supreme Court justices. -must hear all cases brought before them. District Courts. -94 districts and 3 territorial courts. -also a court of appeals **STATE:** (vary state to state) State / Trial Courts. -often held in county courthouse. -judges may be appointed or elected. -hear both criminal and large civil cases. **MUNICIPAL:** Large cities (city & county cities) hear minor criminal and civil (small claims) cases. Small city and town courts probably only hear traffic cases.	It varies between England, Scotland, Wales, and Northern Ireland. In general, the hierarchy of English Courts is... Supreme Court: Like America's Supreme Court, it is the Highest Court of Appeals. England's Supreme Court the–*Law Lords*–only replaced the House of Lords Appellate Committee in 2005. Privy Council: The highest court of appeals for specialized ***Commonwealth*** issues. Court of Appeals: -two division, one for civil and another for serious criminal appeals. -its decisions are final. The High Court: -civil court of the first instance and appellate court reviewing lower court decisions. -3 parts: ***Queen's Bench***, Chancery, and Family Court. Crown Court: -criminal court of both original and appellate jurisdiction. -the ***Old Bailey*** is the famous criminal Crown Court that shows up in literature and is a very bad place to find oneself. Magistrates Court: -lay (amateur) courts, but specialized trained magistrates hear local cases involving licensing, minor criminal cases, youth crimes, and some family matters. County Courts: -district or circuit judges hear civil

	cases including divorce. Despite the confusing list of courts above, the English use a wider variety of specialized courts and tribunals including military, ecclesiastical, maritime, and election courts. There is even one for chivalry, but this court hasn't convened in a very long while.

Regulatory

America	England
.Consumer Product Safety Commission Environmental Protection Agency Equal Opportunity Employment Commission Federal Aviation Commission Federal Communication Commission Federal Deposit Insurance Commission Federal Reserve System Federal Trade Commission	.Over and above the following categories of authorities, England has had to follow the European Union's regulations and its trans-national regulators. At least till they finish separating themselves from the EU. To England's credit, however, many of these organizations are made up more of practitioners within certain fields, than America's career bureaucrats. Charities -one each for England, Scotland and Ireland.
Food and Drug Administration Interstate Commerce Commission National Labor Relations Board Nuclear Regulatory Commission Occupational Health and Safety Administration Securities and Exchange Commission	Education -one for all three parts of the UK and two more besides. Environment -three for each of the three kingdoms plus a forth for the environment as a whole. Finance - six assorted authorities. Health -fifteen councils concerned with the various specialties and professions. Law -six including one for Ireland and another for Scotland. Social Care -four and one each for Wales, Scotland, and Ireland. Utilities -six somewhat overlapping regulators re. water, electricity, phones, gas, sewerage, and nuclear energy. Other -21 other authorities covering everything from advertising to casinos.

Monarchy

America	England
None. This is rather the whole point of what made some English colonists into Americans back in 1776.	While the monarch King Charles is largely a ceremonial figurehead. Even so, the Brits are not quite sure what to do with royalty, so the Government is formally referred to as *His Majesty's Government* and the **Prime Minister** trots back and forth from **10 Downing Street** (like America's White House) to Buckingham Palace (where the king lives) to advise him and get his (ceremonial) blessing on the government's goings-on.

Executive

The President -elected every four years from one of two parties by an electoral college.	**Prime Minister** -selected by which ever party in Parliament has the majority. Lately, there has been no single party with a majority, so a **coalition government** is formed and they pick someone.

Cabinet:
The English has a cabinet like America to advise the PM and tend to matters divided up much like America's various departments and administrations. The English cabinet, however, is made out of **MP**'s (Members of Parliament), and therefore political. They are advised by non-political experts in their fields, the **Permanent Under-Secretaries**.

Legislative

America	England
Two houses: the Senate -fewer of them serving for longer terms, and the House of Representatives -more of them and serving shorter terms. The Senate is presumed to be the wiser and more conservative crowd and the House of Representatives are the more rambunctious and more beholding to the people.	The **House of Lords** and the **House of Commons**, but do not confuse these two bodies with America's division. The House of Lords is now largely ceremonial being as it was made up entirely of rich people back in the day. The House of Commons, on the other hand, is where it's at. The majority party in Parliament IS the government. The word *Commons* as in the *House of...*, does not mean it concerned itself with the common man, but rather that these legislators served everyone in a given district *in common*. As for the House of Lords (more correctly the *House of Peers* -as in *Peers of the Realm*) being largely

	ceremonial now like the monarch. There is, however, one important job for the House of Lords / Peers. They are the source of the Law Lords / Supreme Court Justices.

Judicial

America	England
FEDERAL: Supreme Court -9 justices appointed by the president w/ the consent of Congress. -hears cases at its own discretion. US Courts of Appeal -Justices are appointed like the Supreme Court justices. -must hear all cases brought before them. District Courts. -94 districts and 3 territorial courts. -also a court of appeals **STATE:** (vary state to state) State / Trial Courts. -often held in county courthouse. -judges may be appointed or elected. -hear both criminal and large civil cases. **MUNICIPAL:** Large cities (city & county cities) hear minor criminal and civil (small claims) cases. Small city and town courts probably only hear traffic cases. 	It varies between England, Scotland, Wales, and Northern Ireland. In general, the hierarchy of English Courts is... Supreme Court: Like America's Supreme Court, it is the Highest Court of Appeals. England's Supreme Court the–*Law Lords*–only replaced the House of Lords Appellate Committee in 2005. Privy Council: The highest court of appeals for specialized *Commonwealth* issues. Court of Appeals: -two division, one for civil and another for serious criminal appeals. -its decisions are final. The High Court: -civil court of the first instance and appellate court reviewing lower court decisions. -3 parts: *Queen's Bench*, Chancery, and Family Court. Crown Court: -criminal court of both original and appellate jurisdiction. -the *Old Bailey* is the famous criminal Crown Court that shows up in literature and is a very bad place to find oneself. Magistrates Court: -lay (amateur) courts, but specialized trained magistrates hear local cases involving licensing, minor criminal cases, youth crimes, and some family matters. County Courts: -district or circuit judges hear civil

cases including divorce.

Despite the confusing list of courts above, the English use a wider variety of specialized courts and tribunals including military, ecclesiastical, maritime, and election courts. There is even one for chivalry, but this court hasn't convened in a very long while.

Regulatory

America	England
.Consumer Product Safety Commission Environmental Protection Agency Equal Opportunity Employment Commission Federal Aviation Commission Federal Communication Commission Federal Deposit Insurance Commission Federal Reserve System Federal Trade Commission	.Over and above the following categories of authorities, England has had to follow the European Union's regulations and its trans-national regulators. At least till they finish separating themselves from the EU. To England's credit, however, many of these organizations are made up more of practitioners within certain fields, than America's career bureaucrats. Charities -one each for England, Scotland and Ireland.
Food and Drug Administration Interstate Commerce Commission National Labor Relations Board Nuclear Regulatory Commission Occupational Health and Safety Administration Securities and Exchange Commission	Education -one for all three parts of the UK and two more besides. Environment -three for each of the three kingdoms plus a forth for the environment as a whole. Finance - six assorted authorities. Health -fifteen councils concerned with the various specialties and professions. Law -six including one for Ireland and another for Scotland. Social Care -four and one each for Wales, Scotland, and Ireland. Utilities -six somewhat overlapping regulators re. water, electricity, phones, gas, sewerage, and nuclear energy. Other -21 other authorities covering everything from advertising to casinos.

Americans. While the history is important and interesting, for the reader, a brief comparison of the English and American systems as they are now, might better serve the reader. Be ever mindful that before the Romans came to Britannia, 'government' was nothing more than the oldest and wisest most no-nonsense man or woman in the tribe.

governess   She is concerned with the education of older children. Gothic-romance literature has a lot of governesses because their sad state makes for interesting love stories and plot lines. A governess is the very picture of **genteel** poverty with one foot in the working-class and another in the upper class and not at home in either place -often a sad and lonely place

governor   There are no states as such in England, but they get good use out of the word *governor*. He or she is not likely to be a part of any local government but such a person might be...
   - the representative of the crown in colonies or dominions.
   - the head of a prison.
   - the boss as slang among employees.
   - a respectful term used by Cockneys etc. 'guv'nor' or simply 'gov.'
   - the head of a charitable organization -much like an American
     Chairman of the Board of Trustees.

gown   -much like an American woman's nightgown or evening-gown, but with a few exceptions and a lot more history. In England, a man might wear a dressing gown or what the Yanks call a bathrobe. The black dress-like gown worn by professors and students at some universities have fallen out of favor except for graduation and similar ceremonies. Barristers and justices (judges) still wear them, as do American judges. see **wig** and **barrister**

Grace, Your -the proper address for a bishop or duke.

grammar school   Before WW II these were more or less England's high schools. Students were tested at age 11 and sent off either to trade schools, or tracked for college. These schools were funded by the government or church and were not boarding schools; rather their students were local kids. After the war, they were largely replaced by the *Comprehensives* or converted to fee-charging public schools which Americans would think of private or boarding schools. see **schools**

grant -scholarship

Great Fire   In 1666 most of London burned down. This was everything within the old Roman city walls. It missed Winchester and Whitehall, but burned almost 14,000 homes, and 87 churches. 70,000 out of 80,000 people were left homeless. There were surprisingly few deaths, perhaps because the common folk didn't count; literally, they weren't counted. It was rebuilt quickly, but this was because what burnt down were mostly **wattle-and-daub** timber buildings. It might have started accidentally, or by a retarded Frenchman who was supposedly an agent of the pope, or by Catholics.

Great Vowel Shift   Among people who study how things were pronounced between Medieval English and Middle English, the GVS is terribly important.   Think first of Chaucer whose writing needs some serious help in translation, and then Shakespeare who wrote and spoke *Early Modern English* or more or less the way we do now -with a little help from English teachers anyway.. Between 1400 and 1600, the English went mad for long vowels. *Bit* was good enough for grandpa, but the youngsters pronounced it *bite*. The GVS is also largely responsible for much of the hopelessly confusing spelling we live with today in English, but the fact that the English have taken more words from more other languages than any other language (except maybe the Americans) has undoubtedly contributed to this confusion.

Great War   Until World War II came along, this is what they called World War I.

green fingers	-a green thumb.
green gage	-an ugly little green plum used to make chutney and jam.
green-grocer	-seller of fruit and vegetables.
greens	-usually cabbage or sprouts in England.
green	-an open area in the middle of a medieval village. (The *commons* surrounded the town.)

Greenwich   A borough on the edge of London that is hugely important to navigation and therefore, to the Royal Navy. It is also the site of *zero-longitude a*nd the anchor of Greenwich Mean Time *(GMT).* The Royal Observatory was built there in 1675 to sort out just where the navigational stars were -and *when* they were there- so that ships at sea could figure out where *they* were. Time is so important that this is also the place where today becomes tomorrow for the very first time. see *GMT* and *Navy*

grenadier   -a soldier who threw grenades. The best grenadiers were strong and tall (the requirement used to be 6' 2" !) and hence the word came to imply a particularly big attractive soldier. 'Swearing like a grenadier' was the last word in colorful and expressive speech

grog   -a mixture of rum and water given to sailors every day from 1750 until 1971. Diluting rum just before it was rationed out meant is would spoil before a sailor could save up enough to really tie on on.

ground nut   -an American peanut or goober.

grouse   -a little bird like the American partridge. They were hunted in huge numbers thru most of the Victorian era. It was often a part of massive social affairs put on by the gentry at their country homes.

gruel   -oatmeal cereal on the watery side. You may recall Oliver Twist got in a trouble because he wanted more gruel. see *food*

Guards, the   Now they are more correctly referred to as the King's Guards and stand immobile outside **Buckingham Palace** in old fashioned red uniforms and big funny hats. Originally, they stayed home to guard the monarch while the Expeditionary Forces were for fighting outside of England. see **regiments, army, commission**

guild   From the medieval until well past the time of Shakespeare, whatever part of the economy that wasn't controlled by the crown, was controlled or regulated by the guilds of the various trades. see **work, apprentices,** and **the industrial revolution**

guinea -£1.05 as of 2017. see **money**

Gunpowder Plot   -an attempt by Guy Fawkes and friends to blow up Parliament in 1605. Fawkes was a Catholic and therefor opposed Parliament. He and some friends (from Spain and also Catholic) packed a cellar under Parliament full of gunpowder but were caught before it could be blown up. He was tortured & promptly executed. Now the Brits celebrate Guy Fawkes Day burning him in effigy with bonfires, fireworks and just a little civilized rioting.

There are contemporary images of Guy Fawkes, but between 1982 and 1989 the graphic novels by David Lloyd, V for Vendetta drew a highly characterized version of his face.   A 2005 movie of the same name then popularized this image and it became the Guy Fawkes mask. It is now sometimes worn as part of anti-establishment protests in England and elsewhere in the world. It is also called the 'Anonymous Mask' and thereby useful to protesters.

Guy Faulks (1579-1606)   Guido "Guy' Fawkes was a devout Catholic at a time when this was a problematic religion. He had dealings with the Spanish who were also Catholics and were at war with the Dutch who were England's allies at the time. He and some friends, who were variously Spanish, Catholic, and / or just generally opposed to James I, rented a cellar beneath Westminster Palace and filled it with gun powder—the Gunpowder Plot. Fawkes was discovered before they had a chance to blow it up and he was tried, tortured, and executed about 90 days later.

gutter snipe   Snipes are small marsh birds that are sometimes seen in the city eating out of the gutter so the term has come to mean an orphan or a street urchin.

H*aithces* (and yes, that is how you spell the letter H) It may also be spelled *aitch* in Ireland. In England, dropping the H is for the commoners. It also comes down to a Catholic (aitch) and Protestant (haitch) thing. It's a shibboleth. This means it's "a word or custom whose variations in pronunciation or style are used to differentiate members of in-groups from those of out-groups, with each receiving value judgments of superior or inferior."

haberdashers   In England, haberdashers dealt in what Americans would call *notions* like buttons, thread, ribbon etc. The best and fanciest of these items came from Milan, Italy, and a Milan haberdasher was a *milliner* and this word came to mean someone who made women's hats.

hackney / hack   -originally something rented out like a horse or coach. It would come to mean someone who rented out his or her labor. Later still, the word came back around to mean a horse and carriage, and finally, by the 20th century, it was a taxi.

Hadrian's Wall   About 120 AD, the Roman Emperor Hadrian financed a wall about 70 miles long to keep the barbaric Picts in Scotland and out of civilized Britannia.

haggis   A traditional Scottish dish consisting of oatmeal, suet, spices, bits of mutton, and a sheep's heart, liver, & lung all packed in a sheep's stomach and boiled. It sounds disgusting, but if you were to leave out the lung and cram it all into a pig's intestine, you would essentially have regular sausage.

half-pay   During the comparatively rare times England was not at war, the crown kept officers in reserve and on half-pay.

hangmen -were formally referred to as 'Finishers of the Law.'

ha'penny -half a penny or one 240th of a Pound. At its highest exchange rate with the dollar about 1835, a ha'penny would have the buying power of about $0.50 in 2010. see *money*

hare -larger and tougher creatures than rabbits. Their meat is so tough that the correct way to cook a hare was to roast the thigh and make stew from the rest of the meat with gravy made from its blood. Finally, the hare's speed gives the Brits the expression *haring* meaning to move very fast.

Harrods -a huge department store in London. Goes back to 1849 and now has 200 or 300 departments in a one million square foot store covering five acres of prime London real estate.

Hastings A village on the southern coast of England important for the *Battle of Hastings* where *William the Conqueror* defeated the Anglo-Saxons and brought the Normans to England.

hatters -made hats, but just how mad was "mad as a hatter"? It turns out that beaver pelts were cured and tanned with mercury. There were some processes in making hats that involved the hatter chewing on the pelt a little. No one made the connection in the day, but the symptoms of mercury poisoning were insanity and facial deformity. Witness the Mad Hatter from Lewis Carroll's 1865 novel *Alice in Wonderland,* but the expression goes back to the 1700's

hauler -a trucker in America. His truck is called a lorry.

have on -tease or play a trick on someone.
have a go -do or try one's best.
have up -haul into court or the police station.

headmaster -school principal.
head boy -a senior student used as a good example and usually roundly hated by the other students.
head lad -head stable-man / woman.
headlamps -a car's headlights.

heath -originally a large open area where heather grows. Sometimes it refers to a large flat commons, or to a soggy forbidding moor.

Heathrow -London's largest and most important airport about 16 miles to the west of the city. Like all airports, it isn't a popular place. It's sometimes called "Hell's Waiting Room."

hedgers   -grew, pruned, intertwined, and just generally made hedges that were cattle proof and sometimes even people-proof. Hedging became important after the ***Enclosure Acts*** starting in 1604.

Henry VIII (1491–1547)   Henry was crowned in 1509 at age 18. By all accounts, he was a pretty decent young man; well educated, funny, keen on music & dancing, very tall for his day and considered handsome. Early in his political career, he took council from some of England's best. This would change as he came to dispense with anyone who disagreed with him or displeased him or failed to provide him with a male heir. By the end of his life, he was a total autocrat. He was also a sad figure of a man. He was isolated except for toadies who agreed with him. When he died at age 56, he was syphilitic, bloated, probably diabetic and possibly had a gangrenous foot. Along the way, he fought an assortment of wars –usually unsuccessfully– against the French in 1513, 1515, and 1544, and against the Scots in 1547.

Perhaps Henry Tudor can best be understood by his enemies, real or from his paranoid imaginings. Here are the more famous unfortunates.
> ***Anne Boleyn***
> Robert Aske & 200 of his Catholic friends
> ***Thomas Wolsey***
> ***Thomas Cromwell***
> John Fischer –a Catholic Cardinal opposed to the Church of England
> ***Thomas More***

His marriages ran as follows:
> ***Catherine of Aragon*** -married in 1509 -she died 1533
> ***Anne Boleyn*** -1533 - beheaded in 1536
> ***Jane Seymour*** -died after child birth
> Anne of Cleves -married in 1540 divorced 6 months after marriage
> Catherine Howard -executed for adultery -with younger men and
> Katherine Parr 1543 - widowed 1547

Nonetheless, he deserves some credit; among his achievements are the establishment of England's Navy which would be come the greatest in the world, if perhaps not in his time. Whatever his reasons might have been for starting the Church of England, the dissolution of the monasteries freed up a lot of capital for better use than the pope in Rome might have used it.

hereditary property / title   Wealthy people who owned their stuff so completely they could give it to their kids, were actually limited to the highest levels of the peerage. Knight, for example, were non-hereditary. Upon their deaths, it all went back to the king. In the medieval, knights were supposed to gather any yeoman volunteers they could from the countryside, go fight the king's wars. Between times, their job was to make the countryside productive and pay taxes to the land owner who was probably the king or a duke.

herring   -the fish, but an important source of protein for the common man thru the Middle Ages and beyond

Highlands, the Scottish   The *highlands* are the northern half of Scotland and the *highlanders* are the people who live there. It is beautifully mountainous, rugged, and desolate, but averages only about 1000 feet above sea level and its highest point, Ben Nevis, is 4409 feet high. (America's Georgia is higher on average and has higher mountains.)

The highlanders, however, are not to be dismissed so easily. They gave the Romans fits, the Norman French didn't even bother with them. Edward I tried to take over with various invasions -mostly unsuccessfully between 1298 to 1303. Edward the Third tried in 1335 and again in 1356. Richard II took a crack at them in 1356 and again in 1385, and Henry IV had the good sense to try only once in 1400. No less a personage that Oliver Cromwell also tried in 1650.

Finally, the Brits gathered the southern end of the place into the Kingdom in 1707 with the ***Act of Union***, but this had more to do with James VI of Scotland inheriting the throne than it did warfare. The highlanders to the north were having no part of it. They wore kilts, played bagpipes, made great liquor (and still do) and spoke their own flavor of Gaelic until the 1850's.

hire -to rent. A hire car is a rental car and a hire firm is a rental place.

History, English   *A VERY Brief Overview*
Sometime around 25,000 years ago some maybe-not-quite-modern-humans carved a little fat woman called the Venus of Willendorf in Germany, and then about 17,000 years ago, some entirely human people painted horses on the walls of a cave in Lascaux, France. Not much else happened till the Romans spread themselves all over Europe and made the Mediterranean Sea

a "Roman Pond." This was about at the time of Christ. This period is very interesting to the people who study language but was otherwise rather dull. The Romans petered out about 450 and the Ages got very Dark. The Four Horsemen of the Apocalypse rode rough-shod all over Europe for about a thousand years. As unpleasant as it must have been for the people, not much big history happened till about 1400 when the Renaissance kicked off. A very important thing, this *re-birth*, but it may best be studied in an art-history class.

Long about 1600 the Spanish ran things with a little help with the Portuguese. It's about now that America is mentioned, but the really exciting things were some islands south of China where spices could be gotten and South America where gold could be stolen. North America was good for codfish and not much else. Yet.

In the 1700's England fought with everyone, especially the French, and in the 1800's, things were fairly calm, largely because the English were in charge. This was the time of *The sun never sets on the English Empire* -India and colonies everywhere. In the 20 Century, the Germans fought with everyone and Russia went crazy,

A Slightly Less Brief Overview:

People -or something very much like people, came to England about 40,000 years ago. Then they left because glaciers covered up everything, but the glaciers went away again about 13,000 years ago and the people came back. They had themselves some "ages" -Meso-lithic (middle stone age), Neo-lithic (new stone age), and bronze age. Stonehenge was built in about 3000 years before Christ and was built with big stones but built during the early Iron Age.

The Celts (who would only become English much MUCH later) were just getting started on their Iron Age when the Romans came. Things were fairly quiet when the Romans were in charge, but language got very confusing. The native Celts, occupying Romans, and German(ic) Angles & Saxons all contributed to the mix that would eventually come to be the English language. The Romans left with more of a whimper than a bang along about 450 AD.

It's about now that the legend of King Arthur, Merlin the Magician, and Excalibur etc. were supposed to have happened. It's hard to say for sure. The native Celts, Angles, and Saxons muddled along with occasional visit from the Vikings until the French came in 1066, but they were called the 'Franks' and another language got stirred into the mix. William the Conqueror might be considered England's first king and his 'dynasty' did a reasonable job of running things until it all fell to pieces in 1135. The next ten years were knows as "The Anarchy". Interesting word *anarchy*; it implies mayhem, tumult, and turmoil, but it really literally means *no king* . A monarchy, for example, means one king.

After the *no-king* period, the House of Plantagenet came to be in charge, and it was off to the races with kings, and their thrones, intrigues, wars, and all manner of the stuff that makes for great literature. Confusing as all hell too.   see *Monarchy, Norman Conquest, Protestant Reformation & Restoration, Colonies,* the *Commonwealth, Government, Napoleonic Wars* and battles of *Agincourt,* the *Atlantic,* and *Britain*

HGV   -heavy goods vehicle -an American semi-tractor trailer. Trucks in England are generally smaller than in America being that it's a smaller place with lots of narrow 500-   year-old streets.

High Court   -deals with difficult civil matters, slander, and appeals from county courts.

hiking   -an expression borrowed from America to replace *rambling.* The British have always   been quite keen on having a quiet casual *constitutional* and there is some beautiful countryside to hike / ramble / walk thru.

HMS   His / Her Majesty's Ship / Submarine. *HMAV* is His/ Her Majesty's Armed Vessel. Charles Darwin went to the Galapagos Islands of the HMAV Beagle

Hogmanay   -New Year's Eve. It's very important in Scotland and perhaps even more important than Christmas. Gifts are given, visitors are fed, and *Auld Lang Syne* is sung.

Home Guard   -during WW II, the home guard was a volunteer force made of men too old or otherwise unable to serve in the armed forces.

Home Office   -the ministry in charge of domestic affairs. It is headed by the Home Secretary and deals with police, prisons, fire, immigration, and elections.

home rule   -independence for what would become the *Republic of Ireland.* It was a long time coming; it almost happened in 1886, again in 1896, was approved by Parliament in 1914, but was postponed until 1920 because of WW I.

Home Secretary   Along with the *Prime Minister, Chancellor,* and *Foreign Secretary*, the Home Secretary is one of the four Great Offices of State. This Cabinet Level position is responsible for internal affairs. Like much of the UK's government, the Home Secretary's duties are different in England, Whales, and the rest of the UK. You might think of England's Home Secretary as the head of American's FBI, Secrete Service, and Homeland Security all mixed together. (MI 6 is part of Foreign **Office**'s Secrete Intelligence Service -like America's CIA.)

homely -not ugly as it is in America, but rather comfortable and domestic.

Horsehair / horsehair workers   -used horse and ox hair as well as pig bristles to make an astonishing variety of things including brushes, violin bows, wigs, military plumes, whips, fishing nets, and even window blinds. It was woven to make linings, or curled and used to stuff mattresses & upholstery. The funny looking costumes from olden-times where people had big hips, arms, bottoms etc. are all stuffed with horsehair.

hosepipe   -hose or more currently, a garden hose.

hot ice   -dry ice
hot pot -mutton stew
hot cross buns -an Easter treat -a sweet bun with a cross on the top

householder   -head of the household, but only after about 1832 when men–and only men–who owned a house could vote.

house / home, the English   To understand what the Brits mean when they describe the various parts of their houses, it is necessary to go back a long ways. The oldest castles were fortifications, administrative centers, and storehouses. If you didn't live (and work) in the castle, you probably lived in a *wattle and daub* cottage outside of the castle walls. As homes got bigger, they kept some of the vocabulary from earlier times.

   Halls were a central large room in a castle where most of the indoor goings-on went on. There might have been a throne, feasts, dancing etc. but most of what went on here was household work that was not otherwise done in the kitchen, stables, or armory etc. There were sometimes little chambers along the sides where people slept behind curtains.

   As time went on, the word *hall* came to mean any large room with or without a castle attached. Later still it meant a large home -with or without a large room, and still later, it was a place where England stored its students. The American idea of a hall -as in *down the hall and second door on the right*, would be a *passageway* or *hallway* in England.

   To understand the English need for *conservatory,* which originally were what Yanks would call green-houses, readers need to remember that nearly all of England lies north of the American / Canadian border. London gets about seven and one half hours of sunlight on the winter solstice. (Northern Scotland gets just over six.) By the 18th century, conservatories were attached to nice country homes often as part of the *drawing room* and were for ornamental plants and daytime entertainment. During the sixteen hours of summer days, the conservatory was for after-dinner doings.

The *parlour* or *parlor* is another confusing room in an English house. It comes from the French *parler* -to talk. For a good bit of domestic history, the parlor was a smallish room for quiet family conversations and the drawing room was for larger gathering. Among families that couldn't afford so large a house, and didn't have a drawing room, it was just the opposite. The parlor was for guests but not for the family. The family gathered in the room between the parlor in the front, and kitchen in back which was sort of a combination of dining room and what Yanks might think of as a family room.

To complicate the whole thing even more, under the Norman (French) influence, the parlor was the second room in a two-room cottage–the one without the kitchen and fireplace. It may also have been the room where the family lived when work was done in the other room. (Bedrooms just for sleeping etc., were a long way off for the little guy.) The word *parlour* is now old fashioned -it's been replaced with either **lounge** or the American *family-room*. The **lounge** was originally a separate (more expensive) room in an inn where guests could enjoy a little more privacy than in the public room.

The *sitting room* was for sitting not dining, and not much different from the drawing room, parlor, or lounge, except it often applied to a comfy little room for the family in poorer homes. In wealthy nineteenth century homes with the full compliment of other rooms, the sitting room was probably for women and probably a room that caught the morning sunshine.

Finally, there is the *drawing room* which has the longest and most confusing history. Originally it was called the *withdrawing* room where the family withdrew from the public goings-on to enjoy some privacy. Later it would be where the women withdrew after a dinner party, and then it became simply, the *drawing* room. The confusion arises in what the word means in homes of various levels of wealth and status. Among the wealthiest, the drawing room became the most public room in the home for afternoon tea among the women and then it was where men rejoined the women after they did the after-dinner cigar and port thing. In the royal household on the other hand, the large drawing room in a palace was where women were formally and ceremoniously presented to the monarch, but this room was by no means a *room-of-state*. These days, when a contemporary character refers to his or her drawing room, the author is probably implying he or she is a bit pretentious.

House of Commons   -the theoretically lower of the two legislative house that make up Parliament. It does not mean it represents the commoner, but rather these guys represent various communities *in common*. Originally, they met only when the king needed to come up with a new tax but they were made to meet in the much simpler room that was quite separate from the *House of Lord's* fancier meeting room.

England's long march to democracy, or what Yanks think democracy ought to be, arguably began with the **Magna Carta** (1215), and then bumped along thru the Civil War & the Reformation, and picked up a little speed with the *Reform Act of 1832*. As it did, government got bigger and more complicated and the House of Commons became increasingly important. It also came more and more to represent the common man. Even so, most of its members were wealthy up until the 20th century when Labor Party became more important, but even then, it was largely made of lawyers etc. as it is in America and, like in America, pretty wealthy people. see *government,* the *monarchy, House of Lords* and *political parties*

House of Lords

-the upper legislative body. This is the original Parliament and they advised the king when he asked them. One king, *Charles I*, didn't ask them often enough and it didn't end well for him.

The House of Lords is also called the House of *Peers* -as in Peers of the Realm. It was originally 80 *Lords Temporal* and 25 *Lords Spiritual* (bishops etc.). They pretty much amounted to everyone who owned all the land in the England. (For a long time, a lot of what people might think of as owning a home or building, meant someone may have owned the building, but they paid a ground rent.)

In 1909 King George sided with the little guy and the *House of Commons* on a tax proposal. He threatened to appoint so many liberal Lords it would ruin their conservative majority. The exclusivity of their club proved to be more important to them, so they gave up their right to veto the lower house and their role has been mostly ceremonial ever since.

Today they are in charge of the courts, and they review proposals from the House of Commons, but the Lords can only advise the lower house and slow things down a little. see *House of Commons, government, political parties*

HP Sauce

-named after the House of Parliament and a very popular steak-sauce sort of condiment the Brits pour over roast beef and lots of other things.

hulk

-an old ship with its masts removed and moored in a harbor. They often kept prisoners on hulks; both the ones they decided not to hang, and sometimes French prisoners of war. Once they had collected up enough of them, they put them on real ships and *transported* them to barbaric places like America and Australia.

Humane Society

-volunteer life-guards by the water.

hunt   -riding horses all over the countryside presumably after some poor fox. (Hunting birds is done with shotguns and dogs, and is called *shooting*.) A *hunter* is a special fast horse that could jump fences.

Hussar -a mounted soldier who fought primarily with a saber.
.

**St. Patrick
The Patron
Saint of
Ireland.**

The letter i is closely related to the letter *j* and both were used interchangeably until the middle of the 1500's. The dot over the i? Called a ***tittle***. Why is ***I*** as in *me, myself, and **I*** always capitalized? It goes back to about 1250 in England's written manuscripts so a little pen-scratch of a line wouldn't get lost; much the same reason the lowercase *i* and *j* were given their tittles.

ice -ice-cream. England's *water ice* is sherbet, and *dairy ice* is ice-cream made with actual cream.

incapable -drunk, but not causing any problems, Drunk *and incapable* is quite different from *drunk and disorderly.*

Inclosure Acts see ***Enclosure Acts***

income tax The English have been paying income tax longer than have the Americans. Their first crack at it came in 1799 to pay for the early Napoleonic Wars. The tax ran two shillings a pound, or 10%. The American first got to pay a smallish (at the time) portion of their income during WWI, and it was at about this time that England came up with a two-tier system, a higher one for the wealthy and lower for the not-so-rich. It is currently as follows:

Polite Name	Taxable Income	Tax Rate
Personal Allowance	Under £11,000 ($13,420*)	-0-
Basic	£11,001 to £43,000 ($13,421-$54,460)	20%
Higher	£43,001 to £150,000 ($54.461-$183,000)	40%
Additional	Over £150,00 ($180,000)	45%
* Dollar values as of 2016.		

industrial revolution   While it occurred all over the western world to one degree or another, England was in the middle of it. Many factors contributed to this. A reasonably early bookend and first cause might be the ***Enclosure Acts*** starting in 1604 that were all about vastly improving agriculture that lead to more food and fewer farm workers. What looked like unemployment for these workers, was really more about freeing them up to do the work of making things.

There were rivers, not only for navigation, but some rivers could be dammed up and the water sent over big wheels to make rotary motion to drive machine tools. England had iron and coal, and later, coal was used to make steam that did what waterwheels had previously done with steam engines after about 1776.

England's working population was better educated than the rest of Europe's (but not America's!), and the very well educated inventing class was even smarter yet. Some of these chaps included the above mentioned James Watt, but also James Hargreaves (spinning jenny -1770), Richard Trevithick (railway locomotive -1804), John McAdam (asphalt and road construction -1816 -good roads are not a small thing in an industrial world.), Robert Fulton, (actually, an American, but he invented the steamboat in 1807), William Cooke and Charles Wheatstone (telegraphy -1830's), Henry Bessemer (steel 1850's), and the list goes on.

Then we have ***Adam Smith*** who explained and justified the economics of it all. Over and above all the expensive inventing and prototyping, and making of fancy productive machinery, England has both a stable economy and an excellent banking system to pay for it all. For example, London's Stock Exchange was established in 1770 and America's in 1790. see ***mercantilism, Navy, work***, and ***colony***

India   -"The Jewel in the Crown of Empire." In chronological order, it's history was about spice, opium, tea, cotton, soldiers, and finally, math & computer majors.

In 1623 the Dutch kicked the English East India Company out of the Spice Islands further east. The company then set up trading

posts in Bengal and fought a war with French merchants and traders. The company, being a for-profit organization, hired merinaries to fight for them and finally finished with the French in 1763. By this time tea was a huge money maker. It was so profitable not because the English were particularly good tea farmers, but because they controlled the sea trades and had the better military. Only half of the country was controlled by the Brits and the half they didn't control directly, they controlled by making the local rulers richer.

      Mahatma Gandhi was an Indian educated as a lawyer in London and an entirely loyal subject of the crown, at least originally. He would begin leading India to its independence with passive resistance in 1915. England packed it in 1947 under ***Lord Mountbatten***, and left behind two countries, Hindu India and Muslim Pakistan. It has not gone well between the two ever since.

Inland Revenue   -England's IRS see *income tax*

inns & taverns   These show up in literature of many eras because the neighborhood inn was often the center of news, gossip, commercial dealings, as well as the place to catch a coach to the next town or even to London. Over and above their commonality among the common people in the surrounding community, they were useful settings for intrigue, romance, and drama in literature. From the 15th century onward, they were licensed to sell various sorts of things. It worked out as follows:

Inn	-lodging, food and all sorts of liquor. If a town had only one place, it was an inn and it was *the* place to be on Saturday night.
Tavern	-sold food, ale, beer, and wine
Alehouse / Tippling House	-brewed and sold ale and beer, but not liquor
Beer House	-sold beer and ale, but didn't brew it, and were not licensed to sell hard liquor
Public House / Pub	-(Modern) food, all sorts of alcohol to be consumed on premises and they sometimes offered lodging.
Off-License	-retailer of liquor to be taken off premises -England's equivalent of American liquor stores

IRA   The *Irish Republican Army* is not to be confused with the legal army of the ***Republic of Ireland***. The IRA was an armed militant force resisting what they felt was England's occupation of Ireland. see ***Ireland*** and ***Orange, the House of***

Ireland   People came to this island about 12,500 years ago and by about a hundred years after Christ, they were the Gaelic subset of the Celts. The Roman did not have a lot of luck colonizing the Gaels, nonetheless, Ireland was thoroughly Christian by 500 AD. (***Saint Patrick,*** a real person, had much to do with this.)

    Normans were not much more successful than the Romans, and the English took a shot after the Norman's left. It didn't workout too well for the Brits either until about the 1500's and even then, sovereignty was a dicey thing. In 1690 the Protestants came and that's what finally did it. They simply kicked the Catholics off their land. Rebellions, occupations, battles, a horrible famine, the ebb and flow of rights & the vote for the Catholics followed.

During the potato famine between 1845 and 1852, some million Irish Catholics died, but the Protestant English did just fine. Another million left mostly to come to America. In 1920 Southern Ireland separated itself from England and became the *Irish Free State* and later, the *Republic of Ireland*. (This end of the island actually sat out WW II as a neutral nation.) Northern Ireland was more Protestant than the southern end and remained a part of England, but not a peaceful part. Between 1960 and 1990 there were **The Troubles** which were some serious civil unrest and more occupation by the Queen's soldiers driving about in combat vehicles which were occasionally blown up by the **IRA**.

The Irish contribution to America very important, but out of the scope of an explanation of the English to readers. What is, however, well within this scope, is Ireland's contribution to English literature. This goes way back to the medieval times when the Catholic monks living in Ireland were about the only literate people outside of Persia. The following is a brief list of important authors and poets born in Ireland. Whether they are *Irish* writers, or really English writers born in Ireland, is best left to the literature professors.

Jonathan Swift	1667 - 1745	A Modest Proposal
Edmond Burke	1729 - 1797	On American Taxation
Bram Stoker	1847 - 1912	Dracula
Oscar Wilde	1854 - 1900	The Importance of Being Earnest
G. B. Shaw	1856 - 1950	Pygmalion (aka My Fair Lady)
W. B. Yates	1865 - 1939	Lake Isle of Innisfree
James Joyce	1882 – 1941	Ulysses
C. S Lewis	1898 - 1963	The Chronicles of Narnia
Edna O'Brien	1930 - ~	The Country Girls

ironmongers   -not so much individual people, as the department stores of the day, and the day was the comparatively modern Victorian Era. You would go to the iron-mongers because you wanted some metal hardware or machinery for the home as well as china, pottery, glass, wallpaper etc. Moreover, they would not only sell it, they would install and repair it as necessary. The important take-away here is that the ironmonger crossed many of the responsibilities and *protected territories* of the various guilds. They were evidence of the economy moving from the guild / apprentice system to the more modern mercantilism.

English has no respect for *j*. It is more popular than z, q, & x, but other than showing up in names like Jack and Jill, *j* is a sad bastard child from other lands. Words like fjord and jalapeño have a *j*, but England has neither fjords nor jalapeños and so they don't bother with pronouncing the *j* in such words. In words like *hedge* and *budge*, the -*dge* serves as well as *j*. In fact, it was only in 1633 that any English book on the language even made a distinction between *i* and *j*.

Jack   This perfectly fine first name shows up a lot in English fables and fairy tales. This is because it is the iconic common name for someone who is clever but lazy. Consider Little Jack Horner, Jack the Giant Killer, Jack and the Bean Stalk, and the House that Jack built. Jack Nasty is a man who is nasty & rude. Jack Saucy is insufferably saucy. A jack-a-napes is even worse. Every-man-jack is every last man. The Whitechapel Murderer killed and mutilated five women in London's East End in 1888. He was never caught and so no one knows what his name actually was, but Jack-the-Ripper seemed to suit.

James Bond see ***Bond, James***

James I   -the king who wasn't killed by ***Guy Fawkes*** and friends. By most accounts, he was a pretty good king and probably the smartest one ever. His immediate predecessor was his cousin Elizabeth I.

Jane Seymour   Henry's third wife. She was born about 1504 to an old but obscure Norman family. She was considered a beauty and of somewhat loose morals so she became a pawn in Henry's court. The intrigues were successful and at about age 32, she married Henry shortly after Anne Boleyn's execution. To Jane's credit, she learned from her predecessor that it was best to be seen and not heard and not seen to too great a degree either. In

1537, she gave birth to Edward VI and died shortly after. Her son would be king after Henry VIII died from age ten to age fifteen when he also died.

Jelly -American Jell-O. American jelly is called *jam* in England, *marrowbone jelly* is American aspic, and a *jelly baby* is a fruit candy favored by Dr. Who in one of his incarnations.

jersey -a long sleeve pullover type sweater, warm and rugged, usually with a high collar. An English *singlet* is a sleeveless undershirt, and a *doublet* is a short-wasted snug jacket worn from the 1300's to about the time of Shakespeare. see *clothes*

Jews Clearly a fraught issue, but Shakespeare's Shylock from The Merchant of Venice is not the only Jew to show up in English literature. Jews were expelled from England in 1290. (Spain did much the same thing between 1492 and 1502.) They began trickling back in from Holland during the Civil War. Cromwell of all people, rescinded the 1290 expulsion law in 1656. Charles II was protective and supportive of the Jews because he "seemed to be happy to find one group that did not want to convert him to their religion."* There were still significant restrictions on them until the mid 1800's. Shakespeare's *Merchant of Venice* is a compelling picture into the situation of the Jews in the 16th century but takes place in Venice -not England. It is often performed by local theater groups and is worth seeing as such, but there is also a 2004 movie with a terrific cast. Al Pacino of all people playing Shylock. It's worth seeing if only for this performance.

British English for American Readers. Grote, David, Greenwood Press, Westport, Connecticut, London 1992. This is a great reference for more in-depth study on the subject of the British language.

Jock -a nickname for a Scott -not an athlete like in America.

John Bull A little like America's Uncle Sam, but while Uncle Sam is the government, John Bull represents the citizenry -hale, hearty, and patriotic. While he goes back to the 1700's, he shows up a lot in recruiting posters during WW I much like Uncle Sam at about the same time.

joint   -a roast. It is usually made with all the trimmings and carved at the table with some ceremony. A steak, on the other hand, was easier to prepare & serve and was not at all the same thing as a joint for a proper Sunday supper.

joint-stock company   an old-fashioned version of a publicly held company. Now they are called *Limited Liability Companies* or *LLC's*

jointure -money the inheriting son gives to his mother.

jolly   -a wonderfully useful word, but one whose meaning changes with time and use. From Shakespeare's time, 'Jolly good.' meant pretty good indeed. By the 20th century, this use is more common among Yanks trying to sound British than actual Brits. The word *jolly* in the sense of "You will when I jolly well say you will.", is more like *dang* as in "You dang well will..." Today, a jolly is an expense paid business trip with little work to be done. It would be a boondoggle or congressional junket to Paris to study the lack of rain in Arizona. Finally, to jolly someone in England is to *butter them up* to them in America.

JP's   -a Justice of the Peace. They are not necessarily trained lawyers, but are elected or appointed for intelligence, common sense, integrity etc. They may have assistance from a Justice's Clerk who probably is a lawyer. Judges in highest courts may also be called Justices of the Peace, but are trained as barristers or solicitors. As with all of England's local governments, it varies between boroughs, counties, municipalities and England's possessions. For American readers, think of ***JP***'s as slightly more sophisticated than Sheriff Taylor in Mayberry in the old Andy Griffith TV show, but without the sheriff's duties.

judge   Higher than a Justice of the Peace (a ***JP***) or Magistrate. Judges as professionals are appointed for life and preside over complex civil cases, and serious criminal cases.

It is Greek (Kappa) and stands for kilo or 1000. English is the only Germanic language wherein the *k* sound is always hard -except when followed by *n* in words like knife, knight, knot, etc, when it is ignored altogether.

Kew Gardens   -a 300 acre park* on the southwest edge of London with lots of exotic botany. It started as a park in 1759 and was formally made into the Royal Botanical Gardens in 1840. It has some 30,000 different plants including some James Cook brought home from Hawaii and other tropical islands. It will occasionally show up in literature as the setting for horrible crimes in an otherwise quiet and peaceful setting.
*San Francisco's Golden Gate Park is a little over 1000 acres.

kilt   Yes, it's a man skirt, but with history. Originally it was just a long woven rectangle of dyed wool wrapped around the waist with the loose end thrown over the shoulder. Useful as a warm raincoat, small tent, or even as a 17th century sleeping-bag. After the English finally defeated the Scot Clans in the Battle of Culloden in 1746, the kilt was outlawed -in Scotland. The Scottish Regiments in England (and they were not necessarily actually Scotsmen) were allowed to continue wearing the kilt. It's about now that the kilt turned into just a pleated skirt. BTW, a kilt is properly worn with a tasseled sporran and dirk which is a wee dagger. A sporran was essentially a purse worn on a belt around the waist because the kilt didn't have pockets. See *plaid*

king   For so common a word, it's complicated. King comes to old English from the Germanic to no great surprise. King, queen, and simply *monarch* are all more or less interchangeable. (*Your majesty* is not actually used in England to address the monarch and *your highness* is for prince or princesses. It's much more complicated than this, but if you find yourself waiting to be presented to the queen, someone will explain it all to you first. Otherwise, Americans needn't worry about it.)

In the very oldest literature, a king might be little more than a tribal chieftain particularly in Ireland and Scotland. This explains why any Irish or Scots American doing genealogy inevitably finds they are a descendant of a king somewhere along the line.

The notion of an all powerful king is misleading. They were perceived as filthy rich, but even this is misleading. They were often in debt and sometimes hugely in debt. War is an expensive undertaking when lost, and sometimes even unprofitable for the victor. European history is full of wars and kings playing games with private property, the tax system, and debasing the currency (coining bad money) to pay for those wars.   The ascendance of Parliament did some interesting things; it began to pay some small notice to the little guy -who paid taxes- and limited the monarch's power. Most importantly, it controlled the national purse-strings. During the 1800's nationalism even put government in charge of fighting wars, or more accurately, paying for wars. Kings were increasingly now able to enjoy simply being rich because they owned all the land.*

Even this would change. Going back as far as *George III* (1760 – 1820) the crown began to give royal land, which is to say *hereditary property†*, back to the 'government' in exchange for a fixed but very generous salary and expense account. As expensive as the queen is today, by some measure she and her family are a bargain for the UK. She has terrific diplomatic and PR value.

* Owning land is all fine and well, but its income comes in over time. Soldiers etc. need to be paid right now. The history of borrowing to fight wars is very important to economic history and money.

† In some sense, property and land–even royal land–belongs to someone. Someone who might reasonably want to pass it on his or her children. see ***hereditary property / title***

King's Bench   -not to be confused with the king's court filled with courtiers and hangers-on. When someone was sent off to debtor's prison in an 1800's story, they were there because things went poorly for them in the King's Bench. This court concerned itself with common criminal law up until about 1870 when it got stirred up with some other courts and ministries and became the *High Court*. Thereafter, it tended to large civil matters like suing newspapers for libel and big personal injury cases. It is not the ***Supreme Court*** -but close.

King James Bible / Version   In 1604 King ***James I*** authorized and financed a project to translate the Bible from Greek, Hebrew, and Latin into English, the King James Bible. The job was finished by 1611. This Bible is responsible for an upward trend in English literacy, and their literature arguably becoming the best in the world, but **Shakespeare** probably deserves some credit too.

kipper   Kippered (dried and smoked) herring and tea are a classic English breakfast usually among the urban working class.

knickers   -woman's underpants of the same era of American woman's *bloomers*. (What Americans think of *knickers*–the knee length men's pants worn by skiers and football players–are called *breeches* or *britches* in England.) see **combinations**

knights / knighthood   You will bump into knights in almost all eras of English literature. It's worth trying to get a handle on the subject, but it is a subject of some complexity and confusion. It really only matters to the Brits and it confuses them too. The following will get you through most English writing, but don't use it to settle an argument with any British nobility you happen across.

The most valuable and expensive fighters in the early middle ages were mounted and armored. They all were more or less mercenaries, but some of these warriors were knighted if the king felt they were loyal and capable enough to be sent off to look after things in the countryside. This was in consideration for the knight's willingness to fight. It was only in the 14th and 15th centuries that Christianity and a courtly code of honor get stirred into the minor nobility that were the knights. The Knights Templar personified these virtues, but they were more French than English. But even these knights had more in common with thuggish security guards than heroes of medieval literature.

Historians say that the term *blackmail* comes from armored fighters who couldn't afford a full-time servant (a **page**) who did nothing but polish his armor, so they burnt oil into it to rustproof it much like a cast iron skillet is seasoned. These guys were known as the *black-mail knigh*ts from the color of their armor and chain mail. They were not likely to have a manor to look after and made their livings between wars by jousting. In a tournament, if you knocked the other guy off his horse, you got to keep the horse. Now if the guy went home without his horse, it would be clear that he was a looser. It was likely that he was a rich old guy who *could* afford a full-time armor-polisher but was too old and fat to do well in the joust, so the black-mail knights would ransom his horse back to him at an excessive price. 'Black-mail'–then as now–means extracting money from someone who wants an embarrassing secrete kept secrete. These knights were probably closer to reality than the evil 'black knight' vs. the white knight or knight errant. *Errant* means an itinerant or wandering knight searching for adventure and damsels in distress, or more likely, out looking for a job and his next meal.

By the time, Columbus took off for what he thought was China, the knighthood had become obsolete. There were a few interesting reasons for this: first were national professional armies that were cheaper to train and outfit, as well as easier to mobilize. Second were improvements in guns that were powerful enough to pierce armor. Teaching a soldier to use a gun was faster and cheaper than teaching him to ride around on horses and kill people. Finally, they figured out that a bunch of relatively unskilled guys armed with pikes could mess up mounted knights quite thoroughly. The trick was to have everyone stand close together, jam the tail end of a pike into the ground, and stick the pointy business-end of the pike outward. A pike was a wooden spear that you didn't throw. It had a steel tip and could be up to 25 feet long.

There is an important point to remember about knights going back to the day when the king gave them a manor as payment for military service. These holding were not *hereditary*; the guy's kids were more or less out in the cold

when dad died unless they were knights too. This is unlike the dukes and earls who had wealth to pass on to their heirs. This was not the case on the continent -French, Dutch, Swiss, etc. knights usually got to pass the manor on their heirs. All of Europe and a lot of Asia was feudal for a good long time and as such, the king needed knights to keep the taxes coming in.

;hts around and makes more of them every year to this very day, bu and tradition surrounding the knighthood, and a lot of *this* guy being more impressive than *that* guy.

Knight / Order of the Thistle

The thistle is the national flower of Scotland and entirely appropriate given that a thistle is a prickly thing not to be messed with.

Knight / Order of the Garter

A garter is a belt presumably to carry a sword, preferably a sword blessed by the pope, at least until Protestantism came along.

Knight / Order of the Bath

Yep, bath as in bathtub. Before the ceremony conferring knighthood, the guy took a bath as a symbol of purification.

Knight / Order of Saint Michael and Saint George

A comparatively modern order for diplomats and people in the colonial service.

Knight / Order of St. Patrick

This order is 'obsolete.' When Northern Ireland joined Great Britain and the Southern Irish were either starving or leaving for America, the need for mercenaries stomping around disappeared. So, while the order still exists, it has no members.

Knights Bachelor

The Bachelors are not strictly a Chivalric Order. This is to say you are a knight, and can call yourself "Sir." but you can't join a specific order. You aren't in a club.

There are lower Chivalric' levels that are either 19th or 20th century inventions and usually honorary rather than an indication of military lethality. They include:

Distinguished Service Order -military.

Royal Victorian Order -general services to the crown.

Order of Merit -military, art, science, literature, culture.

Order of Imperial Service -being in the civil service for 25 years. (Yikes!)

Order of the British Empire -miscellaneous military and civil.

Champions of Honour* -arts, science, politics, religion, and industry.

*Yes, that IS the way the English spell *honor.*

Orders of Empire

This is the second broad category but a small one. It is separate from the Chivalric Orders. There are three Orders for India and one for Burma.

Decorations

This is a separate category altogether, but it deserves mention. Readers will meet people proud of things like The Victoria Cross, Military Cross, Distinguished Service Medal etc. They are pretty much all 20th century and all military.

In Literature:

What is the reader to make of the knighthood? In the whole hierarchy from common man up to the monarch, knights are somewhere in the middle. In modern literature, authors use them as self contained and handy characters to spice up a plot line. When the reader bumps into a knight, he or she is probably meant to be an impressive figure. The relative status of, for example, a Knight Bachelor and a Knight of the Bath, is likely only to be meaningful to the chaps in question.

In 17th and 18th century literature, a knight straddled the line between strictly military and courtly. Going back further, for example the Knights Templar and the Crusades, knights were strictly military men or mercenaries.

The romantic chivalrous knight like Sir Lancelot for example, was a fixture in the oldest literature back when literature was either spoken or written in Latin because no one but the clergy could read. Geoffrey Chaucer's *The Knight's Tale* is an important exception, not because of the knight, but because Chaucer wrote in the vernacular that more people could read, rather than Latin. BTW, *The Knight's Tale* is not a story about a knight, but rather a story told by a knight.

know (his / her / your etc) onions -to understand.

The English take a lion as a symbol;
the Welsh favor a dragon

L is a very vexatious letter. Everyone, except for some of the good people from the Orient know how to pronounce it, but the problem arises as to how many of them to use, particularly at the end of words. As is the nature of spelling rules, there are as many exceptions as there are rules. In general, the Brits are in favor of using *ll* while the Yanks often get by with just one *l*. But not always. L is also the abbreviation for *liter* for the metric crowd, as well as *10* in Roman numerals, but the Romans never used it this way.

lace makers   -some of England's best paid working women. Lace came from Holland when the Flemish came to England in the 1560's for religious freedom. It took hours and hours to make and the stuff and it served to show the world just how rich you were. Lace can be seen in rich women's portraits on their gloves, aprons, fans, hats and elsewhere on their clothing. Men often had a little lace peeking out of the top of their high boots. Those silly looking neck-tutus you see in their portraits? They serve some small purpose. They kept your fleas from jumping from your body to your head.

Labor Party   -England's new *Liberal Party*. When the *Liberal* party fell apart between 1905 and 1918, the Labor party emerged by aligning itself with labor unions. They would oppose the Conservative party between the two world wars. After WW II, they supported nationalizing many of

England's industries (notably coal) and National Health. see *political parties*

lacquer -hair spray.

Lady   -either the wife of a Lord or more recently, simply a term of respect for any woman.

Laird   -a Scottish Lord. The chap who occupies a Lairdship or a Scottish manor.

lancer   A mounted soldier who fought with a lance which was a rather primitive weapon that wasn't much used after the 1600's, but lancers and their lances still still part of royal parades etc.

Language, History of the English: There is a lot of it. First there were the Celts who didn't write anything down, or anything that survived anyway. Then the Romans came speaking Latin. In short order, the Angles and Saxons came from West Germany, the Norse Vikings, and finally the French all tromped thru England before the locals would be able to get on with building their own language. They did this a little haphazardly particularly as involves spelling, by stirring it all together into Middle English. (Old English was more German that any recognizable form of what we might think of today as *English*.) Middle English was all the rage from the *Norman Conquest* about 1066 till the 15th century. This was the language of *Chaucer* but the rich people spoke French and the clergy spoke Latin or at least did so during services and ceremonies.
    The transformation from Middle English to Early Modern English, the language of Shakespeare, happened at about the time of the *Great Vowel Shift*. The GVS was the invention of long vowels. That 'e' on the end made all the difference and led to even more irregularities and confusion in English spelling.
    Some experts insist that the publication of King James's Bible in 1611– in **English** no less, rather than Latin, lead to increased literacy in England and thereby contributed to England's wonderful literary history. Shakespeare deserves a little credit too.   see *accent, English*

larder -the pantry. The *butler's pantry* was where the valuable silver was locked-up. The butler supervised the other servants and his pantry served as his office.

lashings -lots, as in *lashings of clotted cream.*

laudanum   -alcohol and opium. It was a good pain reliever. So good in fact that for a good bot of the 1800's, a lot of people, particularly women were addiceds.

laundresses   It may have been a lifetime's work for a woman, but it was as likely to be part-time work done to supplement the family's income. Mechanization to clean fabric came surprisingly late to England (gradually from 1860's thru 1890) but a woman who 'kept a mangle' (a wringer) per parish records, probably took in laundry.

Law Lords -England's supreme court from 1876 till 2005, but this is an over simplification. These Lords were correctly called the *Lords of Appeal in Ordinary* and acted as the supreme court in domestic matters. They were also members of the **House of Lords** until 2005 when England followed America's example by setting up the **Supreme Court of the United Kingdom**.

laying-in hospital -the maternity ward. It derives from the old practice of women staying in bed for anywhere from 9 days to 2 months after giving birth. *Laying in* was also a polite Victorian euphemism for being pregnant.

lease / leasehold Because almost all land was owned by a very few people up until recently, most property was rented rather than bought & sold. A *leasehold* was a rental for as much as 99 years. At the end of the lease, it all went back to the owner. After WW II, *freehold* properties came to be more common and ownership was more or less forever -provided, of course, you pay your property tax every year.

Liberal Party -generally opposed to the Conservative party. The Liberal party grew out of the much older **Whig** party circa 1850 which was in favor of free trade, social reform, and welfare. It all fell apart during the 1910's when it was replaced by the **Labor Party** which was a political view in favor of even more social reform. see ***political parties***

license Reference to a license in English writing probably refers to selling beer or liquor in one way or another.

Life Peers These people straddle the line between the old hereditary *Peers of the Realm*, and the people who actually have knowledge or experience to offer to the **House of Lords**. Now having a fancy title is no longer automatic entry to this House.

line -a regiment in the army. In the Navy, it was wooden men-of-war all sailing into battle in a line.

line-out -in ***rugby***, after the ball goes out of bounds, the teams form two opposing lines, the referee throws it back in, and they push, shove, and just generally politely fight over it.

lines -punishment in school, i.e. writing 100 lines of "I will not hit girls."

lightermen Lighters were shallow-draft cargo barges that were used to unload—or lighten—ships that were not brought to a wharf because they were too deep, or the docks were too crowded otherwise.

literacy in England In 1500, pretty much everyone was illiterate. This is no great surprise. It ran about 99% for women and 95% for men. The 5% of literate men were either the king, very rich, or in the church.

Literacy trended upward slowly but pretty steadily from then on, with more men being able to read than women throughout.

Around 1700, England lead France in literacy (40% to about 30% in France), but well behind Sweden at 90%. Amsterdam & the New England colonies both ran at about 70%. Between about 1725 and 1825, the gap between men and women widened.* In round figures, 65% of English men could read, but only 35% of women could. This gap closed up completely in 1900 to only 4% illiteracy among both men and women.

To put things in perspective, in America today 14% of the population is illiterate and 21% read below the 5th grade level. In England, 16% of adults are *functionally illiterate*, but it must be remembered that these numbers all come from different definitions of exactly what is meant by literacy and grade level, etc.

*Jane Austen published her first book, <u>Sense and Sensibility</u> in 1811 and died in 1817 with one book unfinished (<u>Sandidton</u>), and two to be published after her death, <u>Persuasion</u> & <u>Northanger Abby</u>.

Living   -the income form a parish paid to a rector derived from the 10% tithe. It was a lifetime income that didn't even require him to live in the parish. see *see*

local -one's favorite pub. It may not be the closest, but it is the favorite.

London   The *City* of London is a tiny little part of the whole thing. The 'city' is about a square mile that was actually the Roman fortress of

Londinium, and later, the medieval walled town of London. This is to say that you might have read that someone who was **in** London but was about to go off to 'the city.' Americans might say 'I'm going downtown,' or up-town as the case may be. This little square mile was all there was of London and the rest of London was what Americans might think of as suburbs.

At least until the middle of the 1800's when London started gluing itself together in various ways. Today it has formed into an independent county. The political ***divisions*** of England are terribly confusing, even to the English. An American might think of London as a combined city and county much like some big cities in America like San Francisco, but with one more combination added to get to city-county and all the way up to city-county-state. (States do not actually exist in America.)

It is also the national capital of the UK. London has both a Mayor and a **Lord Mayor**. The former is political, the later is kind of a one-man chamber of commerce at least today, but the Lord Mayor is also the oldest elected position in all of England. He or she is one of the old-fashioned and oddly dressed people in the parade behind the queen's carriage. The regular (political) mayor may be in the parade too, but toward the back and dressed in a regular business suit.

London is so central to all things English and English writing that references to -and places within London- are scattered throughout. Historically, and even before the Romans, it might be named after King Lud, but no one is sure. (For that matter, King Lud himself is a little hard to pin down.) London became an important center of trade (wool mostly) until Queen **Bodecia** burnt it down sometime around AD 61. When the Romans left in about 450, Londonium went down hill largely because it was a good target for the Vikings. This changed a little bit when the Vikings dreamed up Dane Law starting about 800. Dane Law is entirely English and is all about Viking raiders becoming more or less law-abiding English farmers. By about AD 1000 owning valuable things like houses and farms (things that could not be hidden when the Vikings came along) got to be a reasonably good bet once more and so London started growing again. The **Normans** came and built elaborate ornamental things like cathedrals and the **Tower of London.** They also started what would become **Westminster Palace**. The French Normans left in 1066. London bumped along thru assorted wars, religious upheavals, plagues starting in 1348, another big fire in 1666, lots of doings of kings and a couple of queens and just a whole bunch of history. It grew the whole time.

It was the largest city in the world until about 1925 when New York surpassed it. Today it is a little like Yanks might think of it as New York, Washington DC, Boston, and Hollywood all rolled into one. It had a population of a million as far back as 1800, more that two million in 1850, six and half million by 1900. In about 1939 it peaked at a little over eight and a half million but this had to do with WW II. It declined to under seven million in 1981. It has since recovered to eight point six million now.

> **London Bridge**   The original one is in Lake Havasu City in Arizona. The new London Bridge is now a bland concrete thing. Do not confuse the London Bridge with the **Tower Bridge**
> **London Library** -the biggest and oldest library in England.
> **London School of Economics** -with a socialist leaning.
> **London University** -a good school. It admitted poor kids throughout, and even women starting in 1878.
> **London Zoo** -among the oldest and biggest in the world. It's also reputed to be the most humane toward the animals.

loo -a polite word for the toilet. Probably from French *l'eau* -the water.

Lord, the word   Usually followed by "of the Manor" The rich guy in charge of the farm's workers and tenants. It's etymology is interesting. It comes from the Old Germanic *hlāfweard* meaning "loaf-ward" or "bread keeper." In other words, the guy who provided food to his subjects. This meaning would change. Now it is a somewhat slippery generic term for a rich guy, but not necessarily a member of the peerage. Barons -the bottom of the peerage heap are often addressed as 'Lord'. The **House of Lords** might more technically be called the *House of Peers* and its members might be addressed as 'Lord', but there are Lords who are not members of either House of Parliament nor are they peers. It gets more confusing when the judiciary is considered. England's Supreme Court is made out of **Law Lords** and the chaps in charge of the Her Highness' Navy are various **Sea Lords**.

Lords, the people (assorted)   Lords are made out of both the nobility and the gentry. The nobility were guys who could pass their estates on to their kids. In order of the peerage they run dukes, marquises, earls, viscounts and barons. Barons are at the bottom of the nobility but they were eligible for the Parliament. Scottish barons, were non-peers. Below the nobility, were the gentry. These included Baronets, the hereditary knights who *could* pass their estates on to their kids, and regular knights who could not. There were also Scottish clan Chiefs or Lairds included at the bottom of the lower pile of Lords.

There are a whole series of Lords of historically important matters, but now they are usually ceremonial, honorary, and a sinecure. (This means a well-paying job with no actual work to be done.) In general order of importance (or status), they are...

Lord High Stewart -used to be first of the Great Offices of State, but today exists only for coronations. This is the guy who does the thing with the crown when the time comes for a coronation.

Lord Chancellor   -the second highest Crown Minister and responsible for running the courts.

Lord Chamberlain -looked after the King or Queen, particularly the private *chambers* upstairs where only the special people could go. Curiously, the Lord Chamberlain also censored theater from 1737 to 1968.

Lord of the Privy Seal -in charge of the monarch's seal for official documents. (The *Seal of the Realm* is kept by the Lord Chamberlain for agreements outside of the monarch's purvey.)

Lord Chief Justice -second o the Lord Chancellor in judicial authority. He (or she) wears an extra silly *wig* and bright red dressing gown.

Lord(s) of the Admiralty No surprise here, they were in charge of the Royal Navy. They go back to 1628.

Lord High Mayor The mayor of London and the oldest elected office in England. see **London**

Lord Haw-Haw   William Joyce was born in America but grew up in

Ireland. He was what today might be called a political radio personality, but one working for the German's propaganda effort during WW II. His radio show was broadcast from Germany and opened with "Germany Calling." He would then rant on and on in a highly affected upper-class accent. He was captured as the war ended, tried, and hanged for treason in 1946. It is worth noting that (Southern) Ireland was neutral during WWII, but because Joyce was half American, it was treason.

Lords Lieutenant   Back in the day, he was the monarch's local representative. If you encounter one in your reading, he is likely a retired military office or some other old big-wig who now has a largely ceremonial role, but during WWII, he was the chap who might organize some other old guys into the county militia—the ***Home Guard***. Going back to ***Henry VIII's*** day, the Lords Lieutenant took over the military functions and the local ***yeomanry.*** This was formally done by the ***sheriff,*** but with when the Lords Lieutenants came along, the sheriff came to concentrate on maximizing agricultural output and tax revenue.

lose the plot -be exceedingly confused.

Luddite   -angry workers whose jobs were displaced as the industrial revolution brought machinery and mechanization. Between 1811 & 1816 self-employed and highly skilled wool and cotton weavers were pushed out by power looms operated by less skilled and lower paid factory workers. They organized, broke into factories, and destroyed the machines. It all had more to do with the austerity brought on by the ***Napoleonic Wars*** than a genuine hatred of machines. It got so bad in the northwest (England's manufacturing center) that the military was called out to put it down. Similar things happened in the agricultural field surrounding threshing machines.

    The word survives in common lexicon meaning someone who is opposed to, or annoyed by, fancy machines and electronic do-dads, not to mention computers. see ***work*** and ***police***

lumber   -stuff that should have been thrown out, but wasn't. (*Lumber* in America is *timber* in England) A *lumber room* is a large closet. It is also the place the bodies are hidden in a certain genre of English mysteries. Such a room may also be called a *box room.*

lunch   Yes, now it's a comparatively light mid-day meal, but it hasn't always been so. It had to do with candles. Lunch didn't require them, but dinner did so lunch was the larger more elaborate meal. With industrialization, workers couldn't go home for a full midday meal and so they started bringing a portable light meal to the factory. see ***meals***

Scapa Flow

North Sea

North Atlantic

Scotland

Northern
Ireland

Edinburgh

Glasgow

Belfast

Isle of
Man

Pennine Hills

Dublin

L:iverpool

Birmingham

Ireland

England

Cambridge

Wales

London

Cardiff

Thames River

Dover

Southhampton

Brighton

Calais

Portsmouth

Cornwall

Isle of
Wight

English Channel

Gernsey
Jersey

France

The letter **m** comes from the Greeks by way of the Semites by way of the Egyptians. Draw a wavy line and you have water. Chop off all but two waves and you have **m** -and this is probably how **m** came about because the word for water began with **m** in one of these languages. BTW, the use of the Roman numeral M to mean 1000 is a modern invention. The Romans never used it this way. It's doubtful they could count that high anyway, math not being a favorite subject among the Latin crowd.

M   -the designation for motorways like America's freeways. They have limited access, a 70mph speed limit or 112 kilometers per hour, and are bigger than the *A* roads.

Mac...   -Scottish for *Descended from...* For example, all of Donald's kid would be MacDonalds.

machinists   Up until the industrial revolution, the blacksmith, founder,* and carpenter made the tools people used in their work, usually on the farm. As manufacturing mechanized, the increasingly sophisticated tools and machines required a different set of skills -the machinists.
**Founding* is the craft of melting and casting metal

Magna Carta   In 1215 England's nobility -barons actually- had it up to here with King John so they got the Archbishop of Canterbury to write up a set of rules. It covered some protection of the church, protected the barons from imprisonment without a little due process (the king could still do whatever he darn well pleased to the peasantry), some limitations to taxation, and just a hint of what would come to be England's legislative body, the Parliament. Both sides pretty much ignored it and the pope back in Rome annulled it a year or so later. There were some wars. King John died and his son's regents (the boy was so young he needed grown-ups to tend to matters for him) edited it and re-issued The Magna Carta -Mark II. There were some more wars, and the agreement was ignored slightly less than the first time around, but it would not be until 80 years later in 1297 that it became a real part of law. Throughout, it was just for the nobility -the little guy was still unimportant and expendable.

manor -the land under the control of a rich man. He was probably a peer or maybe even a knight, but after the 18th century when the ***middle class*** got rich, they could have manors too.

market -originally these were informal regular open-air gatherings of farmers to sell their output to wholesalers and traders. These markets would come to include industrial output like cloth and manufactured goods. Later still, the towns where the markets convened would support permanent stalls and later still, shops. *Market towns* were given permission to hold a market which was an important thing for a growing town in the medieval era. Markets are the ancestors to *fairs* which were larger annual markets for a specific commodity.

Marques / Marchioness \Number two in the peerage, below a Duke, but above Earl. These people were often used in England's colonies, particularly in Asia because there were similar positions there. The difference between Marques and other peers is a little vague, but it has to do with a vassalage (a property the king has given / lent to a rich vassal) on the border and therefore charged with a more defensive role against invasion than, for example, an earl who was safely inland.

Marquise of Queensbury Rules
Rules of boxing, but may also refer to other sports. Not to be confused with *According to Hoyle* which applies to card games.

marriage Like a lot of English things, the reader might best understand marriage in England with a little history. Not much is known about how the Celts did it. They left no written records. The Romans did it the way the Romans did it. This was a comparatively enlightened view of marriage by today's standards, and more so when compared to what would come later. After the Roman left, the Angles and Saxons held a view of women and marriage that would seem even more reasonable to modern folks. Women could own property, divorce was possible for various causes, and women had a lot to say about whom they married, and most contrary to the way things would come to be under Christendom, they shared -for want of a better word- *ownership* of the kids.

By the medieval, marriage was a transaction of property. The good news—such as it was— was that if neither party had any property, marriage wasn't really necessary. Marriage was also taxed and expensive at certain times and places so a lot of otherwise committed and loving couples didn't bother with it. Not being married makes divorce simple for the poor. None of this is to say people didn't love one another and look after their children tenderly, but things were different. Childbirth took a lot of women, war took away a lot of men, plagues came and went, and took everyone. This explains why we read about people who might have had three of four spouses. Add to this the fact that a 14 or 15-year-old was considered old enough to be out working and making his or her own way in the world. A stepmother, evil or otherwise, might be younger than her stepchildren. Such things that the modern reader might think of as part and parcel of fairy-tales, were everyday realities during the Middle Ages.

On the other hand, if there was wealth involved it got terribly confusing. A daughter was not so much property as she was a liability and if dad wanted to get rid of a liability, he had to be to pay someone to take on that liability. This is why *dowry* shows up in English stories so often, but it was not paid to the groom, but rather the groom's family who assured that the girl would be able to continue to live in the fashion to which she had been accustomed even if the groom ran off with a more attractive woman.

The church also weighed in with a long series of steps leading to a wedding. First there was a contract between the parents. Next, the **banns** had to be read on three successive Sundays in the church were the bride and/or groom live. This would come to be the "let them speak now or forever hold your peace" part of a modern wedding. Then the couple had to exchange oral promises in front of witnesses. This was a minor part of the whole rigmarole that today we think of as the heart of the wedding ceremony. There was often a ceremony in the church but it was not necessary. It was followed by a feast if dad had any money left after the dowry was paid. Finally, there was the all-important consummation. Shakespeare's plays, or the romances anyway, often end with a marriage and often a secret one, but no priest shows up .

So it went for the merely rich. To some degree, all marriages were about making and rearing children and ideally a male heir, and thereby protecting & improving the families' wealth. For the royal families, it was so very much the case as to get even weirder. Charles II (the guy whole father was executed by Cromwell and friends) married Catherine of Braganza, a Portuguese Princess. Her dowry was India. An entire sub-continent with millions of people was the price-tag to get a king to take on the liability that was this single woman.

Given the confusion of just who the next king might be, and who his father might *really* be, the bride and groom doing the consummation thing often had a witness or two– no less than there needed to be a witness when the bride and groom did their wedding vows.

Despite *Henry VIII* having invented the Church of England largely so he could set aside some wives, divorce was not otherwise a possibility even among the rich. The Protestants and certainly the Catholics were against *divorce*, but when you consider the complexity of untangling property and negotiated inheritance, one wonders if this was not so much an ethical position as it was an economic decision just not to bother.

In 1753 Parliament passed the *Marriage Act* that made the Church of England the point man in getting marriage standardized in England and Wales. The church also took on the responsibility of record keeping to the eternal gratitude of historic demographers. It also made very sure the parents gave their permission which in turn made for poignant stories of lovelorn young people, forbidding recalcitrant parents, elopement, disinheritance, and confusing melodramatic scenes like the one where Romeo thinks Juliet is dead, but she is only drugged, so he kills himself, and then Juliet wakes up and finds Romero dead and so she offs herself too. (Shakespeare used a lot more words to get it done though.) Finally, the church made getting a divorce even harder for everyone up and down the economic scale. It was only in 1837 another Marriage Act finally legitimized Catholic weddings.

Thru much of English history, the average folks tended to postpone marriage till they were well established in careers etc. This was pretty much the same way in America but the Brits tended to wait a little longer. The average age for marriage thru the 1800's in England was 25 years of age. What is interesting is that during this time and despite the absence of reliable contraception etc., illegitimacy ran about only 4%. It all made for some stories about long, indeed, very long courtships.

To bring it all to the 20th century, an 1870 law permitted women to keep their wages, and after 1882, they were allowed to keep the property they brought into the marriage, but because divorce was virtually impossible until 1937, it didn't do women as much good as might be hoped. see *women, dowry, divorce, servants*

Martinmas -one of the quarter-days (every three moths) when rents were due during the medieval. It comes on November 11 when the crops are in, animals are slaughtered, and then, after harvest festivals and feasting, people settle in for winter, or at least they did until the industrial revolution and urbanization put them to work year around.

masons More than brick-layers, masons were stone cutters, dressers, and setters. *Free masons* did extra fancy work in *freestone* or soft sandstone. The society (club) of the Freemasons has lots of history, but today is has little to do with actual masonry, other than to suggest that this was a high-status and well paid profession back in the day.

meals Breakfast has always been breakfast, but lunch, supper and dinner are terribly confusing. Before about 1850, the regular people ate their largest meal, dinner, at about 3:PM and usually called it *lunch*. After 1850 and well into the industrial revolution and factory work, *supper* was a light mid-day and the pubs served sandwiches and meat pies at all hours.

Rich people on the other hand, and ate a large *dinner* at noon. Then later, in 19th century, Victorians had a light *lunch* at 1:PM and *dinner* had moved from mid-day to 5:PM and gradually moved still later in the evening during the 20th century. Children might be served a *tea* earlier. Supper was now a late-night snack after the opera etc.

measurement   It's not quite as simple as metric system and the *other* one. There is also the Imperial and US measurements that only involve volume. Americans base their system on the English system of the 18th century, but then the English changed their system in 1824. Cubic inches, feet etc, are the same, but the measurements used in the kitchen work out with 1 US gallon equaling 0.8 Imperial gallons. Both gallons are still four quarts and eight pints, but the English P's & Q's are smaller especially when involving beer. Bushels (9 US gallons) and pecks (2.3 US gallons) are also different.

  Inches, feet, yards and miles are the same between the Yanks and Brits, but a nautical mile is 6076 feet or about 15% longer than a statute mile. There are three different systems of measuring weight that a reader might come across -one for precious metals, one for medicine, and a third for everything else. Weighing big things like ships and barrels of grain involve pounds as a fundamental unit, but pounds gathered into tons, tuns, and tonnes. Other things were weighed in stones -14 pounds. In literature, people are describes as being so many stone i.e. *She weighed every bit of 12 stone,* (12 stone would be 168 pounds and it's always singular 'stone,' not 'stoneS.') In your reading, if you encounter someone described as weighing so many stone, you can either do the math or just conclude they are fat. Bigger than stone(s) are hundredweights -which are not 100 pounds, but rather 112. see ***ton***

merchant   This was rather broad occupation. It ran from *merchant* in the language of the medieval era who was a businessman of any sort. Later it would come to mean an importer or exporter who likely owned or was part owner of ships like Shakespeare's *Merchant of Venice*. Stores as we might think of them today, were owned and operated in good size towns by *retailers*, and way out in the sticks, there were *peddlers or **chapmen***.

mercantilism   -the economic view that wealth derives from trade. This view holds that the correct role of government is to protect a nation's markets thru tariffs etc., and to protect its trade routes to foreign markets and sources of raw materials with warships when necessary.

  Mercantilism is a controversial word like *capitalism* and *imperialism*. Raw materials were turned into more valuable finished products and exported. Importing finished goods was to be limited thru protective tariffs. It was all about what we would call a favorable balance of trade to bring gold and silver into the country. In England, we see the first mercantilistic policies arise as early as the 1500's. When history is viewed thru this lens, exploring the world to get things like pepper, spices, tea, and cotton begin to make more sense. Going to war to protect the merchant class also comes to make more –if sad–sense. It must be remembered that from the 16th century to about the 19th, the word *merchant* meant a guy with ships (like Shakespeare's chap from Venice) who was an importer / exporter and not the guy with a store. see ***colonies, work, Navy***

mess   -originally any group of people who ate together, but the word now refers to military meals. As are many things English, mess is carefully divided up into class, one for officers, one for the middle manager like sergeants, and yet another for the private soldiers. This is not to make light of it; mess serves important social functions of communication and what would now be called *team building*. A *mess jacket* is an officer's formal dinner jacket and a *mess kit* is the less formal dress for dinner, but if you are or were an American Boy Scout, then a mess kit is a collection of dishes, pots, utensils etc for cooking & eating while camping.

meter   -not the meter that is a little more than a yard, but rather what Yanks might thing of as a vending machine in the home or apartment. In England, if you were feeling chilly, you would drop some coin into the heater and enjoy a metered amount of heat from either electricity or natural gas. Since the late 20th century, the system has been changing to the American way with the meter outside and the meter-reader coming by periodically followed by a bill in the mail.

Methodism   -a Protestant sect that split off from the Church of England beginning in 1738. It was a fairly strict sect, but not quite Calvinism. To its credit, the Methodists missionaries reached out to the lowest levels of society in England. see *religion* and *baptists*

mews   -originally a stables, but it might also have been row-houses, and later the alley behind the houses and a small house for a horse or two, a carriage, and quarters above for the chap who tended to it all. With the coming of the auto, little carriage-houses in/on the mews were converted to loft or even little two-story homes. Because they were in wealthy old neighborhoods, an address in/on the *mews* suggested a trendy little home for literature's artists and eccentric characters after the beginning of the 20th century.

MI-5   -Military Intelligence, Section 5. This is for domestic counter-intelligence and security. It got its start in 1909 to oppose the Imperial German navy on behalf of the Admiralty. Today, it's a little like America's FBI

MI-6   -Military Intelligence, Section 6, aka *SIS or* the Secrete Intelligence Service. This office gathers foreign intelligence for Her Majesty's Government like America's CIA, It is also *James Bond*'s employer in most of his incarnations.

midden -a garbage dump.

middle class   -hugely important and often misunderstood term. In America, for example, middle class means in the middle of the income or wealth distribution. In England as the *industrial revolution* and *mercantilism* progressed and made people rich who did NOT own lots of farmland. They did buy manors and elegant homes in the countryside, but this was not at all the same as having inheriting it from a long line of dukes, and barons, and such. The English middle-class stood between -in the middle of- the nobility and everyone below them and were very wealthy indeed; they were just not *Peers* of the Realm.

Midlands   -the middle band of England running east to west. ***Birmingham*** is its largest city in this area, and the second largest in all of England. The Midlands were important to the Industrial Revolution, so literature about the Midlands in the 18th and 19th century might be thought of as like the big industrial cities in America's Midwest during the 19th and early 20th centuries.

midshipman   -a boy or very young man who was being trained as an officer in the Royal Navy. He was usually the son of a wealthy family and acted as a servant. George Washington (an English subject at the time) wanted to be a midshipman when he was 15, but his mother forbade it. His older step-brother served under Admiral Vernon who was the inventor of ***grog***.

Milk Tray   -a box of chocolates made by Cadbury, and often a given to a woman.

milliners   -first a subset of haberdashers who dealt in fancy notions from Milan, Italy, and later became makers of ladies' hats.

millwrights   -made and dressed the big stones used to grind things like corn (what Yanks call *wheat*), barley, oats, beans etc. Each product needed a stone shaped and dressed in a particular manner.

mince   -means almost the same thing in American as it does in British; to mince words is to chop them up small, chose them carefully, and perhaps not say much of anything as a consequence. *Minced meat* is chopped up extra fine like American hamburger (note the D in the word.), BUT *mincemeat* is chopped fruit used to make things like fruitcake.

Minister   -a ***MP*** from the ***House of Commons*** and in the ***political party*** that is the majority. He or she is the head of a government ministry and may also be refereed to as a ***secretary***. Some non-conformist churches are careful to call their clergymen ministers so no one confused them with Catholic priests.

ministry   -like America's federal departments of this and that. While these departments in America are headed by secretaries, in England they have ***ministers*** or secretaries.

minor   -like in America, someone under 18, but in schools, where they address students only by their last names, two related kids, or kids unrelated kids but with the same last name, are distinguished one from the other as, for example, Smith Major and Smith Minor.

Miss.   -a more discerning word in England than in America. For example, in the 18th century Smith family, the eldest daughter, Sally Smith, would be addressed as Miss. Smith, and her younger sisters, Linda and Betty, would be addressed as Miss Linda and Miss Betty. Furthermore, the American distinction between married Mrs. and unmarried Miss blurs for a 20th century tradeswoman or shop assistant who was addressing a patron who might be young enough to be unmarried. A student would address his or her female teacher of any age, married or single, as Miss.

mister   In medieval times, a mister was the *master* of his craft. Master is Middle English from the Germanic *maister* going full circle back to *master.*

Mockney   -mock Cockney.

moderns   -an old-fashioned word for those new classes at university that did not involve Greek and Latin. A *modern* education lead to careers in things like medicine, engineering, accounting etc..

Monarchy   When viewed thru the lens of big history, our modern world without kings being in charge, is a brief experiment. Divine kings go back to the Porto-Indian Era that were even before the Mesopotamian and Egyptian civilizations. To put it mathematically, and using the Yank's 1776 as a historic marker, for every 20 years with kings, mankind has had one year without.

Today the world's only absolute monarchies are religious. There are 5 or 10 Islamic *absolute* or *semi-constitutional monarchies* in the mid-east. The Pope technically is the king of the Vatican. There are some *sub-national monarchies* in Africa, Indonesia, and the South Pacific.

A few *constitutional monarchies* are scattered about Europe, often in little tiny rich countries with casinos. Monaco comes to mind with Albert II, but he is a Sovereign Prince; he's not quite a king. Sweden keeps Carl XVI Gustof around and Japan has Emperor Naruhito. These gentlemen are helped out with the usual mix of Parliament and assorted Minsters of State and wear suits and ties to work. A few other "constitutional" monarchies include Jordan, Kuwait, and Bahrain, but one wonders just how constitutional these places really are.

Queen Elizabeth is also a constitutional monarch, but her realm is a **commonwealth** so outside of England, it doesn't count. It doesn't count for much inside of England either, except for ceremonial occasions, and besides that, they are all quite fond of the old girl. The following might help a reader pin down who was in charge and when.

House / Dynasty	King / Queen	When	Literature	Events
Norman (French)	*William I* (William the Conqueror)	1066 - 1087	King Arthur and Merlin were supposed to	The 1st Crusade 1096

			have fought against the Normans.	
	Henry 1	1100 -1135	A complicated mess re. succession of French vs. English kings begins in 1101 and lasts till 1154	
	Matilda	1141		
Plantag-enet	Henry II	1154 - 1189		
	John	1199- 1216	Robin Hood[1]	
	Richard I	1189 - 1199	Much confusion here. Robin Hood, Evil King John, and Richard the Lion Hearted are all tangled up together.	
	Henry III	1216- 1272	*Chaucer*	
Not quite Plantag-enet, but neither Lancaster nor York	Edward I	1272 - 1307	1343 – 1400 Canterbury Tales-1380	The Last Crusade[2]
	Edward II	1307 - 1327		
	Edward III	1327 - 1377		Black Death 1348 - 1350
	Richard II	1377 - 1399	Another Robin Hood possibility, and a Shakespeare play. Richard's head cook writes England's 1st cookbook, The Forme of Cury ('cury' derived from the French 'curie' -to cook).	
House of Lancaster	Henry IV	1399 - 1413	Shakespeare would write plays about all three of the Henrys, skipped Edward, and did Richard III many years later.	Battle of Agincourt 1415
	Henry V	1413 - 1422		
	Henry VI	1422 - 1461		Joan of Arc burned at the stake 1431
House of York	Edward IV	1471 - 1483		The War of the Roses 1455 - 1484
	Richard III	1483 - 1485		
	Edward V	1483 (never crowned)		
Tudors	Henry VII	1485 - 1509		Columbus doesn't find India in 1492
	Henry VIII	1509-1547	First *New Testament* written in English 1526	Martin Luther published his 95 Theses in 1517 and Protestantism begins.
	Edward VI	1547 - 1553	William Shakespeare born 1564	
	Mary I	1553 - 1558	Reformation (Literature was mostly Catholic vs., Protestant.)	Mary, aka 'Bloody Mary' executed lots of protestants.
	Elizabeth I	1558 - 1603	Shakespear: *Hamlet* 1600, *Romeo & Juliet* 1594	The the Great Plague of London kills 80,000 people between 1665 and 1666.
	The Tudors are a short-lived bunch, but did lots of interesting stuff and fought a lot of wars. Henry Seven's daughter was Lady Jane Grey and			

1. The legend of Robin Hood is scattered all thru the middle ages. The first recognizable writing about the archer outlaw shows up in 1377. It has been embellished and improved to this day in everything from middle English ballads to Technicolor movies.

2. The numbering of the Crusades is a complication beyond this Yank's understanding; there were eight or nine of them -unless there were seven.

was thought to be the rightful queen.

Henry Eight -the guy with the turkey leg- married Catherine of Aragon, Anne Boleyn, Jane Seymour, and a few others. Things did not go well for these women and Henry died without a proper heir. Henry Seven's grandson (Eight's nephew) James I would be the first of the Stuart kings

House / Dynasty	King / Queen	When	Literature	Events
Stuarts	James I	1603 - 1625	William Shakespeare died in 1616.	Shakespeare's MacBeth & King Lear -1605
	Charles I	1625 - 1649		Chuck1 was beheaded by Cromwell
	Common Wealth 1649 - 1660 After beheading Charles I, **Oliver Cromwell** was appointed Lord Protector of the Commonwealth of England, Scotland, and Ireland. Very confusing, but very important. See the **English Civil War.**			
	Charles II	1660 - 1685	British take over New Amsterdam and it becomes New York.	
	James II	1685-1688	Newton published his book on real fancy math in 1687.	
	William III Mary II	1689 - 1702 1689 -1694	*Pilgrim's Progress* 1678	Scotland + England = Great Britain in 1707
	Anne	1702 - 1714		
Hanover	George I	1714 - 1727	Enlighten-ment	Jane Austen 1775 - 1818
	George II	1727 - 1760	(political) writing, i.e.:	The magazine was invented in 1731.
	George III	1760 - 1820	Alexander Pope, Johnathan Swift, David Hume, & Jane Austin	The king who so annoyed the American Founding Fathers and who was was possibly mad.
	George IV	1820 - 1830	*Pride & Prejudice* in 1813	Napoleon dies in 1821.
	William IV	1830 - 1837	Dickens, *Oliver Twist* 1837	Slavery is prohibited throughout the British Empire in 1833.
	Victoria	1837 - 1901	Darwin, *On the Origin of the Species* 1865	The source of all things "Victorian."
Windsor (Saxe-Coburg & Gotha)	Edward VII	1901 - 1910	H. G. Wells, *The First Men in the Moon* 1901	England launches the world's first Dreadnaught battleship 1906
	George V	1910 - 1936	Conrad, *The Secrete Agent* 1901	World War I 1914 - 1919
	Edward VIII abdicated his throne. in December of 1936.			
		1936 -	Huxley,	World War II

House / Dynasty	King / Queen	When	Literature	Events
	George VI	1952	*Brave New World* 1937	1939 - 1945
	Elizabeth	1952 - 2022	J. R. R. Tolkien, *The Lord of the Rings* 1954 - 1956	… and life goes on.

money   English money was so confusing that in 1971 they 'decimalized' it. This means that now it's pounds and hundredths of pounds or pennies. Up until then you needed three numbers to put a price on things. Worked out roughly like this: the fist number (£) refers to pounds or something more than a dollar. The next one (s) is shillings and these are one-twentieth of a pound or a nickel. The third number (d) is for pennies –except that there are 240 pennies to a pound, so a shilling is actually twelve and a half pennies and an English penny is smaller than an American penny.

Slang   There are also various nicknames and slang terms Brits use to talk about their money, but in fairness, Yanks have their share too, i.e. buck, saw-buck, five spot, Hamilton, Franklin, etc. From smallest to largest, the English have…

farthing   ¼ of a penny.

ha'penny   half a pence or half a penny.

tupence   two pence or two pennies.

thrupence   three pence or pennies.

tanner   six pence or pennies.

sixpence   half a shilling

shilling   12 pence or pennies or 1/20th of a pound.

bit   "

bob   "

two bob   2 shillings

two-bob bit   2 shillings + 6 pennies.

half-crown   "   "

crown   5 shillings or 60 pence / pennies.

quid   a paper note for 1 pound sterling.

sovereign   a gold coin equaling a pound sterling.

Abbreviations (and some Latin):

£ Pound sterling -from the Latin *libra*. Gives us *lb.* as our abbreviation for pound today.

s Shilling -from the Latin *solidus* -solid –as in solid metal coin.

d Penny -from the Latin *denaro*.

In the medieval times, you would buy your nails 100 at a time. Big nails like the ones used to nail together your house might run you 16 pennies per 100 or 16d, while smaller ones used to hang a picture on the wall might be 6 pennies per 100 or 6d. Now we buy nails by the weight (pounds in America) but their size is still described in pennies.

History   To make things even more confusing, the English Pound has deflated as has the Dollar, and a single Pound back in the day of the three-number system was some serious money. For example in Charles Dicken's time (he published Oliver Twist as a series between 1837 and 1839) a Pound was worth a little more that $5.00, and this was when a Dollar was also some serious money. A 1837 Pound would have about $130.00 of buying-power in today's market. *see **banking, Bank of England, mercantilism, coiners,** and Chancellor **of the Exchequer***

monopoly   In the days of the powerful **guilds**, monopolies were granted by the monarch for a cut of the profits. They were thought to be good things that kept prices and employment stable for the monopolistic guilds. The public on the other hand, had to pay whatever the guild said. The industrial revolution and the notion of free trade began to erode the monopoly's power. By the time Adam Smith published The Wealth of Nations in 1776, monopolies were seen as bad things and so they remain today. see **mercantilism**

Sir Thomas More (1485 – 1540)
One of Henry's advisors who came to bad end when he displeased Henry. He was a remarkably talented man. He was a lawyer, judge, social philosopher, author, and statesman He also served Henry VIII as Lord High Chancellor of England. He was also a Catholic and this wasn't necessarily a bad thing at the time -at least until Henry demanded everyone declare the King's Supremacy over the English Church. This was a step too far for More, so he was accused of treason, given a brief trial with all manner of court intrigues (No less then Thomas Cromwell played a part), and witnesses of doubtful honesty, and was decapitated in 1540. His last words are well documented and telling. He said that he "died the king's good servant, and God's first."

    The 1966 movie A Man for All Seasons won many Academy Awards including Best Motion Picture. It is said to be very historically accurate.

mote and bailey   -not to be confused with the picturesque water filled moat, a mote is a ditch surrounding a fortification of some sort with a wall (wood or stone) on top. The bailey is an open place or a court yard within the mote. Going way back before fairy-tale times, there was often a hill, usually artificial and often made with slave labor, with a **castle** on top.
MP's see **Member of Parliament**

mummers   In America, mummers are attached to either New Orleans' Mardi Graw, or New Year's celebrations, but in England back in the day, mummers were mimes or amateur actors doing small scale performances. They were often performed in inns and often on religious themes during Christmas or Easter. The clowns in Shakespeare's *A Mid-Summer's Night's Dream* were mummers.

mushy peas   -peas cooked in marrow fat and made extra mushy with a little baking soda. They are a popular accompaniment to fish and chips and a lot of other English dishes. Imagine thick split-pea soup with ham on the side rather than cooked in.

mutton   -meat from a sheep a year old or older. It may also refer to goat in India. It is tougher than lamb, but a little more flavorful, and a lot cheaper.

In ancient Egyptian, the word for *snake,* begins with a *n* sound, so the Semitic letter *n* is a squiggly drawing of a snake. Unless it's a fish as it is in Phoenician, Hebrew, and Arabic, but it's harder to see how a fish looks like an *n*.

Napoleonic War(s)   -a series of wars with France between 1803 and 1815. England fought many MANY wars, but given that their victory over Napoleon in 1815 was the beginning of the almost 100 year long *Pax Britannica*, this war -or this series of wars- might have been the most important. Furthermore, and more important to readers, there is a lot of heroism, tradition, and literature arising from these twelve years.

Americans must be forgiven for thinking that the uprising in the western colonies might have been pretty important along about 1776, but to the English, it was a minor nuisance that took resources away from the more important wars with France. It's a fairly straight line from the French and Indians on one side, with the English and the American Colonists fighting together on the other side in 1750. Then, about 25 years later, the English crown tried to tax the Colonists to pay for it all. The Americans traded sides and then revolted against the mother country. Yanks have to understand England's position–if only a little. Once England got itself out of the American quagmire, the English got serious once again fighting with the French.

Continuing on a straight line from 1776, the colonies, and on to the Napoleonic War, with a quick review of French history, Louis XVI and Marie Antoinette were killed in 1789. France had themselves a Revolution that led to Reign of Terror that eventually led to Napoleon. In 1803 Great Britain, Spain, and a few other countries formed the First Coalition to sort it out. Napoleon won, and would continue to do so for the next three Coalitions. The Peninsular War went badly for Napoleon when he lost to the English,

Spanish, and Portuguese. But he went on to win the Fifth Coalition, and then made one of histories greatest blunders; he invaded Russia in the fall of 1812. The French expected to be home again in time for All Saint's Day (November 1) and they just packed sweaters and an extra pair of socks. By the middle of December, 400,000 men out of the 520,000 invaders died, most of them from cold and starvation.

Note the year -1812. The English were blockading France throughout, and needed sailors to do so. Being a sailor in the British Navy was the very definition of a miserable job and recruiting them got so difficult that the Royal Navy simply took them off what ever ship their men-of-war happened across on the high seas, including American merchant ships. This lead to Act Two between America and England -the *War of 1812*. It was considered a draw. The American Navy raided all up and down the Atlantic and the Brits burnt down the American's brand-spanking-new Washington DC. In the end, everyone decided to more or less call it a draw and just go home.

Returning now to Europe, it went downhill for Napoleon from about then. The Sixth Coalition (England, Prussia, Austria, Sweden and a few others), was another loss for Napoleon. He was exiled to the Island of Elba but escaped in 1815 and put together another army of about 280,000 men. The Brits assembled the Seventh Coalition made from the usual suspects -Britain, Russia, Prussia, Sweden, Austria, the Netherlands and a few small German city-states. This was literally Napoleon's Waterloo. see *Nelson Column, Trafalgar Square*

Napoleon de Bonaparte (the man) Born 1769, he was a French military leader from 1799, the emperor from 1804 to 1813, died at age 52 in 1821. Hard to say why he goes by his first name -Napoleon and not his last name, Bonaparte, but there it is. He was born on the Mediterranean Island of Corsica. He fought in the French Revolution at age 20 and was so good at military strategy and leadership that by 1799 he was France's top military guy and then the Emperor of France in 1804. To some degree, his success was a function of the mess that the French Revolution made where-in anybody who was anybody got their heads chopped off, and ultimately, anybody who knew anybody who knew anybody who was rich faced a similar fate.

His record as a military leader was impressive enough even if it made him England's greatest villain, but the guy did some important things quite aside from what the English call the Napoleonic Wars. He implemented liberal policies in France and much of the various countries he conquered. His legal code, the Napoleonic Code influenced legal systems all over the modern world.

According to the English historian Andrew Roberts, "The ideas that underpin our modern world –meritocracy, equality before the law, property rights, religious tolerance, modern secular education, sound finances, and so on– were championed, consolidated, codified and geologically extended by Napoleon. To them he added a rational and efficient local administration, and an end to rural banditry, the encouragement of science and the arts, the end of feudalism, and the greatest codification of laws since the fall of the Roman Empire." This from an English historian!

There are a couple of interesting myths about Napoleon. Contrary to popular tradition, Napoleon was not short, but of about average size for a Frenchman of the day. The French were just a little smaller that the English back then. (see *food*). There is also a lot of interesting, if speculative, writing as to how Napoleon died at a mere 52 years of age. Was he poisoned? By who? Why? And so it goes.

National Health   Health care in England has been paid for by a combination of health insurance deducted from employee's paychecks and general tax revenue from about 1948. Most healthcare workers are salaried government employees. People may seek out private care for better service, or for procedures not covered by insurance, but they have to pay for it privately.

navvies   -from the word *navigation.* These were the people who first dug canals, then built railroad grades, tunnels and bridges etc. They were a huge army of rough laborers from all over England and Ireland. In 1850 there were more navvies than personnel in the Army and Navy combined. In building one particular tunnel, the odds of a navvie being killed on the job were greater than a soldier in the Battle of Waterloo being killed in action. They were well paid by the standards of the day, but hard drinkers, hard fighters and lived in appalling conditions. They were also viewed as barely human by most of the rest of society.

Navy / Royal Navy   As far back as the 11th century, English folks who owned ships could get out of paying taxes if they let the king borrow their cargo ships to move soldiers from place to place. (It's not clear what sort of shape the ships were when they got home again.) It was *Henry VIII* that really put together a functioning professional navy with real and designated fighting ships, cannons, officers, and a budget in the early 1500's. From then until at least WWII, the Royal Navy was the best in the world. It would be hard to say if the Royal Navy was responsible for England's success in her colonies, or the other way around, but they certainly went together.

The navy had the added distinction of being far more professional than the army even if the navy had less status. This was because of a peculiarity of the English mindset. The navy needed skillful educated people running ships and navigating by doing math. Such people were selected based on their ability rather than who their fathers were. On the other hand, the army was where the rich people sent their younger sons who were not suited for the clergy. Furthermore, sailors also were often away for years at a time and couldn't come to the required parties. James Bond, for example, is/was a Commander in Her Majesty's Navy.

Nelson, Lord Horatio -

England's greatest naval hero was born to an upper-middle class family in 1758 and died at sea in 1805. Nelson perfectly demonstrates the Navy's odd practice of promoting talent rather then social rank the way they did it in the army. He entered the navy as a common seaman at the age of 13, shortly began training as a midshipman, and had his own command at age 20. He rose thru the ranks, but was left unemployed at the end of the American Revolution. The French Revolution and Napoleonic Wars put him back to work in the Mediterranean and Atlantic. His greatest victory was the **Battle Trafalgar** against the French & Spanish off the coast of Spain in 1805, but he was killed by a sniper during the mopping up operation. The English people were so grateful, that they built *Nelson's Column* in *Trafalgar Square*.

Nelson's Column -a 170 foot tall column erected in 1843 in Trafalgar

Square as a memorial to Nelson's victory at Trafalgar. There are four large bronze plaques at the base made from French cannons that the Brits captured and melted down.

Newton, Isaac (1642 – 1726) Newton

had a tough life as a boy. He was born prematurely and his dad died before he was born. He didn't get along with his step-dad, but nonetheless, worked out lots of important physics (optics and his famous laws of motion), astronomy (gravity, the planets & their orbits),

and math (calculus). He also dabbled in theology, biblical chronology, and even helped the Royal Mint track down counterfeiters after he did his scientific work. He actually disguised himself as a drunken wastrel and went undercover.

Newgate originally a gate to the old city of

London. It was a prison for London's worst criminals from 1188 to 1902 and held them in deplorable conditions. From 1783 till 1867 it also held public executions.

nonconformist Shortly after Henry split the

Church of England off from the Catholic Pope, Protestantism split itself off from the Church of England. Then some varieties Protestants like the Presbyterians, Quakers, Methodists, Puritans, and Baptist did not conform and also split. They were suppressed like the Catholics, but for slightly different reasons.

Norman Conquest   In 1066, the Norwegians invaded the north of England and the Normans, Brentons, and French (but they were all French) invaded the south. This all had to do with an Anglo-Saxon king dying without an heir. William the Conqueror came out on top and ran England. He did this by kicking out all the rich landed Anglo Saxons (see The *Doomsday Book*) All of 8000 Normans settled in England, but they replaced the exiled landowners. Historians are conflicted as to whether the Normans were better or worse than the ruling Saxons. Slavery went away, but was replaced with serfdom, which was not much better.   see *women, history,* and *language*

North Sea oil   -largely a modern thing, but oil was mined on Scotland's coastline as early as 1850. *Mined* is the appropriate word here. Drilling for deep oil would have to wait for the 20th century. Today England shares the North Sea oil with Norway, Germany, Denmark and Netherlands but declining production has lead to England once again becoming a net importer of oil.

Northern Ireland   part of the United Kingdom and home to about 1.8 million people who are mostly, but not entirely Protestants. Northern Ireland split from what would become the (independent) Republic of Ireland in 1922. Friction between the Catholics and Protestants grew to the *Troubles* between 1968 and 1998. see *Belfast*, & *Ireland.*

Number 10 Downing Street / Number 10   -England's executive residence, their White House. Historically, it was the official residence of First Lord of the Treasury, but in 1905, the *Prime Minister* and Treasury roles were combined. Today it is the *PM*'s home and headquarters of Her Majesty's *Government*, given that in England, one party IS the government and the other party is the *Loyal Opposition*. The building is 300 years old and has over 100 rooms. The Prime Minister lives on the third floor, and it's close to *Buckingham Palace* (the queen), and *Westminster Palace* (Parliament).

nurse   -the servant who cared for the wealthy *middle class*'s very youngest children. A wet-nurse nursed babies. From the nurse, the child would be passed off to a *nanny* and later still, a *governess.*

nursery school   -like America's pre-school, it was prior to infant school or America's elementary school.

Scapa Flow

North Sea

North Atlantic

Scotland

Northern
Ireland

Edinburgh

Glasgow

Belfast

Isle of
Man

Pennine Hills

L:iverpool

Dublin

Birmingham

Ireland

England

Cambridge

Wales

London

Cardiff

Thames River

Dover

Southhampton

Brighton

Calais

Portsmouth

Cornwall

Isle of
Wight

English Channel

Gernsey
Jersey

France

It's been a circle just about forever. The Phoenicians thought of it as an eye and drew-wrote it accordingly, but it was probably a consonant back then. The Greeks made it a vowel–Omega. Non-Semitic languages like English, write the letter like a little mouth making the *oh* sound.

oak   Yes, it's a tree, but the British Navy made their ships out of oak, so it is a symbol of the toughest, bravest, and altogether the best of all things British.

oakum picking   Oakum is the individual fibers of worn out rope that are unraveled and used in the seams of oak ships as caulking. Tedious, but not very challenging work performed while sitting down and often done in prisons.

OAP   -old age pensioner

oat(s)   -grown in the north and a staple food for the Scots. In England, it was usually fed to horses, except in porridge or watery gruel. see *food*

OBE   -Order of the British Empire. Sort of a catch-all for the non-noble people who needed or deserved a little appreciation and recognition. Everyone from civil servants to rock-stars might get this order, and be addressed Sir or Dame. It comes in five levels. From highest to lowest, they run...
    GBE   Knight / Dame of the Grand Cross
    KBE   Knight / Dame Commander
    CBE   Commander of the British Empire
    OBE   Officer of the British Empire
    MBE   Member of the British Empire

Observer -the world's oldest Sunday paper first published in 1791. It's well respected for its liberal view. Conservative Brits read the *Sunday Times* which sells slightly better.

OC -Officer Commanding like the American CO or Commanding Officer.

Official Secrets Act -goes back to 1911 and criminalizes revealing anything the government doesn't want revealed. It has been amended regularly, most recently in 1989.

Odds and sods -Americans have *odds and ends.* The English also have *bits and bobs.*

old boy, old thing, old man, old son, old girl, old chap etc. - are all expressions of affection or respect.

O-Levels -exams given to students of about age 16 from 1950 to 1988. The *forms* vary from school to school and have varied thru the years, but what has not changed is that these exams indicate whether a student was going to university or into the trades.

OM Order of Merit. These are handed out by the monarch for distinguished service in military, science, art, literature. There are only 24 members of this club at any one time.

113-B Baker St. -Sherlock Holmes's fictional home he shared with Doctor John Watson.

opportunity shop -a second hand store. It is often a charitable operation like Goodwill or the Salvation Army in America.

Opposition / Loyal Opposition -members of the minority party in Parliament. Given that the majority party selects it own Prime Minister and all the cabinet members (Ministers etc,), the opposition doesn't do much.

Orange, the House of -William III's home in Northern Ireland along with his buddies before he became king in 1795. It's more important meaning was about the Protestants. Orange was the opposite of Green (Southern Ireland), Protestantism is the opposite of Catholicism, and Northern Island is the opposite of Southern Ireland. The *Orangemen* were a political society supporting the Protestants and unity with England. It was relatively benign until the 1880's when the idea of Irish independence took hold in the south. Things went down hill from then and reached a head with the ***Troubles*** between the early 1960's and 1998. It was all but full-out guerrilla warfare between the Orange and the ***IRA*** - the Irish Republic Army.

orangery -a greenhouse used to protect ornamental orange trees that were fashionable in wealthy homes in the 19th century.

ordnance -a detailed and accurate map or set of maps of the whole country.

OTC -Officer Training Corps -like America's ROTC

outhouse -either what Yanks would call an outbuilding on a farm, or what it means in America. Once sanitation (sewer systems) came to a town, the pipes often went down the alley and no further than the back wall of the garden, so the British outhouse was not a merely hole in the ground under a seat, but rather almost-a-bathroom. But it was still a separate little building in the back yard.

Outsize -XL, XXL, etc, -clothes

Oxford A nice town in central England about 60 miles NW of London on the River Thames. Oxford University is probably the oldest in England (***Cambridge*** is a close second) but exactly what is meant by *university* is historically fluid and fuzzy. Something vaguely like a university in Morocco goes back to 859, but Oxford's birth in the 1100's is impressive. In 1225 we see the first *hall* emerge, but a few years later, *colleges* phased out mere halls. Both were originally where monks copied books and translated from Latin and Greek. Between then and the early 1800's, education in Oxford and all of England for that matter, served mostly to train clergy. As the industrial revolution got going, there was a need for more educated people, both in the trades, as well as in the head-office, not to mention the need for people to go off and attend to matters in India.

Today, so many Oxford grads have entered high levels of government that the simple expression *Oxford* implies the British Establishment. It is necessary to mention Cambridge in a discussion of Oxford. Cambridge leans more to science while Oxford is the more liberal of the two.

The Sottish Thistle.

The letter p -**π**- is a handy thing when dealing with circles, circumferences, and diameters and all, but for the Germanic Angle Saxons, the letter *f* was the way to go. Words beginning with *p* are foreign and almost entirely French, Latin, Greek, or maybe a little Slavic. *P* also used to abbreviate pence (a penny) back when a penny was real money. When a Yank would say *50 cents*, a Brit would say *50 Pee*.

PA -personal assistant. What Americans used to call a secretary is now an administrative aid / assistant, or simply an *admin*.

packet -a ship traveling a regular route and originally carrying the mail.

pack drill -punishment in the army. The guy had to do regular drill wearing a full pack or one filled with rocks.

packed-up -broken down as in a packed-up machine.

Paddington / Paddington Station A neighborhood in northern London and a railroad & canal hub back in the day. Now it is a lower middle class neighborhood, but is undergoing gentrification with artists and hip young computer people.

Paddy -mildly derisive nickname for the Irish -from the name *Padraic*.

padre -no such clergy in England as such, but it has come to be a military term for any sort of chaplain.

page -originally a knight's servant and maybe a young knight in training. He was often the son of a noble who sent him off to the castle at the age of seven to learn what passed for manners of the day. He would act as a minor but elevated servant while doing so. The next step up at age fourteen was to become a full-time knight's servant, a **squire.** After the middle ages, a page became what would be a messenger or go-for to the modern mind.

paint makers   -made paint. Not surprising perhaps, but it was only in 1866 that two men by the names of Sherwin and Williams hit on the idea of premixing paint and selling it in cans. Up until then, if you hired someone to paint your house, he would show up in a horse-cart with bags of colorful powder (dirt), some turpentine, linseed oil, and such. He then mixed whatever color you wanted -as long as you wanted a bland earth-tone.

pajamas/ pyjamas   -American pajamas, but more. They have always been a loose comfortable garment -from India no less, but worn by Muslims rather than Hindus. During the Blitz, men and women wore pajamas not only for relaxing on weekends, but also to bed because they might be rousted out of bed in the middle of the night if the Germans were bombing the area.

Paki   -an old-fashioned word for someone from Pakistan. In general, words like *Paki, Wog,* etc. were not as fraught in England and show up in certain literature of the 19th and early 20th century. This is changing in modern speech.

pale   -a wall of sharpened stakes quickly erected around English colonies during the various invasions of Ireland. *Beyond the Pale* means out there where things were uncivilized.

Pancake   There is no such thing as what an American thinks of as a pancake in England. What they call a pancake, a Yank would call a crepe and their flapjacks are robust things made from sugar, butter, and oats.

pants   -not what you think, pants in Britain are underpants. They wear trousers. When they say *pants,* it is mildly naughty.

paper makers   Go back to about 1490 and paper was an expensive commodity, but no one could read anyway, so the cost was not critical. In the 17th century, rag pickers would sort all manner of trash into big vats and beat on it till it could be made into paper. It was not until the 19th century that they hit on the idea of making it from wood waste and by then it became capitol intensive and no longer a craft. Before paper, if something was important enough to be written down, you would get yourself a...

parchment maker   -part of the paper-making industry, but parchment was made by carefully slicing off the top layer of sheep-skin. Much after the 17th century, parchment was used only for certificates and deeds.

parade   -both the street show with marching bands & floats, as well as what Americans would call a pedestrian mall.

paraffin   -kerosene. *Liquid paraffin* is mineral oil or baby oil in America and is used as a laxative.

parish   Originally it was the community surrounding a single Catholic church and its priest (A cathedral was the hang-out of a bishop.) As the

Catholic church came to share things with the Protestants, the Church of England followed these divisions and after the **Civil War,** the civil or *non-secular* government worked within these boundaries, but with the comings and goings of the Catholics and Protestants, the borders were drawn and redrawn to a fair-thee-well. In 1888, they tidied things up and did **counties**. Until then, parishes were more than a town, but less than a county. After that, the *administrative* parish became the lowest level of civil authority that mostly just looked after the poor. see **divisions** of England.

parish school   During the 1700s and 1800's the parish schools were usually (but not always) run by the church. They taught the local kids a little math as well as reading and writing, but the reading was to be done in the Bible. They were limited to the local kids and hence were called **private schools**. **Public schools,** on the other hand were open to anyone whose father could afford the tuition.

parish pump   -gossip gathered while getting water from the parish well.

park   -both what Americans would think a park ought to be, but also a wild area where the noble's deer were available for hunting and where only the nobleman could hunt them. see **poach / poacher**

Park Lane   -terribly wealthy road along **Hyde Park**. The authors who have set scenes on Park Lane include Arthur Conan Doyle (Sherlock Holmes), Agatha Christy (Hercule Poirot), John Galsworthy (various Forsytes), and many more, not to neglect the game of *Monopoly*.

parlor   -originally a monk's visiting room, It comes from the same French word *parler. Parlay* means to talk or negotiate. Later, it was a small room off to the side of the medieval great hall, then a private room for the family, then finally it became a formal place to receive guests. In this last iteration, the family, or the children anyway, did not otherwise enter. In the modern home, the parlor would be the *front room* and the *family-room* would be where the family hung out and watched television. see **homes**

parson   -originally a Catholic parish priest, and later a rather generic and sometimes snotty term for any clergyman. A more formal address would also be more specific like **vicar** or **rector**. A parson's home is a *parsonage*.

party-piece   From the time before TV, people entertained themselves at parties with skits. Someone's party-piece in England would be their *shtick* in America.

pastie / pasty / Cornish pastie   -a meat pie made with game. In time past, they were made with partridge, pheasant, venison and / or hare. Now they are usually beef, but the fancy ones may still have rabbit, venison, or pigeon.

patience   -America's solitaire. English *solitaire* is played with marbles.

Pax Britannia   From the end of the Napoleonic Wars in 1815 until the beginning of WWI in 1914, the world was relatively calm and this was because of the British and ***mercantilism***, hence the *Pax Britannica* or the *Peace of the British.*

PAYE   -pay as you earn. It's withholding for income tax and national health insurance.

pay packet
-a little envelope with cash and a slip noting deductions etc. Many English workers do not have checking accounts and so receive their pay in cash. As late as 1989, unions have fought any move toward pay checks. This practice is slowly changing, particularly among the salaried workers, but the English ***Post Office*** is still the common way for bills to be paid with cash. see ***banks*** and ***giro***

PC   -***Privy Council*** of the United Kingdom

pea   -THE most important vegetable in England. Eaten all the time despite the availability of various other vegetables frozen, canned, or fresh. *Mushy peas* are boiled with baking soda and then pureed and to make sure they have no texture. *Peas porridge hot* from the nursery rhyme is just that.

pea soup   -a mixture of very dense fog and pollution that is/was actually yellow colored. The first reference to pea soup fog shows up in 1820. People actually died of various lung diseases until they replaced soft coal with natural gas in their ***fires.***

peat   -partially decayed vegetable matter. Bury it deep for a few million years and it becomes coal. Bury it even deeper, give it even more time, and it becomes oil. But just as it is, it can be dug up and put in your garden as a soil amendment or dried and used as fuel.

pecker   -as in *keep your pecker up.* In England, a pecker is a bird's beak. Best to keep it up when one hits a bad patch.

peckish   -a little hungry

peeler   -a policeman, bobby, or constable.

peer (as an individual)   Given the Brit's preoccupation with knowing who is better than whom, a Peer of the Realm is an equal or a peer to the entire kingdom. This is to say that the proper order of the peerage is–and will ever be–first king, duke, then marques, earls, viscounts, and finally, mere barons. Knights do NOT make the cut.

Peerage, English (as a group)   -basically, rich people. The Peerage of England was replaced by the Peerage of Great Britain in 1707 with the Act of Union with Scotland. (Ireland and Whales would have to wait.) Up until 1899 and the House of Lords Act, all peers could sit in the ***House of Lords***. (Women peers were admitted to this club only in 1963.)

These positions are hereditary; the oldest kid got the title. Baronets are hereditary, but not peers. Knights, Dames, Ladies etc. don't rate. These peerages come from long ago and have confusing histories that are made all the more so by different rules between England, Scotland, and Wales. In order from high to lowest, together with the appropriate address:

	Address	How many of them are there now.
Duke / Duches	Your Grace (by inferiors) Duke (by social equals)	24 -but the Royal Dukes -the children of the king or queen- don't count.
Marquese	My / Your Lord Your Lordship / Ladyship	34, but most of them are also dukes
Earl		191 including 4 countesses
Viscount		115 but not including 'courtesy' viscounts
Baron		426 including 9 women, but not including courtesy baronies and lordships)

Knights, Orders, and recipients of certain Decorations may be addressed as *Sir / Madam* or *Dame,* usually followed by their Christian name.

peg   -either a clothespin or coat hook on the wall

Penal Colonies   America was a penal colony for the English for a long time. Some 50,000 convicts went to the Chesapeake Colonies in Virginia. Georgia, for example, was settled by a 17th century entrepreneurs who bought many people out of debtor's prison and shipped them off to Georgia. These were not what we would think of as criminals, but people who couldn't pay off the 17th century equivalent of 20th century credit cards. But not just debtors, also Scots and Irish or anyone undesirable in the eyes of the English at various times in history.

After the American revolution, the English turned to Australia and added advocates of Irish Home Rule and Labor Unionists to the list of folks to be gotten get rid of in the southern hemisphere.

pence   -2 1/2 p or the plural of penny. see ***money***

Pennines / Pennine Hills   -the mountains running up the center of northern England. The highest one is Cross Fell at 2930 feet above sea level.

penny-farthing   The high wheel bicycle popular in England from about 1869 till 1880. It was so named because the large front wheel was like a farthing, and the little back wheel was the size of a penny. If, for some unfortunate reason, the big front wheel stopped turning, inertia would toss the rider onto his head rather violently. This gives the expression *header* for a bad forward fall. In 1880 the 'safety bicycle' was introduced and that was about the end of the penny-farthing. The penny-farthing had a short life but is very iconic of the Victorian era. Also, something done in a *penny farthing* manner was something done in a sloppy way.

pension   -much like America's social security but with some funding differences. It is arguably more soundly financed than America's FICA.

pensioner -either a retiree or a student who pays his own way

pepper rent   -token rent so low that it could be paid with a single pepper corn.

Pepys, Samuel (1633–1702)   Pepys was a **MP** and administrator in the **Royal Navy**, but he is best known for an extensive diary he kept from 1690 to 1699. His work has been a valuable primary source for **Restoration** history when it was first published about a hundred years after he died. He covered the **Great Fire**, the plague, a couple of wars, and some gossip.

perishing   -general purpose modifier for very or complete, i.e., it's *perishing hot*.

periwinkle   -a tiny blue flower, or small sea snails / whelks that are not eaten much anymore. As a verb, to *winkle out* something would be to pull it out as if pulling a periwinkle out of its shell.

Permanent Secretary / Undersecretary   Because the ministers / secretaries of the English government come and go with elections, the actual experts in matters of state, foreign relations, economics etc., are the under-secretaries. They are presumed to be non-political and advise their elected boss who sets broad policy. They also tend to the small day-to-day details of government.

perry   -cider made from pears rather than apples.

petrol   -gasoline

Petticoat Lane -the nick-name for a market in Middlesex Street in east London that dealt in used clothes going back to Shakespeare's time. It is held only on Sundays because it was in a largely

Jewish neighborhood as their sabbath was on Saturday. After about 1880 Jewish immigrants from Eastern Europe settled in the area and were even more active in the garment industry. Today it's a touristy place to go after brunch.

phaeton   -light four wheeled carriage with an open top pulled by one or more often two horses. All carriages were owned by wealthy people during the Regency era and Jane Austen's crowd favored this sort of carriage for purposes of seeing and more importantly, being seen. It is indeed as ridiculously high as it is shown because it lifted the passengers high above the street to protect their clothes from mud. A woman needed a step ladder and footman to get in and out.

Piccadilly Circus   No clowns or elephants, a *circus* is a circle, or an American round-about or traffic circle. Piccadilly Circus sits in London's West End and is the middle of shopping, theater, and nightlife. It is also lit up even more than New York's Times Square. The Brits are terribly fond of it as the symbol of all things exciting and trendy.

Picts   -a subset of the Celts living in Northern Scotland from well before the time the Romans came. They survived on to the early medieval era. Much of what is known about them comes from Roman writing and their beautiful and intricate stone carvings.

pie   -a pastry usually filled with meat. Such a pastry eaten for desert is called either a *flan* which is filled with custard, or a *tart* which is filled with fruit.

Pilgrims Way   -a road running from Winchester to Canterbury. While it shows up in Chaucer's writing, it is not clear exactly where it was. The Pilgrims in question were on their way to get miracles from **Thomas Becket's** tomb.

pillar box -a red five foot tall mailbox that goes back to about 1850.

pinafore / pinny   -a 19th century smock-like garment pinned over a little girl's dress to keep it from getting dirty. Later a pinafore came to refer to what an American might call an apron. Its use in the Gilbert & Sullivan's comic opera *The HMS Pinafore* is for comedy and satire.

pinchbeck -fake gold showing up on the uniforms of poor naval officers needing to look the part, so it came to be synonymous with poor and/or cheap.

pip -fruit seeds. Consider Sherlock Holmes's case involving *Five Orange Pips*. A pip may also be the little metal do-dads worn on the epaulets of British officers higher than a Lieutenant Colonel. The more pips, the higher the rank. The spots on dice are also called pips.
pip emma -military-speak for PM. *Ack emma* is AM.

pirate stations When rock and roll arrived in England from America (and before going back the other direction with the ***British Invasion***) the BBC didn't respond to the demand from young people for this sort of music, so a number of unlicensed radio broadcasters set up shop on ships anchored close offshore.

pish -nonsense. *Pish-posh* or *pish and toss* are more of the same and often dismissive. It's sometimes used by the lower class trying not to sound vulgar.

plaid -does not refer to the pattern, technically, that's a tartan. A plaid is a large bit of wool cloth worn over the shoulder and wrapped around the waist. See ***kilt***

plaster / sticking plaster -an adhesive band-aid.

platoon -an army unit consisting of three ***sections***. Four platoons make a ***company***. Platoons are usually commanded by a lieutenant. see ***army***

plimsoll(s) -a shoe with a rubber bottom and a canvas top. It's a tennis shoe. They are so named because they are thought to look a little like a...
Plimsoll line In 1872, British MP Samuel Plimsoll devised a law requiring ships to have a mark on their hulls that indicated the greatest depth to which they could be safely loaded.

Plough / Plow
The constellation that is so clearly the *Big Dipper* is equally clearly a plow to the English. The Greeks thought it was a bear –a big bear– *Ursa Major.*

plowman's lunch -bread, cheese, and often beer.

plugs / points / power points The English were slow to adopt and standardize household electricity and so they use a variety of different plugs or what Yanks would think of as outlets. Appliances are usually sold with bare wires to be attached into whatever plug fits. Of greater importance to Americans who might plan to visit England with their own electrical devices, is the fact the electricity coming out of the walls is 240 volts vs. America's 110 to 120 volts.

plus-fours   What Americans would call knickers, but having another four inches below the knees.

Plymouth   Literally the mouth of the River Plym, and a very historically important harbor. It was the embarkation point for many ships going off to the colonies, the Mayflower being among the first and perhaps the most important. Much of its shipping activity was commercial but it also has a Royal Naval shipbuilding facility. (The Royal Navy did most of its non-building thing in Portsmouth to the east.) It was heavily bombed during WWII but nonetheless, it served as an embarkation for the D-Day invasion.

poach / poacher   After the *Enclosure Acts*, it got a little harder for every-man to feed his family after Lord Whomever claimed all the land and all the game for himself. Snaring a rabbit for the stew pot would get a man *transported*. Rather a nasty thing all around and the sadistic game-keepers you find in some writing from the 18th and 19th century are not uncommon.

police   It depended on how large the community was, but what we might think of as policing activities were done by the *beadles* in the earliest times. Up until the Civil War and Protestant Reformation, the church took it upon itself to put people in the *stocks*, pillory, or lock-up if the church felt they needed it. The Parish Constables was appointed a year at a time and did the dirty work in these cases. Again, it depended on the size of the community, but a Petty Constable would enforce manorial law. These were laws that derived from the Lord of the Manor. Justices of the Peace and / or the Chief Constable might have larger duties including what we might think of as being much like today's police duties. These were like keeping things calm down at the taverns and ale houses, as well as running off vagrants, dragging in unwilling jurors & drunks, chasing down the fathers of bastards, and so forth. Certain civil matters fell to them as well, like collecting taxes, organizing elections, raising the local militia, finding places to sleep for any soldiers who happened to be marching thru, keeping track of weights and measures, and occasionally even sorting out commercial conflicts.

In 1812 the *Luddite* upraising had gotten so out of hand that it prompted the crown to send out the army. This seemed a little bit of an overkill so there began to develop the idea of something more intimidating than a one-man Justice of the Peace but less so than a Division of His Majesty's Cavalry. In 1829, a Justice of the Peace and *MP* Robert Peel set up a small detective force to combat the general lawlessness of London. After that an act of Parliament created what we might think of as the beginnings of a modern police force with constables who carried a truncheon (club) and whistle. They had to be at least 5'7" tall, under 35 years of age, literate, and of good reputation. But they worked only in London. They were initially resented by the commoners as traitors to their class. (The high collars on their uniforms were protection against garroting.)   Within a few years, they were thought of as friendly but firm disciplinarians and were nick-named *Bobbi*es or *Peelers* after Robert (Bobby) Peel.

Between 1835 and 1856 various laws were passed to duplicate London's Bobbies outside of London. There were also some specialized police forces like the Marine Police who protected property on the River Thames, Railway Police who covered all England's railways as well as the London Underground, and dockyard light-rails. There was also a separate Royal Military Police. Women joined the Bobbies in 1919, but could not arrest anyone till 1923.   see *Scotland Yard*

Political Parties   England's political parties are another subject of surpassing importance to English writers and American readers, but also a subject of equally vast confusion. America has had a couple hundred years to argue about which side of the aisle was right in its thinking, and which side was made entirely out of self-serving nitwits. England has had considerably longer to sort it out and it seems they are still at it. A consideration of history might help the Yank get a grip on it, if only a little.

The *English Civil War* might be as good a place to start as any, but the two sides were by no means political parties. They were opposite sides of a war that killed almost 200,000 people. It was between the Catholics who supported the pope & the monarchy, and the Protestants who felt the Parliament was the way to go & felt the pope had to go. This is of course an oversimplification, but let's say the Catholics (nick named 'Cavaliers' because they dressed flamboyantly), were in favor of things staying the way they were on the conservative side of the aisle. The Protestants were called *Round-heads* because they cut their hair short and dressed in somber black. They wanted things to change in a progressive direction.

Dates	Left Leaning "Liberal"	Right Leaning "Conservative"
Roman Occupation. AD 43 - 410	Nope. No political parties then. The Romans on top and the locals on the bottom. Julius Caesar topped off his Gallic Wars with a swing thru Britannia between 55 and 54 BC.	
Between the Romans and the Franks	Because politics–such as it was back then–was essentially about issues only the aristocracy cared about, alliances were formed and dissolved to serve the various goals of individual rich people.	

Norman Conquest / Occupation 1055 - 1204	It was only slightly more complicated now. We have about 8000 the Normans (French) displacing the Anglo-Saxon rich guys. Various revolts, wars, and such, but for the little guy, not much changed. Nor was there much of what we would think of as political polarity.
1215	The English nobility force King John to sign the **Magna Carta**
1265	England has the world's first Parliament meeting. It still had to do with matters only the rich guys cared about.
1642 - 1651	English Civil War: Now we see some real division of opinion -still rich people having the opinions and the little guy playing the role of canon fodder, but it's a start.

Protestants Parliamentarians	Catholics Royalists

1680 - 1850	1678 - 1681 The Exclusion Crisis leads to **Whigs** and **Tories.** Very confusing and religious. Charles II was restored to his executed father's throne (see **Charles I, & Cromwell**), but his uncle James, Duke of York who was a Catholic and could'a should'a might'a been the king. This did not sit well with the Protestants who weren't too enthused with ANY sort of a king to being with, so they exclude him. This gives us the...

Whigs: Protestants -supported constitutional monarchy	**Tories**: Catholic -supported the Stuart kings and absolute monarchy
American Revolution 1776 - 1781: Americans tend to forget that some good people were not enthused about splitting from England. The first *American* political divisions might be said to be the Loyalists (loyal to the king and to England) and the Patriots in favor of revolution.	
The Whigs and Tories were still not so much political parties as we might think of them today, but rather loose alliance of interest.	

1850 - 1900	**Liberals** (evolved from the Whigs)		**Conservatives** -evolved from the Tories -they haven't changed or evolved as much as the liberals - the majority in His / Her Majesty's Government for 57 years of the 20th century.
At long last, we see some concern for the little guy. At least the little guys in a labor union.			
1900 - 1920	regular Liberals	Liberal Unionists -closer to conservatives	
1920 - 1939'is	Labor Party -the Anti-Tories -labor movement, labor unions, and socialism		
1929 -	From somewhat before WW II and on to 2010, things sloshed		

Dates	Left Leaning "Liberal"	Right Leaning "Conservative"
2010 (?)	back and forth between Labor and Conservative Parties. (see ***Churchill, Winston***)	
2010 - ???	No single party could claim a majority, so this becomes the age of ***Coalitions.*** Some of the various parties that hooked together to form these coalitions, include: Liberal Democrats: -third largest party until 2015. Scottish National Party -third largest party in terms of seats. United Kingdom Independent Party (UKIP) -third largest in terms of votes	

Poor Laws   To the credit of the English, the notion that government ought to do something about the poor arose sooner there than in most of the rest of Europe. It goes back to 1536 under ***Elizabeth I***. In 1834, they tightened things up in order not to encourage indolence and laziness. They did this with workhouses that were were miserable and prison-like. (Think of Dicken's <u>Oliver Twist</u> saying "Please sir, I want more.") The modern system of welfare started after WWII and set aside the Poor Laws.

pop   -as in *pop in*
in pop   -in hock
poppers   -party favors / crackers, or clothing snaps
poppet   -doll or a cute small child

porridge   -hot cereal and usually a breakfast food. In the old days, it might have been all there was to eat. Oatmeal is one example of porridge, but any grain can be boiled into porridge, for example wheat, grits, rice, or even peas. During comparatively good times in the otherwise bad times of the dark ages, porridge might have a bite or two of meat.

     Today 'porridge' is what is given to babies when they start eating solid (mushy) food and in this use of the word, it might be made from things other than grain.

Porters   -show up in a lot of English stories, but not all were simple carriers of any old stuff. As far back as 1604, it was a matter of guilds that defined who got to carry what. Alien porters dealt with imports and collected duties on these goods. Billingsgate porters had a monopoly on schlepping corn (wheat), coal, salt and a few other commodities. Wine porters carried only wine, and street porters carried goods to and from the waterfront. Tackle House porters were the first crowd licensed to haul almost whatever they wanted and only in the 19th and 20th century. Today a porter carries luggage around train stations, airports, or in the better hotels.

portion   The eldest son was given the bulk of the estate, but younger son might inherit a much smaller ***portion***. Daughters were also given a portion but in the form of a dowry and probably before dad died.

Portsmouth   The port where **Henry VIII** built his navy; perhaps his greatest contribution to the kingdom and England's first 'professional' navy. Today, Portsmouth IS the British Navy. Here we find Nelson's flagship the HMS Victory and the *Mary Rose*, hauled off the bottom in 1982 and restored from where she sank in 1543.

Henry built the worlds first dry-dock in Portsmouth. It was the world's most fortified city from the 1700's onward. It had the world's first mass production line and was the world's most industrialized city for most of the 1800's. It was both heavily bombed during WWII and an important embarkation point for the D-Day Invasion. As far as literature goes, any Napoleonic War story involving the navy inevitably has one or more scenes in Portsmouth, as do various crime stories. Charles Dickens was born here in 1812,

PS   -Permanent Under Secretary. The non-political expert advising the thoroughly political **Minister** that **Parliament** has selected to fill the role.

post -the mail, **to post** -to mail, **post code** -zip code, **postman** -mail man
postal order -money order

Post Office   The English Post Office is considerably more than a place to stand in line to buy stamps or mail a package. It goes back to 1635 and has taken on various tasks including:
- 1840 -built the first 'modern' postal system with the help of the rail roads and a fixed rate of an 1d self-adhesive stamp for all letters.
- 1861 -opened the Post Office Savings Bank.
- 1868 -acquired private telegraph companies and was responsible for all telegraphy by 1870.
- 1878 -began telephone services.
- 1880 -sold government bonds.
- 1904 -controlled radio broadcasting until 1922 when the BBC was formed and took over.
- 1960's -offered general banking services thru the National **Giro** for the working man.

potato   -arrived in England from South America sometime between 1588 and 1593. It was more popular in Ireland for reasons having to do more with being able to get enough to eat than with taste, but they were big in England too. Potatoes have long been served almost every day either fried as chips or mashed. The popular notion that the were brought to England by either Sir Francis Drake, or Sir Walter Raleigh doesn't hold up. It is more likely they got to England from Spain or even Amsterdam. see *food*

potato famine   While it is called the Irish potato famine, it actually hit Germany with similar, but less dramatic results. There had been something of a population explosion in Ireland *because* of the potato; the Irish were almost entirely dependent on them for food until a mold wiped out all the potatoes. Between 1845 & 1852 about a million people died and another million left Ireland, usually to America. The sad fact is that Ireland was a net *exporter* of food the whole time -mostly to England. see *food*

potted   -in a can (food) or a growing in a container (a plant).

potter   -as in *pottering about.* Like American *puttering around* is doing nothing of compelling importance.

potty   -a little nuts, but if you are rich you are just eccentric.

pound   -a *Pound Sterling* was never an actual pound of silver, but rather 240 old silver coins. A transaction large enough to need pounds of silver was usually done in gold *sovereigns*. see *money*

prang -a crash -usually in a car.

pram / perambulator -a baby carriage

prat
-originally the bottom -hence *pratfall*. Later a prat came to mean someone who was an annoying ass.

Prefect   -someone, usually an older student, in charge of maintaining discipline in a public school.

prefects / prefectures   This sort of geographic division occurs in many part of the world particularly in Roman Colonies and Asia. Fortunately, for the American reader, its use in England is probably related to church matters. In general, a religion's *territory* may be divided into districts, smaller parishes, and the smallest, the prefects.

prelate   -a bishop or other high-ranking clergy. It may refer to a person, or an office (the P*relature*), or the territory over which a given prelate has jurisdiction. Keep in mind that as the English were sorting out the whole Catholic / Protestant thing, Parliament was made out of assorted prelates, bishops, and arch-bishops; the **House of Lords** still is.

prep school   -a public school charging a fee for boys from the age of about eight to twelve to prepare them for admission to a public boarding school so beloved by the British aristocracy and writers, and so hated by students.

Presbyterian   Originally, this was a non-conformist and somewhat Calvinistic splinter of the Church of England. It tended to be more popular among the wealthy and Scottish.

press gang   During various wars–not the least of which being the Napoleonic wars–the Royal Navy needed men and because there was no draft, so they simply sent out gangs of thugs to kidnap whatever men they could find. These poor souls would then be dragged back to the ship where they were virtual prisoners until the ship sailed off to war. The poor guy had no choice but to learn to be a sailor, and if he were slow in learning, the cat-of-nine tails (the lash) would hurry him along. It was a brutal practice that lead to the mutiny of 1797 in *Spithead.*

There was a similar means of acquiring capable sailors that involved taking American sailors off any American merchantmen that an English warship came across on the high-seas. This lead to the War of 1812 which was sort of an encore to the American Revolution.

pretender / pretender to the throne   -someone claiming a throne or other powerful position occupied by another. Given the confusing laws of succession regarding the throne and given further the confusion surrounding, for example, *Henry VIII* and his various wives and children, there have been several instances of pretenders in English history. see *Bonnie Prince Charles*

primary school   -basic tax-supported schools for students from about age five to eleven. These are roughly equivalent to American elementary schools.

Primate   -the most senior bishop or archbishop in one of England's Anglican Church Provinces. A Catholic Primate is entirely honorific.

Prime Minster   -like America's president, but with some exceptions. He (or she, Margaret Thatcher and Teresa May have filled this role) is selected by the members of Parliament's majority party. Up until about 1700, the king's ministers ran the tedious parts of government. After that, Parliament became increasingly important and had a hand in whom the king could appoint to the various ministries, but with the Reform Act of 1831, the appointment of all ministers -including the Prime Minister- fell entirety to the majority party in Parliament. see *Parliament, government*

prince   -the son or sons of the monarch, but only the immediate sons. The title is not inheritable. This means that while Prince Charles is prince, his sons will only be princes once he becomes king -this despite tabloid headlines to the contrary. The same rule applies to princesses.

Prince Consort   -the spouse of the ruling queen, but only *Victoria*'s Albert was consort. *Elizabeth II*'s husband is the Duke of Edinburgh.

Prince of Wales   -the heir apparent to the throne and now Prince Charles.

prison   The brutality of the old days is well illustrated by the English prisons. Bad people—or those whom the elite viewed as bad, were quickly tried and hanged so a stay in prison was apt to be pretty brief. People who were somewhat less undesirable, were transported. They were shipped off the various colonies. Debtor prisoners, however, kept people locked-up for as long as it took to get the debts paid off. Throughout, they were private businesses wherein guards were largely paid by bribes or tips. There was some reform in the early 1800's with fewer hangings and less transporting, but prisons were still private or run by the local council. In 1877 the crown got involved and things slowly came to look a little like they do today.

private   -much the same meanings as in America, particularly in the army, but with a few extra meanings. A *private gentleman* has no titles. *A private member* is a member of the **House of Commons** who is not a part of any **ministry** and is likely a **back-bencher**. A *private trader* would be a closely held corporation or sole-practitioner in America. see **private school**

private school   -schools (originally parish schools) that limited enrollment just to the local kids, or kids in the parish. This was unlike *public* schools that were open to anyone whose daddies could pay for it. see *schools*

privatization   After being frightened by the General Strike in 1926, the Brits began carefully nationalizing important industries, and did so faster after WW II. They took over the Bank of England, electricity, coal, the rails, iron & steel, and, in short, all the heavy industries. During Margaret Thatcher's term in the 80's, many of these industries were returned to private ownership but with publicly held shares.

privy   -from the French *prive* -meaning private. Its early meaning involved what we might think of as the behind-closed-doors machinations of government. It was only about the 19th century that the privy came to mean the outhouse in the back yard. Later when plumbing moved inside, the name stuck but *privy* is now a little old fashioned. The American word *bathroom* in England refers to a room with a bathtub or shower, that may or may not have a toilet. Slang expressions include the biffy, the loo, the head, or simply, the toilet.

Privy Council   The monarch's Privy Council was his or her inner circle of advisers who would council privately in the Privy Chamber (the *private room*). As the monarchy became increasingly ceremonial along with the ascendancy of Parliament, the role of the Prime Minister increased and he used the Cabinet for advice and administrative chores. The Privy Council then became largely ceremonial. The Privy Purse is the monarch's allowance from Parliament, and the Privy or Great Seal the final –but ceremonial–step in making laws or writing big checks.

Protestant Restoration / Reformation see *Reformation* and *Restoration*

provinces   -the sticks or anywhere outside of London, or outside of any city wherein the speaker lives and thinks is pretty posh or certainly more posh than *the provinces*.

pub   -short for *Public House*. A pub is a neighborhood bar, but with considerably more history. It depended on how strong the drink they served, how may lodgers they were prepared to have, and in no small part, the crown's need for license and tax money. For example, when gin became popular in the late 1700's, pubs that served the stuff were required to be licensed. Therefore, pubs that served only beer became more popular until they too were required to be licensed. They were primarily working-class, but after WWII such distinctions broke down and all classes enjoyed the sense of community that typifies pubs. Most pubs serve simple food like fish and chips and some very few still rent rooms to travelers. All in all, an English, Irish, Scot's, or Welsh pub would seem familiar to an American who spends time in a neighborhood bar, but a pub must NOT be confused with an American disco or nightclub. see *inns and taverns*

public convenience -public restroom.
public oven -a communal bake-house common in the medieval.
Public Records Office -the national archive.
public schools -schools that anyone (but usually boys) may attend, provided their daddy is rich. see *school*

pudding   For the Brits, *pudding* is one of those useful words that covers a lot of territory. Consider plum, figgy, Christmas, bread, and Yorkshire pudding. *Pudding* may mean desert or a specific type of desert. The Brits are very keen on pudding or *pud*, and make a dozen or more varieties. Neither savory *pudding*-pudding, nor *desert*-pudding are anything like the chocolate, banana, coconut, butterscotch, or vanilla goo that Americans make out of the little box. Such would be called *custard* in England.

pukka   -solid and reliable. The word is usually applied to a military person. The word comes from India and in the modern use, it is not only solid and reliable, but a tad dull.

Punch   -a weekly humorous magazine published until 2002. It was noted for its cartoons and satire. It's a little like America's *Mad Magazine*, but for a more sophisticated readership. The name *Punch* comes from the rather nasty little Punch and Judy Puppets popular in the Victorian era.

punch-up -a fist fight

punt   -a small flat bottom boat useful for summer romance among students, particularly at Cambridge or Oxford.
punter -a loosing bettor or otherwise a sucker.

push-bike   -an old-fashioned word for bicycle and distinct from a *motorbike*.
push-chair -baby stroller.

putting-out system   As the industrial revolution got going, and before factories became huge coal-burning soul-sucking behemoths, manufacturing was often done in specialized home shops. An *undertaker* would gather up the raw necessary material and take it to one worker's shop–often in someone's home–for a single process to be performed. He would pick up the finished work he had dropped off previously, do a little quality control, and pay a piece-rate price for that work. Then he would take it to another shop for the next part of the process and so on till the product was ready for market. One example of this process might begin with a bunch of dirty hair sheered off of a sheep, and turning it into clothing. It turns out there are a lot of steps.

Moving from sheep anyway, and turning to manufacturing things made from metal and such, the same system worked. The pay for this work depended on the skills and tooling necessary to do the work. From the undertaker's point of view, costs could be pushed down as far as possible if the steps were broken down to the smallest degree that needed the least skill and the fewest and cheapest tools. Because of this business reality, the putting-out system was sometimes called 'white slavery' with the entire family laboring dawn to dusk at tedious dirty work in the living room and earning a bare substance.

BTW -during WWII, the little pieces and parts used to make fighter planes came form an ad hoc arrangement reminiscent of the putting out system.

Q is a ridiculous letter. There is some use for it in Semitic languages like Arabic and Hebrew, but the English could have gotten along without if it perfectly well if it were not for French. There is also the issue of Q always needing to be helped out by a following U. Zee is the only letter less popular than Q.

Quakers   Most correctly, they are *The Society of Friends.* The name *Quaker*, comes from a Quaker preacher being tried for religious blasphemy in 1650. During the trial, he "bade them to tremble at the word of the Lord.") What is not often understood by Yanks is that the Pilgrims and Quakers came to America not only because the thought they were being persecuted, but also because as the crown increased its authority over assorted miscreants, and the church was not able to slap people in the stocks as often as they liked. They wanted room to persecute others as *they* saw fit.

quarriers   -hauled several things up out of big pits in England, the most important being granite and lime. The former was a building material and the other was the source of cement and mortar, whitewash, bleach, hide tanning solutions, as a disinfectant for graves & garbage tips, and even as a soil treatment. Cotswold stone came from around **Cotswold**. Kaolin (porcelain) came from Cornwall, and coprolite (phosphate fertilizer) was dug up around Cambridgeshire. Flint was very important to prehistoric English cavemen for their arrow & spear heads, later as a building material, and still later in another weapon, flint-lock firearms.

quarter days   -goes back to the Medieval practice of paying rent quarterly, but when few people understood calendars, the four days every year was based on church festivals etc. For example, and depending on the part of the British Isles in question, Christmas, Lady Day, Michaelmas, and Mid-summer. Labor contracts were also based on quarters for working people who didn't pay to rent land to grow crops but rather worked as laborers usually on a farm.

que / queinging -a line or taking one's place in a line.

Queen   A male monarch is simply the king, but the word *queen* is far
more complicated. There have been only five or six monarch queens:
Elizabeths I and II, Victoria, and (Bloody) Mary being the most important
ones. The queen may also be the wife of the current king and technically the
Queen Consort. The widow of the king is the *Queen Dowager*. The *Queen
Mother* is the most complicated. She is the mother of the queen, but there are
no king mothers. Or queen fathers for that matter. Elizabeth II is queen, but
even as the mother of Charles, grand mother of Harry, and great grandmother
of two more, she is not the queen mother. Her mother, on the other hand,
was the widow of George V and she was the Queen-mother throughout the
reign of her son *Edward VIII* (who hung it up to marry an American!) and
then Queen-mother of George VI.

Queen's Bench   -a high level court. It's now the Queen's Bench,
but in due time, it will be the *King's Bench* again.

Queen's / Queen's College   There are three of them and one is
just for girls and one Queen's University is for the Irish. All of them are
expensive.

Queen's Council   An old and presumably accomplished barrister
available to advise the Queen, but they rarely do. *QC* is another title some
Brits like to put on the back of their names.

Queen's Guard   -the infantry and cavalry who guard the royal
residence. (When the monarch is king, they are the King's Guard.) They
wear tall bearskin hats and stand motionless outside Buckingham Palace for
American tourists.

Queen Scout -like an American Eagle Boy Scout.

queer   -feeling poorly -as in *come over queer*. To be living on *Queer
Street* is to be on the verge of bankruptcy, and *queer the pitch* is to interfere
with business.

quilting   -an important home industry to bring in a little extra cash during
the 1600's and 1700's.

quince   -a hard pear-like fruit. It needs boiling before it can be eaten
and even then it is used sparingly in pies or jelly. BTW -the Portuguese word
for quince is *marmalo* and the original quince jam was called *marmalade*.

Quisling   -a traitor, a person who collaborates with the enemy
occupying forces. From Vidkum Quisling of Norway who cooperated with
the Nazis during WWII.

R is a controversial letter. It's closely related to *P* in ancient Greek, but related to *D* in the older Semitic languages. It fell to the Romans to add the tail to rho to get our *R*. (Note that the Greek π already has a tail and a rather fancy one at that.) In English in England, spelling, the *r* in words like *centre* precedes the *e*, but in American spelling, it's *center*.

RAF see *Royal Air Force* and *military*

railway   To understand he English rail road system, it's important for Americans to remember that England is much smaller that America. Getting from one end of the Sceptered Isle to the other end is child's play compared to –for example–getting across the desert from Denver to Los Angeles. Automobiles also came much later to England than they did to America.

They were originally a conglomeration of privately owned railways but they have been connected together in various ways during most of the 20th century. This includes hooking up with Europe thru the *Channel Tunnel*, the *London Underground*, other municipal transit systems and finally, various narrow-gauge tourist junketing lines. Today there are a little more than 10,000 miles of railroad track in England.*

Moving trains also make great settings for murder mysteries and the whole crime-solving crowd so popular in English literature and movies.
* US has 140,000 miles of train track, but depending on how passenger miles are measured, the US trains carry less then one tenth as many passengers.

ranks, military   The subject of military ranks is hugely complicated; so much so that the following addresses—with much oversimplification—the way it is today, and this will have to serve the student reader. This compares the English Army with the American Army and adds the English Navy for good measure. Both the USAF and the RAF ranks sort of straddle line between the Army / Navy ranks. This is because the USAF split off from the US Army only after WWII, whereas the RAF more or less invented itself at a time when the English Army was recovering from WWI.

English Army	American Army	English Navy	Notes:
Officers:			
Field Marshal	General of the Army	Admiral of the Fleet	All of these ranks attain only in times of war.
GENERAL STAFF: The way the English and Americas rank their officers is almost identical. There are three further breeds of General; (regular) General, Lieutenant General, and Major General		There are 3 types of admirals; (regular) Admiral, Vice-Admiral, and Rear-Admiral,	In the army, a division (10,000 – 50,000 soldiers) is commanded by a Major General.
Brigadier	Brigadier General	Commodore	Commands a brigade of 5,000 to 10,000. A Naval Commodore commands a flotilla of ships as part of a larger naval force.
Colonel		Captain	
Lieutenant Colonel		Commander James Bond is / was a Commander.	In the army, a Lt. Colonel would command a battle group of 700 to 1000. A Commander in the Royal Navy might run a frigate, destroyer, sub, aviation squadron, or shore installation.
Major		Lieutenant Commander	Lieutenant derives from the French lieu as in lieu of the tenant
Captain		Lieutenant	-the real boss who is out of town.
1st Lieutenant The Brits pronounce it *lef-tenant*. This is probably because it's a French word and they didn't get along for a good long time with the French.		Sub-Lieutenant	An Army lieutenant may command 30 men, as might a Naval Sub-Lieutenant or Midshipman.
2nd Lieutenants		Midshipman	
Between the officers and enlisted men, there is a confusing gray area of highly specialized–and often highly educated–warrant officers and Petty Officers in the Navy. These people serve important functions -often high-tech functions- that may fall outside of regular military purposes.			
Enlisted Men:			
Army Sergeant Major		Warrant Officer of the Naval Services	These ranks are ceremonial, and in some ways, these men may tell a much higher ranking officer where to get off—and do so none too politely if he is so inclined.

In both the English and American Army's, most of the important work is done by sergeants or in the Navy, it's done by Chiefs. There is a very complicated variety of these people and they don't line up one-to-one very easily. None-the-less, they run as follows:

English Army	American Army	English Navy	Notes:
Warrant Officer Class 1 (Regimental Sergeant)	Command Sergeant Major	Warrant Officer Class 1	Most sergeants have been in the enlisted ranks eight to ten years before they make sergeant. A sergeant will normally advise a lieutenant in charge of a platoon of 30 to 50 men and may directly command an 8 to 12 men Section on his own.
Warrant Officer Class 1 (appointed)	Sergeant Major	Chief Petty Officer (equivalent to an Army Sergeant First Class)	
	First Sergeant		
Warrant Officer Class 2 (Company Sergeant)	Master Sergeant		
	Sergeant First Class		BTW, the word derives from Latin *servient*, meaning serving or servile
Color / Staff Sergeant	Staff Sergeant		
Sergeant	Sergeant		
Corporal	Corporal	Petty Officer	
Lance Corporal	Specialist	Leading Hand	Most of these service men are trained to be specialists in the various tasks or functions.
Private Class 1 to 3	Private 1st Class	Able Seaman 1 & 2	
Private Class 1 (Junior)	Private 1 & 2	New Entry	

rasher -a slice of bacon that is thicker that an American slice.

rat catchers -actually earned more than common laborers. Rat and vermin infestations were a real problem in warehouses, barns, and homes, but there was a market for live rats for blood sports involving dogs or ferrets. Rat pie was a delicacy among the commoners and moles were valuable for their skins.

rates -property tax and among the highest in the world.

rationing America rationed gasoline and a few food commodities from 1942 till 1946 as part of the war effort, but it was only polite patriotism compared to what the poor Brits went thru. England rationed from 1940 until 1954 when the last ration on meat was lifted. (It was rationing in America that left the Yanks with an enduring love of macaroni and cheese as a substitute for meat. One stamp was good for two boxes.) see *food*

reading   In Parliament, a bill must be read three times before the vote.

ready, steady, go   -equivalent to America's *On your marks, get set, go.*

receipt   -a sales receipt as well as recipe, but when it's a recipe for medicine, it's Rx. Both words come from the Latin *accipere* meaning *to receive.*

Rector   In the Church of England, the parish priest is either a vicar, a curate, or a rector, but the rector is paid better. It's a little different in the Episcopal Church where the rector is in charge. The same thing as a *vicar* in the Church of England. An English Academic Rector would be a college *chancellor* in America.

Recusant   -people who didn't go to church as often as the Church of England thought they should. It was largely a means of suppressing Catholicism, but as Protestantism and the nonconformist movement unfolded, it was used to suppress anyone who took a different religious view. Today, the word applies to anyone who disagrees with any currant authority.

Reform Bill (of 1832)   As the industrial revolution unfolded, people moved from the countryside to big cities which until then had been little more than places with markets and occasional fairs for turnips and other agriculture. All well and good, but the Parliamentary representation remained in the countryside where it was further dominated by the rich land-owners. The Reform Act then was the culmination of a long legislative battle toward what Yanks would call redistricting. One member of Parliament might represent 12,000 electors and another represent as few as a dozen in what were called the 'rotten boroughs'; where there may have been little more than his family and his servants. The Reform was an important milestone in England's march to democracy. It was also the end of the *Tory Party.*

Reform Club   -a gentleman's club contemporaneous with the *Reform Act* and as progressive as the *Whigs* of the era. It was so modern that it actually admitted women in 1981. (Yes, 1981 -the same year that Lady Di and Prince Charles married.)

Reformation, Protestant   This all started when Martin Luther nailed his 95 thesis –complaints actually– to a Catholic church door in Germany in 1517. It's hard to say if that was a cause or effect. One of Luther's biggest objections was the church selling indulgences. You could buy a get-out-of-jail-free cards for sin. Unquestionably a doubtful practice and most of Europe was increasingly tired of Rome and the Catholic Church. Luther lit the fuse, but it was probably going to happening with or without him in short order.

England was sort of on the sidelines till *Henry VIII* wanted to set aside his first wife, *Catherine of Aragon*, and the Catholic pope wouldn't let him.

In 1533 he said enough with the pope and gave himself a divorce anyway. He started **Church of England** a year later. So began the **Reformation** in England. Things between the Catholics and Church of England (the Almost-Protestants) bumped along but came to a deadly pass during the **English Civil War** between 1642 and 1649.

regent   -a substitute for the king usually until he reached the age of eighteen. For example, Henry VIII's dad Henry VII shuffled off in 1509 when VIII was only 17. His 23 year old fiance, Catherine of Aragon, would act as his nominal regent for a short time. Then, about 30 years later, his only son, Edward VI, would be king form age 9 to the boy's death at age 16. During these seven years, a Regency Council tended to matters. The most important regency, however, was during the...

Regency Era   From the time **George III** went mad in about 1811, until his death in 1820, his son, George IV served as his regent. There is some argument as to just when it started; there are those who suggest the Regency actually went back to 1795 when III started loosing it.

The Napoleonic Wars ran thru much of the Regency, and this caused a good bit of social, political, and economic change, but despite this, the era was notable for fashion, romance, and elegance as well as significant achievements in art, literature, and perhaps most importantly, **architecture**. It ended with the death of William IV, who was George III's youngest son and George IV's little brother. Queen Victoria was next and so began the **Victorian Era.**

Regiment   To understand the importance and ubiquity of the regiment in English writing, it is important to understand that in England, the word 'army' was a loose abstraction that referred to a collection of independent regiments. From the very earliest medieval, military matters were somewhat economic affairs. The people who had land paid the crown 'rent' in the form of knights and /or soldiers. This gave them the right in turn to collect rent from farmers. This arrangement would evolve into a for-profit industry. As late as the 1600's, a regiment could be assembled by a self-appointed Colonel who paid to equip it out of his own pocket. Then he collected money from Parliament or what ever monarch had need of soldiers. He usually did so at a tidy profit.

Up until 1871, military officers bought their **commissions** from the officers who owned the various regiments much like someone today might buy a going and profitable business. It was only after the embarrassment of the Crimean War (1853 – 1856) that this practice was discontinued and the crown 'bought back its army.' Up until then, officers and private soldiers joined a given regiment, He did not join *the army*. Even after that point, a soldier's membership in a given regiment was very telling of his status if only among other military people.

Today a regiment is still the organizational unit of the Army. In theory, it is more or less self-contained and is responsible for logistics, deployment, and training its own personnel. It depends on the regiment's purpose as to its size and chain of command. In America, the various divisions of the Army -armies, include divisions, battalions, and regiments and such, were numbered or lettered. Not so in England. A cursory reading of the parts that make up the English army today will reveal the *Royal This*, and the *Guards of There*, and *Queens Own That*. The very highest organizational authority was an ad-hock General Staff that gathers only in times of war, otherwise it was, and still is, all about the Regiments.

These regiments still exist, each with its own uniform, insignia, and even its own marching music. An officer of a given regiment is a member for life even if he has retired. It's somewhat less so for the enlisted men, but all of them take pride in their regiment. In times of war, the General Staff might reshuffle personnel as needed, but people are not transferred as in the American Army; rather they are *seconded* (lent) to other groups. This sometimes leads to a situation wherein a given officer might have one rank in his (or her) regiment, and quite another rank when he reports to work at another regiment.   See *commisions*

registrars   -originally were in charge of collecting birth, marriage, and death records. After 1867 they also kept track of vaccinations.

religion   Today religion in England is much like it is elsewhere; people practice whatever religion they like and are pretty much left alone. It wasn't always so.

From about 500 BC to 500 AD the pagan Celts worshiped the forces of nature, occasionally sacrificed people, and did what their priest class, the Druids* told them to do. There are no written records from the Celts and what little is know about them comes from the Romans who got there shortly before the time of Christ. By the time the Romans left around 450, Christianity was well on its way and what little was left of the Celtic religion had changed to resemble the Roman polytheistic deities -Jupiter, Venus, Mars etc. with a little of the Norse stirred in, i.e., Thor, Woden. Odin etc.

But Christianity and subsequent Catholicism were the big thing, at least until Martin Luther pulled the rug out from under the pope in 1517. In 1533 **Henry VIII** wanted a divorce and the pope wouldn't give him one, so he declared himself the head of the Church, not the Catholic Church, the **Church of England**. It wasn't Lutheran nor Protestant quite yet, and other than replacing the pope with the king, relaxing ideas on contraception, and thinking that holy communion was more symbolic than real, the Church of England was pretty much the same as Catholicism.

Henry VIII died in 1547 and his daughter Mary ("Bloody Mary") by his first wife **Catherine of Aragon,** was crowned. Sort of. There were a lot of people who felt she was not the rightful monarch. Mary was a devout Catholic (like her mom) and a lot of non-Catholics died rather horrible deaths, as did those who thought she was not the rightful heir but that was pretty much the same thing as not being a Catholic.

By the time Mary died and Henry's second daughter, **Elizabeth I** became queen in 1558, the Church of England had become thoroughly Protestant. Elizabeth was a Protestant so things turned back the other way. This puts us somewhere in the **Protestant Reformation**, but various flavors of Protestants (Lutherans, Calvinists, and Episcopalians etc.) were growing all over Europe. The Reformation might be said to have ended in 1555 with the Peace of Augsburg which allowed both Catholicism and Lutheranism to coexist, if only in Germany. It ended some more in 1648 with the Treaty of Westphalia that ended the 30 Years War. This was a long hot mess of a war, but didn't settle things between the Protestants and Catholics in England. Nor were they sorted out until the end of the **English Civil War** in 1651, and even then...

In 1791 the policy of excluding, pestering, fining, and otherwise suppressing **recusants** (people who didn't go to the Church of England) were set aside. Today and for the last long while, the Catholics and Protestants have gotten along -but sadly, not in **Northern Ireland.**

* Merlin the Magician, if he existed, might have been a Druid.

Remembrance Day   -November 11 -aka Armistice Day and the end of WWI. After WWII it is to memorialize all the British war dead.

remittance man   -originally an emigre to one of the colonies who received money, a remittance, from back home. In literature, he was likely to be an embarrassment to his family and so the colonies were a convenient place to be rid of him.

Renaissance   England had a renaissance, but it's a lower-case renaissance compared to the Renaissance starting in Italy quite a bit earlier. Picture Queen Elizabeth and William Shakespeare as the English renaissance. In fact, think theater and literature and you are pretty well done. This is not to make light of literature etc., but the painting and other visual arts that Italy did so beautifully were pretty much stomped out by the Protestant Reformation (beginning about 1530) which set aside anything and everything religious, or at least the religious iconography so favored by the Renaissance painters. For the following hundred years, English art was pretty much limited to landscapes and portraits of wealthy people.

rep / repertory / repertoire   In general, it's someone's bag of tricks, but in the performing arts, it is a company's set of plays, operas, or ballets to be performed in a given season.

Resident   -the top representative of the crown living in one of the colonies, particularly India. see *viceroy*

Restoration, Protestant   It's either restoring the (limited) monarchy to Charles II, or less commonly, the restoration of (Catholic) church properties back to the bishops. Historians go either way. It amounted to much the same thing. Eleven years after chopping off *Charles I's* head, they brought his son, Charles II back from exile in France and made him king in 1660, but with the firm understanding that Parliament would have a greater say in the way things were to be done.   As to the bishops getting back their estates, it had more to do with giving some rich guys back their stuff, than it had to do with giving it back to the Holy Catholic and Apostolic Church.

Riot Act / read the Riot Act   In a curios, yet very British combination of brutality and courtesy, the Riot Act of 1714 gave local authorities permission to open fire on any gathering of 12 or more people who would not disperse when told to do so, but only after the Riot Act had been politely read aloud to them.

road / roadway   -any street, or highway in the city or country. The *roads* on the other hand, are a sheltered part of the SE coastline where ships could anchor and marshal -to wait till all of them gathered so they cold head out together.

road making   -didn't much change in England from the time of the Romans until the Scotsman John McAdam invented the modern way to make roads in about 1816. It was much like the way Romans did it, but with tar mixed into the topmost layer to make *tarmac*. It worked so well, it is still done this way.

rod   -a very old measure of length (5 ½ yards) used in measuring land.

rollmop   -pickled herring curlicues on a toothpick.
roll neck   -a turtleneck shirt.
roll-on   -get on with something enjoyable -like America's *let the good times roll,* or the New Orleans equivalent *Laissez les bon temps rouler !*

rook / rookery   A rook is England's crow -large, smart, black, noisy, and prone to stealing. They live in rookeries. When the word may also refer to where people live; it's a slum which is also full of noise and theft.

rooms   -an apartment. A *flat* is an entire floor and a *house* is a house that probably needed servants. The meaning of the word has changed over time. Sherlock Holmes and Dr. Watson had rooms, two bedrooms connected to a sitting room, but no kitchen. (Mrs. Hudson fetched up tea and occasional meals.) see *architecture* and *houses / homes*

rounders   Like American baseball, this game involves hitting a ball and running around four bases to score a point while the other teams chases down the ball, but it's a much older and–for want of a better word–friendlier game. Courtly Tudor men and women played together on nice summer days before they invented croquet. There are however, some differences between rounders and baseball. For one, bat is shorter and usually swung one handed. There are other differences in the rules as to strikes, outs, at-bats etc., but these are fiddly details. American might think of it as a blend of baseball and *cricket* played while sipping wine.

Rovers -boy scouts

rowing   -the preeminent college sport. Rowing those long skinny boats up and down rivers is hugely popular among college students, but it is not as horribly commercial as American college athletics, but rather more like intramural sports run by the students. Even so, it was not all that democratic. The whole thing got organized back in 1886 and excluded both professional rowers and anyone "who is or has been by trade or employment for wages, a mechanic, artisan, or laborer."

royal / royalty   The word shows up so often in England that is has lost all meaning other than having some often tenuous connection to the monarch and his or her family. This being said, there are some royal things that readers might bump into in their reading and therefor deserve a mention.

> **Royal Academy (of Arts)** A conservative and exclusive club of mostly old artists who put RA behind their name.
>
> **Royal Academy of Music** -a very old association of professional musicians and a conservatory that teaches music.
>
> **Royal Arsenal** -goes back to Henry VIII who set it up as the headquarters for his navy's cannons. It still is an arsenal.
>
> **Royal Assent** -ceremonial approval by the monarch to any law passed by Parliament. No king or queen has refused to sign-off since 1708 when Queen Anne decided against setting up a Scottish Militia. (The Scots were mostly Protestant then and Anne was a devout Catholic.)
>
> **Royal College of Art** Unlike the **Royal Academy**, this is an actual school, but it tends not so much toward the fine arts as toward design and fashion, and also unlike the Royal Academy, it is very trendy and modern.
>
> **Royal College of Music** -attached to the **Royal Academy of Music.** It teaches music.
>
> **Royal Court** -a theater in London going back to 1870. It tends toward the avant-garde.
>
> **Royal Geographic Society** -an independent collection of geographers going back to 1870 and bent on mapping the world. Consider the famous "Dr. Livingstone I presume" asked by Henry Morton Stanley when he happened on the good doctor in deepest Africa in 1871.

Both men were members of the Royal Geographic Society.

Royal Highlanders -the Black Watch regiment of Scotland.

Royal Historic Society -a club of historians and writers going back to 1868.

Royal Horse Guards -one of the army's highest status regiment. When they are not parading around on horse-back and presumably protecting the monarch, they drive tanks.

Royal Hospital -one of England's two veteran's hospitals; one is for soldiers and one for sailors.

Royal Household -as Parliament and the Cabinet took over more and more of the issues of government, the royal household came to concern itself with the monarch's safety and comfort. see ***servants***

Royal Observatory The observatory was established in 1673 to sort out celestial navigation for sailors and the Royal Navy. It did this so well that the town where it was originally located, ***Greenwich***, is now the prime meridian where both longitude and time start; it is 0° longitude and Greenwich Mean Time (GMT) is where / when the day starts..

Royal Shakespeare Company -a comparatively recent national and nationally funded theater based in Stratford, but with a touring company.

Royal Society -an important club of scientists going back, depending on whom you ask, to sometime between 1657 and 1667. At one point it was called the "College for the Promoting of Physico-Mathematical Experimental Learning." Fellows and members included Issac Newton, Charles Babbage, Charles Darwin, Albert Einstein, Steven Hawking, and even the woman biochemist Kathleen Lonsdale in 1945. Benjamin Franklin was not a member but demonstrated his lighting rod there in 1751. Their motto is worth noting: "Nullius in verba." -*Take no one's word for it.* see ***college***

Royal Air Force / RAF

England's air force got its start late in WWI and is the world's oldest independent air force. (The USAF separated from the US Army Air Corps only in 1947.) At the end of WWI, the RAF was also the world's largest air force. Its finest hour was undoubtedly the **Battle of Britain** during the Blitz of WWII. It was when Winston Churchill said of the RAF that, "Never in the field of human conflict was so much owed to so few."

An important difference between the USAF and the RAF–and this is controversial–is that the RAF acts to support the army and navy while the USAF can't be bothered. The American Army uses helicopters for ground support and the American Navy operates from big aircraft carriers. see ***military***

royal residences

The queen's homes are grand locations of state, but

usually for non-political functions. All of the residences are open to the public to various degrees and at various times. If this list seems long, remember that Elizabeth II had 60 residences. In general order of importance they are...

Windsor Castle

Buckingham Palace

Kensington Palace: -built in 1769 and where Queen Victoria was born and grew up. It is also the official residence of all manner of dukes and duchesses including the queen's kids, grand kids, and now great grand-kids.

Balmora Manor: Near Aberdeen Scotland, it's the summer place to go for shooting.

Sandringham Estate: Built in 1862, it's one of the newest. It's near Norfolk and a country estate with woodlands, heath, and beautiful gardens.

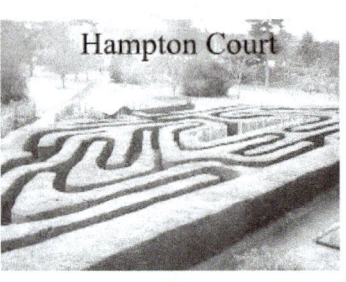
Hampton Court

Hampton Court Palace: Not used much by the queen, but it is very popular with the tourists because of its Tudor architecture and its gardens with huge hedge mazes.

rubbish tip -a dump. The old word is *midden*.

Rugby   If English football is American soccer, then rugby is really English football and it's called Rugby Football to distinguish it from regular football or soccer. It's not played with pads or helmets. It should be, but it's not. Instead of downs, rugby sorts out who really gets the ball with *scrums*. Scrums look like lines of scrimmage, but there is no buffer zone between the opposing linemen; they stick their heads into the other team's shoulders and push as something of a tug-of-war in reverse. Once the ball pops out, they follow various rules that look much like soccer, but they use their hands. *RU* is the Rugby Union.

rum   -spirits distilled from the by-products of making sugar, particularly molasses. Something like rum has been made all over the world from earliest recorded history usually in tropical places that grow sugar cane. In England, rum had to wait for the sugarcane to grow in the Caribbean during the 17th century. One document from Barbados sent back home to England said, "The chief fuddling they make in the island is Rumbullion, alias Kill-Devil, and this is made of sugar canes distilled, a hot, hellish, and terrible liquor." It would improve. It came to be very popular in the American colonies where they first started turning molasses into rum in Boston in 1664.

Rum and the Royal Navy go back to 1655 when they captured Jamaica. Sailors were given a *tot* or 2 ounces every day up until 1970. It may not have been rum, but rum or brandy depending on what was available. Availability was often a function of what ships the navy might have captured recently, or with whom the were they were trading at the time. The word *proof* also involved the navy. The Royal Navy bought rum only after testing it for strength. They would mix it with gun-powder and if it burned, it was said to be proof. (BTW -100% alcohol is equal to 200 proof.) At roughly the same time the Royal Navy was active in the Caribbean, pirates were as well. The connection between pirates and rum is more than apocryphal. Rum was a valuable commodity and as such, pirates were at least as interested in acquiring it as a trade-good, as they were in drinking it.

There is a final story involving rum and the Royal Navy. Sailors were not given a tot of pure rum. If they were to save up their tots over a period of some days, a mild buzz from the tot could grow into a more serious and debilitating bender. The English Admiral Edward Vernon hit on the solution of diluting the two ounces as it was taken out of the barrel at full proof. This diluted run would spoil before the men could collect up enough to really tie one on. Vernon was a pretty decent guy among the mixed bag of often dictatorial and sadistic British navy officers. He had the habit of wearing a grogram coat and was fondly nicknamed *Old Grog* among the sailors. The product of diluted rum came to be named *grog* after Vernon. Vernon had a young cabin boy -the son of a rich English family living in the colonies. This young man remembered Vernon so fondly that when he would go on to achieve a great measure of success, Lawrence Washington would name his estate Mt. Vernon after his old boss. George Washington, his step brother, would later inherit the place.

rushes -a useful grass-like plant with long hollow stems. During the medieval and beyond, they were used in weaving, as a crude candle, and spread on the packed-earth floors for insulation and cushioning.

RWV -robbery with violence -a mugging.

S was a mild and useful letter from its first appearance in the Semitic alphabet (Šîn *teeth*). It bumped along thru Greek and Latin with some minor confusion as to how to handle *s* vs. *ss*. About the middle of the 18th century newspapers got into it. No less an American than Benjamin Franklin wrote to a friend in 1786 that "the Round s .... begins to be the Mode, and in nice printing the Long 'ſ' is rejected entirely." Remember, Ben was a printer and publisher. See *ſ.*

SAE
-either the English equivalent of the American SASE -a *self addressed stamped envelope* or the *Society of Automotive Engineers*. This system of measuring nuts and bolts in fractions of an inch is sometimes called the English system, but it not used anywhere but in America. England went metric in 1965. see ***measurement***

sahib
-an address of respect used in India for an European. A memsahib is a European woman.

Saint
The word S*aint* prefaces even more expressions in England than the word *Royal*. Many saints have churches, towns, or other locations named after them. Some saints have feast days celebrated by the Catholics or the Protestants or both. BTW, places in America beginning with *San, Saint, St.* or *Saint* were probably settled by some flavor of a Catholic crowd like the Spanish. Portuguese, or French.

> ***St. Andrew*** -patron saint of Scotland and the white and red diagonal cross on the flag of the UK. His feast day was originally November 11, but was moved to November 30 and is now a bank holiday.
> ***St. Bartholomew / St. Barts*** -two churches in London, a hospital, and a fair for cloth makers up until about 1850.

St. Blaise -February 3 -important to wool growers. Saint Blaise was martyred in 316 in Armenia. He was tortured and beaten to death with the iron combs used to prepare wool for spinning and so naturally, he became the patron saint of wool combers. BTW -blaise is the fabric that is used to cover billiard tables and came to England in 1525.

St. George -two churches in London -one is in Mayfair -the most exclusive expensive neighborhood in London and THE place to be married. St. George is the patron saint of England and his cross is the red one in the flag of the UK. He was supposed to be a Greek soldier working for the Romans until he found Christianity and was summarily tortured to death. The bit about the dragon was a myth from the mid-east that the crusaders brought back to England.

St. James -A toney neighborhood in London known for Restoration *architecture* and clubs. St. James' Place is Henry VIII's country home, and now the Court of St. James is where England keeps ambassadors. St. James's Park on the edge of London was a deer hunting park until the 19th century when it was landscaped to a fair-thee-well.

St. John -a couple of colleges -one at Cambridge and one at Oxford, an ambulance brigade, and a woods are all named after St. John.

St. Martin in the Fields -originally a church sitting out in a field. The *Academy of St. Martin in the Fields* now refers to the orchestra that plays there.

St. Michael and St. George, the Order of -a ceremonial order for diplomats and civil servants. It's given to anyone who stays in the civil service long enough and its membership has gotten a little large.

St. Paul's -a huge popular cathedral that was used as a prison, burned down at various times going back to Shakespeare's time, and ultimately escaped bombing by the Germans in WW II, and became an icon of England's defiance. There are several other churches named after St. Paul, but none have the fame or architectural gravitas of this cathedral.

Saint Patrick -the apostle of Ireland and a real person. He was the son of a Roman official in England born sometime in the 5th century. He was kidnapped by Irish pirates (sort of local Vikings) at about age 16. He was sold into slavery in Ireland but escaped as a young man and made it back either to England or to Rome, but there is some confusion here. Somewhere he became a Christian and returned to Ireland. The Irish were then a literate crowd -unlike nearly all of Europe at the time- and even then were given to telling stories. Stories surrounding St. Patrick became beloved Irish legends. For example, the one about his banishing snakes is doubtful because Ireland has had no snakes after the last ice-age. His demonstrating the holy trinity with a shamrock is perhaps a little more believable. At one point he was said to have stuck his walking stick into the ground and it became a living tree. This is all fine and well, but there are three locations in Ireland claiming the tree in question.

St. Stephans -a chapel in Westminster used for meetings by the House of Commons between the time of Henry VIII and 1834 when it burned down. It was rebuilt.

St. Swithin's Day -something like America's Groundhog Day that predicts winter. Wet weather on July 15 predicts 40 more days of fog and rain.

St. Thomas Hospital -where Florence Nightingale founded the first nursing school.

salad   -any cold dish eaten with a fork that may or may not have lettuce and tomatoes. It likely involves *salad-cream* -a thinner and blander form of mayonnaise. *Salad Days* referred to youth from Shakespeare's time, and later came to refer to fluffy theater about nostalgia and innocence.

salters   -made salt -usually by evaporating sea water, but sometimes from inland salt springs. In the 17th century rock-salt was mined in Cheshire. Towns ending in -*wich* like Nantwich and Middlewich etc. probably were sources of salt.

salt beef	-corned beef
salt pot	-salt shaker
salts	-Epsom salts
saltings	-a tidal or salt marsh.

samosa   -a triangular deep-fried pastry from India stuffed with meat and vegetables. It is similar to, but spicier than a ***pastie***.

sanctuary   During the medieval, sanctuary in a church was limited to 40 days. It was good against civil authorities at a time when the church was arguably stricter than the civil authorities and perfectly willing to hang, burn, impale, press, dunk and otherwise punish people as the church thought best. The practice was banned for criminals in 1623, and in 1723 it was set aside altogether. This was all part of the civil / secular government coming to concern itself with the little guy, if only to keep the (Catholic) church out of it all.

sand bag   -a *cosh* or American black-jack. To be *sand bagged* is to be mugged or (metaphorically) be betrayed by someone you previously trusted.

sandwich   The story of the 4th Earl of Sandwich -John Montague (1718 – 1792) having a good run at the poker table and asking for a slab of meat between slices, or 'rounds', of bread is evidently true -or true-ish. Nonetheless, the English sandwich is a much simpler affair than the American Dagwood. It is rarely more than a slice of cheese or some cucumber on a single round of white bread.

sardines   -yes, the canned fish, but also a game similar to hide-and-seek. When the seeker found the hider, the seeker would squeeze into the hiding place until it was crammed full of players -usually teenagers.

Saturday   In 1850 textile mills were required by law to shut down at 2:PM Saturday. Gradually other industries and businesses followed suit and the weekend was almost invented for the working class. A modern Friday night's cutting loose, and Saturday's chores, errands, shopping and the occasional sports game all had to be done between Saturday afternoon and Sunday morning when church happened. see **weekends**

Savile   -a London club associated with writers and actors. **Savile Row** is a street in London where the best men's tailors do business

Savoy   -a neighborhood in London where you will find the Savoy Chapel, Savoy Theater, Savoy Hotel, and the Savoy Hill. The last is was where the BBC first set up shop.

sawyers   -sawed wood. Mark Twain's Tom Sawyer? Evidently he was the descendant of a man who made his living in a saw pit. This had to be the very definition of miserable work -particularly for the guy down in the hole looking up at the boss and getting a face full of sawdust. One contemporary source insists that all sawyers were 'drunkards and wastrels.'

Saxons   -not to be confused with **sextons**, the Saxons were half of the famous Anglo Saxon team. Both were tribes from Northern Germany that raided England and then settled there after the Romans left.

SAYE   -*Save As You Earn*. An automatic savings plan -like **PAYE**, but with money coming in rather than going out. It has tax advantages somewhat more generous than America's IRA's

Scapa Flow   The channel between the far north end of Scotland and the Orkney Islands. This is where England kept it Grand Fleet during WW I and where the Germany's High Seas Fleet was scuttled after the war's end. Being almost out of the range of German bombers during WW II, the English kept part of their navy there again. Recently, it has been very important for **north-sea oil.**

Scarborough   -a small fishing village on the North Sea that used to be a fashionable resort. Simon and Garfunkel's lovely ballad *Scarborough Fair* derives form an old (at least as early as 1650) English folk song about a man who asks a woman to perform a series of impossible tasks. In the original version, the impossible tasks went both ways between the man and a woman. An evil elf, a market fair, the plague, and finally, **Robbie Burns** all show up in it the various versions of the lyrics. One 17th century duet runs:

Man:
> *For thou must shape a sark to me. Without any cut or heme, qouth he.*

Woman:
> *I have an aiker of good lay-land, Which lyeth low by yon sea-strand.*

scheme -a plan or procedure There is no sneaky skulduggery involved.

schilling -an Australian coin not to be confused with shilling -the English coin. see *money*

schiltron This is a late medieval battle formation involving a bunch of soldiers with long lances all gathered into a very prickly square. It's a Roman invention, but the Scots used it to great effect against English armored knights on horses.

Schools Public and private schools are exactly opposite of what the American reader might guess. In theory, public schools are open to anyone, or anyone who could afford it. Private schools, on the other hand, limited their enrollment to working men's children who live in a given neighborhood or parish. As is so often the case, a little history might help sort it out.

The French king Charlemagne (747 - 814) was big on culture and learning. He was an indifferent scholar himself, but was responsible for the survival of most of the classic Latin by having it gathered up and copied. The 'Carolingian Renaissance' saw the flowering of art, architecture, literature, and even mathematics. But this subject properly belongs in French history. In England and the rest of Europe, books were copied by hand, usually by monks and often monks who were themselves illiterate; at least until after Gutenberg invented the printing press in about 1440.

Until then, literacy meant being the king, a bishop, cardinal, or high ranking priest. It also meant reading and writing Latin. Literacy among kings goes back as far as Alfred the Great before the Normans. All the kings (and the few queens) could read and write. Many could do so in several languages beside English.

Literacy and the ability to write business letters gave the Catholic Church tremendous power, over and above its purported ability to get people into heaven. To the credit of the church, it made some progress teaching the aristocracy Latin. In addition to the rich kids, some few lads from the countryside might also get an education, but only if they seemed very bright and inclined to enter the clergy. The oldest such school in England was Oxford which probably got started in 1096. In 1167 Henry II forbade English scholars going off to school in Paris and so Oxford grew apace.

On the continent, Gutenberg invented the printing press in 1439 and the Renaissance was picking up steam, but it had more to do with art than literacy. Furthermore, if no one could read, no one would buy books and Gutenberg was a businessman. Rather, it was the Protestant **Reformation** that was really the big thing that put reading over the top. (The Reformation started in 1517 in Germany with Martin Luther, and finished up in England about 1537). Up until then, the Catholic Church appointed itself as the authority on what was necessary to get into heaven. It worked out as follows; people needed to know precious little except what the church told them, what they were supposed to do was give money to the church, and as to what they were not supposed to do was mostly anything enjoyable. If someone slipped up and did have some fun, then they had to give more money to the church for an indulgence. This last thing was what so disturbed Martin Luther. After the Reformation, people began reading the Bible on their own, at least the Protestants who were literate.

So from roughly the time of Queen Elizabeth (who spoke several languages herself and was something of a Latin scholar) what little education

that was available to the masses was reading the Bible and while they were about it, maybe doing just a little business math.

But before we step off to the Enlightenment when the world became enlightened enough to have something to teach, we need to review the pragmatic

apprenticeship system. An apprentice's parents would indenture the lad to a master craftsman for seven years to learn a craft. It depended on the craft, but a little extraneous education had to happen; printers probably had to be able to read and builders might need a little math. This system certainly served a quality control function; buildings ought not fall down and apothecaries ought not hand out poison. In defense of the apprentice system, it must be said that they did provide job-skills to people who went on to build and make and just generally increase the *Wealth of the Nations**.

Along about 1810, the English noticed that there were lots of things that needed dong in the economy that the medieval guilds just couldn't handle, so they repealed the *Statute of Artificers*. This old law defined both who should be doing things, and how things should be done. This was scarcely surprising. With the coming of railroads for example, the need for the guild of long-haul oxen driving teamsters diminished, and contrary wise, the question of what guild was be in charge of those newfangled steam engines arose. But we are ahead of ourselves. We will come back to the educational consequences of mercantilism and the industrial revolution after we revisit religion and education.

The notion of what we might think of as charity is a function of the enlightenment that suggested that life just maybe was about more than suffering and getting into heaven. The parish church took up the role of looking more carefully after the health and welfare of the poor, rather then just their souls. While about it, they came to concern themselves with their minds as well.

Early in the 1800's, non-conformist and / or non-denominational schools began to take students from the purely Protestant churches. These

"British Schools"† were still charitable and still had a religious connection, but they were teaching as many as 25% of the school-age children. In 1833 (4 years before Victoria's coronation) Parliament voted sums of money to build schools. Various acts and state funded programs unfolded thereafter. In 1880, for example, education was compulsory for children between five and ten years of age. The *leaving age* was raised to 11 in 1893 and 12 years of age in 1899. It wasn't all fun and games for children however; any child working full time who was under the age of 13 had to produce a certificate of *education standard* or the employer was fined, but it was apparently not a very steep fine. By the end of the 1800's, there were fee-charging schools for the rich as well as parochial schools which charged fees on a charitable or sliding scale for the particularly devout. Finally, there were state funded schools for everyone else. Curriculum was standardized and modernized, but Latin was still taught throughout.

As all this was going on, England had become the center of the world, She imported raw materials from all over, made fancy expensive things out of the stuff, and shipped products back out to the rest of the world and did so at great profit. Lots of engineering, administering, and merchandising created the need for technical educations and technical colleges which were initially funded by a whiskey tax. (Studying Latin and Greek became something of an elective. Math and science, however, became very important.) There was even a Department of Science and Art which approved the curricula. In 1900 the leaving age for children was moved up to 15.

A few comparisons with education in America are appropriate. School in America are more intensely local affairs than in England, if only up thru secondary school. In 1862‡ the Morrell Land Grant Act provided for agricultural and engineering education. In 1916 the federal government began to provide for vocational education in somewhat the same way England began technical education, but quite unlike England, America faced the problem of race and segregation issues from as far back as 1890.

The 20th century begins a very confusing series of reforms and acts in England that were the consequence of two world wars and the machinations of the conservative and liberal governments. Perhaps the most important one, the Butler Act came along in 1944. This was a three part system consisting of grammar schools, secondary modern schools, and secondary technical schools. It hinged on a test students were given at age eleven that determined if they would go on to what to the American mind would be vocational / technical schools. Better students, would go on to grammar school, or what American would think of as high-school or preparatory schools.

* The Wealth of Nations by the English philosopher Adam Smith, was published in 1776 and is considered the first and perhaps most important book on what would come to be the science of economics. Adam Smith suggested that his famous 'invisible hand' (an internal market-driven control) was the best way for economies to regulate themselves rather than external controls like

government caveats or even the guild / apprentice system.

† The Scots were funding schools for everyone as early as 1660.

‡ At about this time, America was one if the most literate places in the world.

scones   -a little round biscuit made with sugar, and egg wash, and sometimes with fruit, raisins, or sultanas (yellow raisins) but without yeast like ***crumpets.*** These are very important accompaniment for tea and clotted cream.

schooner   -either a glass a little larger than might be expected for sherry, or smaller if for beer.   -or-
-a smallish ship fore-and aft rigged with two masts, the taller one being at the back, or a larger ship with a similar rig of three or more masts all the same height.

Scotch eggs   a hard-boiled egg rolled first in sausage meat, then rolled in egg yolk & breadcrumbs, and deep fried. Classic picnic food. Think of American deviled eggs, but meatier and greasier.

Scot   -someone from Scotland. Scott is either the first name, or the proper name for the *Clan Scott*. ***Scottish*** is the modifier, NOT to be confused with...

scotch   -whisky made form malted grain usually dried over a peat fire. Even the word *whisky* is tricky. Scotch whisky is not to be confuse with Irish whisk*E*y.

Scotland   -to the north of England. It was the second kingdom which, when Wales is stirred in, gives you Great Britain. To understand the English and the Scots, begin with the English view that Scotland was at least as troublesome as Ireland, if not more so. It goes back to the Romans who built Hadrian's Wall to keep out the Scots –the Picts actually– who were a particularly tough variety of Celts.   Things did not improve and there was pretty constant warfare until the English finally subdued them in 1707 when the two kingdoms were unified, at least to the minds of the English. The Scots did not see it that way and kept fighting till 1745 when ***Bonnie Prince Charles*** lost the battle of Culloden. More of Scotland was Catholic than England was and this did not help matters. To put it in terms of American History, the Scots were a little like the South after the Civil War; exploited, impoverished, and increasingly patriotic to Scotland as a consequence. Today Scotland has its own Parliament, church, breakfast sausage, and whisky. They are better engineers and the North Sea Oil was in their back-yard. Every so often, the Scots get together to vote on the possibility of dropping out of the Great Britain / United Kingdom thing. They haven't yet, but they seem to get a little closer every time.

Scotland Yard -a street in London where the Metro Police built their headquarters in 1829. The nick-name has stuck so well that when they moved their headquarters across town to Victoria Embankment in 1891, it was still called Scotland Yard, but it may sometimes be referred to as the New Scotland Yard. Whatever its name, it is not England's equivalent to America's FBI. It is a big city police force with enough personnel to have specialists that from time to time may be called on to help out the local police outside of London. For the big crimes that cross county borders, the **Special Branch** does the sort of things the FBI does in America.

Scottish Highlands Yes, they are high, both in terms of elevation and latitude, but the word comes from Scots Gaelic word *Ghaidhealtachd*, shortened to Heilands, meaning the *place of the Gaels*. There was lots of history, poverty, rebellion, and horrible exploitation by the English. This led to forced mass emigration, first to Ireland and later to the colonies. In literature, someone from the Highlands is to be taken very seriously indeed. It is also beautiful in a wild and rugged way.

scratch meal -made from left-overs.

screw -a twist or *spill* of paper to hold a bit of something, or a prison guard.

scullery -a room behind the kitchen for cleaning pots and pans. A scullery maid was at the very bottom of the household servant's hierarchy. see **servants**

Sea Lords -four members of the Royal Navy's Admiralty along with two civilian members who did large scale planning After 1964 the Admiralty was absorbed in to the Ministry of Defense and five more civilians were added. At the time of the sinking of the Lusitania and America's entry into WWI, **Winston Churchill** was a senior Sea Lord, while across the pond, F. D. Roosevelt was the Secretary of the Navy.

season, the From about May to early August, the trendy swells needed to be in London for all the fashionable parties and to *turn out* their daughters. This meant to dress them all up and present them to polite society for consideration as wives. Think Debutante ball

secondary school -before about 1960, these schools were for students up to about eleven years of age to prepared them for vocations. They were replaced with **comprehensive schools** and now are roughly the equivalent of American high-schools. see **schools**

secretary He or she may be a stenographer or executive assistant, but more commonly it refers to a position in the Cabinet. The term is largely interchangeable with *Minister*, but the later is more current. Originally a nobleman's secretary handled correspondence and the administrative details of running the holdings and may be thought of as a consultant more than a servant. The secretary of a club or society, particularly charitable ones, is probably the administrator and beholding to an elected board of directors.

Secretary of State   -a little like America's Secretary of State -but more complicated. Today this position is one of the four Principal Ministries. The other offices are the Prime Minister, Exchequer, and Defense.

Historically, the king had a clerk and later a secretary who wrote letters for his signature or seal. As time went on, this position morphed into Secretaries of State of the Northern and Southern Departments. Both dealt with Home Affairs but divided into the northern Protestant counties and the southern department dealing with the Catholic southern counties.

After the union with Scotland in 1708, a Secretary of Scotland was added and later two more, the Home Secretary and the Foreign Secretary. The third secretary, the Scottish one, was discarded, but two more were added, one for the War Department and one for India.

Secretary of the Treasury   -the minister just under the *Chancellor of the Exchequer*. Between the two of them, they sort out how much money the other ministers get, how much public employees will be paid, what and how much the government buys, and where the money comes from.

see   -a bishop's territory.

see off -escorting someone out -without their necessarily wanting to go.

see out -more polite. Seeing someone to the door for friendly good-byes.

see over   -to inspect.

see right   -to settle up what might otherwise be a fraught situation.

Selfridge   -a chain of departments store second only to Harrods in size and prestige. It goes back to 1908.

sergeant   -like an American military sergeant, but coming in only two flavors in England, the Sergeant and Sergeant Major. (America slices and dices them up into several different levels.) The English Sergeant Major is the oldest sergeant in a company and the Regiment Sergeant Major is the top enlisted man. An English police sergeant is much the same as an American one, a level up from the constable. Finally, a sergeant is not to be confused with a *serjeant* -an old and obscure term for a high-status and expensive barrister. BTW, to be perfectly correct, it's spelled *sergeant* and not *sargeant* which is a last name.

semi-detached   -a duplex. These are much more common in England than in America and as in America, the owner often lives in one and rents out the other.

seminary   Historically, this was a school for a specific profession like educating the clergy but not necessarily. They acquired a bad reputation among Protestants in the 1860's because the Catholics trained guerrilla priests to infiltrate and spread 'Popery' (Catholicism). The Church of England actually stopped using the word all together. In the early 1800's, *ladies' seminaries* came about and acted as what we might think of as finishing schools today.

sennight   -seven nights -a very old word for week.

servants, domestic   There is much to be said about servants in England. First thing is to say it was a much less enjoyable life than TV and movies would have us believe. Second thing to remember is that it started way WAY back with slavery during the Roman occupation, improved only slightly under Norman feudalism and the middle ages, became the backbone of the monarchy and government during the Renaissance. The occupation of servants bumped along for hundreds more years until it finally reached its starched-uniform-wearing, stuffy, formalized, rigidly hierarchical pinnacle toward the end of the 19th century. Good stuff if you are writing Gothic Romance -not so much for the people involved, but, by WW I, it was well on its way out.

    Begin with the second thing first and consider the Roman Governor of Britannia. He had to report back to his boss in Rome. Even ***William the Conqueror*** had to go back to France now and then on business and when there, he 'owed fealty' to the French (Frankish actually) king. To some degree even the English kings owed something to the pope, at least until ***Henry VIII*** set aside Catholicism and started his own church. Perhaps not the king, but from there on down and throughout history, everyone worked for someone higher up the food chain. The *peerage* -the mystifying order of who was the coolest richest bossiest person really came down to who their father was and thereby, who had to obey whom. It is perhaps to the credit of the American mind that this sort of thing is a little incomprehensible.

    Getting enough to eat was one of the big concerns back then and land was where food came from, so land was the source of power and wealth. Feudalism was the system of land ownership mixed together with the ownership of labor. The modern notion that a worker owned his own labor hadn't occurred to the various land-owning nobility, nor–it must be said–had it occurred to the peasants who were pretty preoccupied with staying alive till they hopefully got into to heaven, so the church was another big concern. (The church had its own land and its own rigid hierarchy of bosses too.)

    The final big thing back in the day was war. War was often between varieties of Englishmen over this religion or that religion. It was often with the French, but Spain and Denmark as well as a few other kingdoms show up in history. The middle managers in all these big things were the **knights** who were useful and owed *fealty* to the nobility and / or the church. Between

 hostilities, this meant they extracted food and taxes from the locals. Occasionally they would go off to war with their own servants -*squires*, and recruits etc. They did so with abundant awareness of who was in charge of what. As a part of this business of service and ranks and hierarchy, we have the military. This was not a small thing, but military **rank** was pretty well nailed down by the Roman and the English took it up where the Romans left off with some help from the Prussians later on.

The plague killed between one third and one half of Europe between 1348 and 1349 so Europe set aside war as it would have been a little redundant. Bad news if you died, but if you survived, it was a good thing because a labor shortage down on the farm led to rising wages. Things got so bad -at least to the thinking of the aristocracy- that in 1351 Parliament passed the Statute of Laborers which was sort of a 14th century wage and price control measure, but it only controlled wages. Prices –particularly for food– went up, so it all fell apart.

After various rebellions and revolts, serfdom was eliminated. Up until then, the surfs were not *technically* owned by the local lord, but rather owned by the land which in turn WAS owned the lord. Pretty thin gruel of a legal fiction, but it wasn't 'slavery.' The big news for onion diggers and stable-muckers was that they now could go down the road if the employment grass looked greener over yonder. By 1450, English workers had the highest wages in all of Europe and this would continue well into the 19th century. We begin to see just a hint of a middle-class about now, but for the greatest number of people, they still had to put in time on the squire's farm or in his household.

At the very top of the heap (in London rather then down on the farm and out in the sticks) was court. *Queen Elizabeth* (1533-1603) had a grand court that provides an illustrative intersection of servants (ceremonial and the actually productive ones) the peerage, and the operation of the government at the time. At the bottom, were the servants who made beds, did laundry, scrubbed pots, and cleaned out the stables. This crowd numbering in the hundreds was invisible at the time, other than showing up in the occasional rags-to-riches story written much later. There were also dozens of career servants who were well paid by the standards of the day, but the queen had the best and most experienced people in the roles of...

- almoners who gave alms to the poor.
- kitchens -various kitchens with various capabilities and specialties, and many of the best cooks in the Realm.
- cellars for wine, as well as butter and cheese.
- acataries who bought and processed meat, fish, and salt.
- poultry for not only poultry, but other white meats.
- laundry for table and bed linen as well as towels (Clothes were done

elsewhere.)
- scullery men and maids.
- woodyard for cooking & heat, as well as rushes that soaked up what we now put in the toilet.
- spicery for spice, fruit, and wax to seal the bottles of spice.
- stables

Each of these departments were so large and busy that the various department heads fulfilled their roles more as accountants and managers than actual cooks and stewards etc. A large part of everyone's job was to impress visiting royalty and diplomats as well as to look after the queen and all her hangers-on. It was good work if you could bet it and it was a lucky peasant boy who got a job shoveling out the queen's stables. He could go far.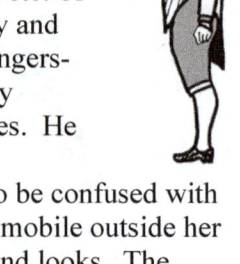

A little higher up were the monarch's guards. (Not to be confused with Queen's Guard -the guys in the big black hats standing immobile outside her residence.) The guards were hired based on their height and looks. The regular queen's guards (not capitalized) guarded the queen and wore pretty uniforms too, but were presumably actually skillful in matters of defense and arms.

Still higher were the government professionals. Usually put into position, once again because of daddy. But not always. Some number of these councilors were actually talented and skillful at things like diplomacy, economics, foreign trade, and what we might today call executive management.

From here on up the ladder, Elizabeth's servants were entirely ceremonial and always the kids of some important personage. These include six Maids of Honor, two or three Ladies of the Bed Chamber, some Grooms of the Privy Chamber, and one Gentleman Usher. All of them looked after the queen. Even at this level, there is a hierarchy. At the bottom were the servants of the Presence Chamber which was pretty much the whole court.

Next up, was the Privy Chamber with its compliment of servants, both ceremonial and productive. This is where she met with her councilors and did most of the business of being queen. ('Privy' means *private*. It came to mean the toilet / biffy only much later -for obvious reasons.)

Finally, there was her Bed Chamber with her most trusted crew. Even here, she was hardly ever alone. Elizabeth acted the role of a virgin her whole life, and historians are doubtful about her virginity, but given the number of people were around her 24-7, it seems they are justified in debating the real state of her chastity.

The ceremonial servants were her bare-bones traveling staff and each of them had their own staff of servants who did some actual work. Each of her 60 (Sixty. Yes, that's a big six-zero) royal residences had another layer of local full-time professional servants. The Queen and her court would typically only stay at a given palace for a few weeks at a time, before it needed 'airing and sweetening.' This is to say they needed to gather up all the used rushes and air the place out.

So it went thru the Enlightenment, Regency, and other eras till we come to the Industrial Revolution. Several things to remember about this revolution; first, there was something to buy besides turnips. Second, land was no longer the only source of wealth. Some people got rich my making things and other people got rich by selling those things to well-paid farm workers. (This is of course a gross oversimplification. People got rich lots of ways that often involved the colonies.) The final thing to remember is another of those things that are very confusing to Americans; actually doing something productive to earn your money was not nearly as cool as having a rich daddy *give* it to you.

But first a few words about 'class' that will also baffle Americans. Yanks view class a function of money or of some combination of education and talent which often leads to money. Stir in pluck, and you have the whole Horatio Alger thing. Brits, or old-time Brits, take a different view. You are what your daddy was and will only ever be only what your daddy was. Period. Full stop. At least until after WW I and for the blue-blood-blue-hair crowd, only after WW II.

You can take some small pity on the English. Until after the **Restoration** (1660 - 1685) there were only two classes, the nobility and everyone else. Actually, this is another over simplification; to over-simplify slightly less, there were the nobility who both owned land and could pass it on to their kids, and then there was the gentry. Useful word *gentry*. Its meaning has changed over the years. Back then it meant the knights who could <u>not</u> pass heir land on to their kids. Then there was everyone else. Briefly, lawyers. doctors, professors and a few other professionals were allowed into the gentry, but this would change.

London was the biggest urban area in the western world from the time of Elizabeth. (New York would surpass it in population only about 1925.) As industrialization and urbanization continued, things changed. Manufacturers and merchants got rich and tried to become middle class, by being what Americans would call snooty; they put on airs. They became so intensely interested in being all social and proper that they kicked the merchant class (who were often their fathers who got rich in the first place) out of middle class and into what is called the 'working class' along with doctors and lawyers. They also got themselves servants just to prove that they had made it. The more servants they had, the closer to the gentry they felt themselves to be.

There were some splinter classes no one knew quite what to do with and whom readers may trip over from time to time. For example, there were independent farmers who owned a lot of land and were rich and important, but they did actual work and occasionally got muddy, so they couldn't be allowed into the middle class. So the middle class simply ignored them, but they ignored everyone who they felt was beneath them anyway. Sometimes these rich muddy farmers do make it into English literature and usually are seen as a better more enlightened sort of Lord of the Manor.

Then there were educated young women who for whatever reason weren't married. They became *governesses* and are the very center of a whole lot of literature. They often are seen as heroic figures of genteel poverty. Romance attains in the books, but rarely in reality because their education didn't fit them into the working class and nor were they of any higher class. Finally, there were the younger sons of the nobility went into the clergy, or if they were too stupid for preaching, they joined a *regiment*. These hapless chaps also show up as useful characters in certain literature staged before WW II.

David Grote* defines the hierarchy vividly and completely as follows:

1. Nobility
2. Genrty (non-inheritable titles, landowners, leisured)
3. Professional gentry (civil servants, clergy, officers -from gentry families)
4. Middle-class professionals (doctors, lawyers, officers, dons)
5. Modern professionals (engineers, architects, headmasters)
6. Middle-class businessmen (industrialists, brokers, bankers, foreign traders)
7. Middle-class merchants (wholesalers, operators of chain stores)
8. Servants of the gentry
9. Office workers (clerks, bank tellers, bookkeepers, schoolteachers)
10. Farmers
11. Shopkeepers
12. Servants of the middle-class
13. Artisans (including actors and musicians)
14. Shop assistants
15. Skilled industrial workers
16. Semiskilled industrial workers
17. Manual laborers (urban or rural)

By far the biggest and most important splinter class was the servant class. Notice where they fall in Grote's hierarchy. We began this essay with the observation that everyone was a servant to someone else, and this was no less true in the 19th century. A great part of the population, as many as two million in London alone, were servants by the end of the century. The curious thing was that not many stayed servants. There were certainly career servants, but because a married servant was utterly unacceptable to the middle class, men and women both passed out of service and on to other work and started families. But if they didn't get married and go on to make other servants, where did the middle class replenish the supply? In a word -the sticks. Young girls fresh off the farm were in big demand. Once she had a little experience under her belt, women servants were the highest paid women in England at the time.

So let's review things as they were when Queen Victoria (1819 - 1901) was nominally in charge. We have the tiny nobility with titles like Baron and Viscount and all. Next we have the gentry who own land, but so do the wealthy middle class by now -if only a summer place and if only to impress the other middle class people. Then there is the professional crowd, and below them, the working class or the poor people 'in the trades', and finally, the servant class. It depends on how you count, but this was probably the biggest class anyway you count it. At the time, England's *middle-class* was a whole lot richer than what Americans think of as their middle-class. They differ from Yanks in another important way. While American struggled to move up the ladder and are admired for doing so, the English were pretty content to know their place and stay in their place. The rich middle-class were content to stay rich-middle-class, but very interested indeed in showing the world just how classy and rich they were.

Now we have at long last laid the ground work to understand butlers, maids, and governesses, of Gothic English Literature. The poorest urban household aspiring to be middle-class, and even many a working class household would have a maid-of-all-work. She was apt be as young as 14. When she learned she was expected to work ten to twelve hours six days a week and only half a day on Sunday, she was delighted to have it so much easier that she had it down on the farm. Better prospects of marriage in the big city too.

A step up and the family would add either a cook or, if children were in the house, a nurse-maid, and / or perhaps a chamber maid or parlor maid. The chamber maid tended to the family's needs in their chambers (bedrooms) and was therefore more intimately involved with the family and was necessarily more trusted and of higher status than the downstairs parlor maid who tended to things downstairs and was therefore of lower status in the chain of command. (The maid between floors, the *tweeny* was an apprentice and was sent to wherever she was needed.) These four or five women were the minimum of aspiring gentility.

There is some flexibility as to what servants got added next, but a butler was considered a very good thing to have. He would supervise all the other servants including the cook who might have been a super-star cook who earned more than the butler. The butler, in addition to being management, acted as waiter, valet, may have looked after the family horse and carriage, and finally dealt with vendors and tradesmen.

A lady's maid or an assistant cook might be added next. If the family was wealthy enough, they might add some combination of a coachman & groom, laundry maid, scullery-maid, upper parlor-maid, another nursemaid etc. Footman were added at the very top end of the urban household's domestic acquisitiveness. If the staff grew large enough (and the lady of the house wasn't inclined to do so) there would also be a house-keeper who managed the female staff while the butler managed the male staff, but he was superior to the house-keeper.

This is for an urban household. A county estate involved an entire different and larger staff, much like a combination of Elizabeth's traveling and non-traveling local servants. Some of the urban servants would travel with the family when they left for the country and cared for the family, but the locals looked after the estate. It might take only a handful of family servants but twenty or thirty servants on the estate.

At the top of this particular heap was the land or estate steward. He was an expert in farming if the estate grew things, and he collected the rents. Just under this position was the house steward who managed things beyond the butler's purvey. Both of these positions were not so much a servant as a professional and respected much like an account or lawyer would be today.

The gardener was as important for impressing the guests as was the cook, and he might manage a staff, but he did not live in the *house* but rather had a cottage on the grounds. There was a head groom or stable master to tend to the horses and perhaps master's dogs, and he might have managed a staff as well. Add a game keeper or two and a grounds keeper and the estate stood ready to impress guests. But not weekend guests. People who worked during the week were necessarily of the working class and therefore were never invited and furthermore, weekends weren't been invented until the 19th century. There were Sundays, but they were for going to church.

This leaves us with the most literary character of all, the governess. She was hired to educate and look after the family's daughters. The boys were sent off to boarding schools as soon as they left the care of the family nurse-maid, but girls were more problematic. The Gothic romances got at least one part right, the governess was typically the well educated but unmarried daughter of a fallen or impoverished ex-genteel family. As such, it would be unthinkable to be a servant, but a girl has got to eat. She was hardly part of the family as having a clouded background. The servants viewed her as no better than they were, despite her education. It was typically a sad & lonely existence for governesses.

It must be remembered that there was no social security in the 19th century. Furthermore, industrializing and urbanization were changing things in England faster than society could easily adjust. A servant was happy to have food and a warm & reasonably dry place to sleep. There is also the English fondness for propriety and knowing one's place. Only the most professional and highest paid servants stayed servants much past the times in their lives when they would marry and start families. Finally, there wasn't much to spend money on. They didn't need cars, or computers. Health care was minimal for everyone, even the rich. Fashion was limited to a nice bonnet to wear to church. The following lists the annual earning of a servant in pounds with a base year of 1860 and 2016 buying power in dollars.

Position and Pay -in historic pounds and in 2016 dollars.					
grounds keeper	Ł10	$1440	cook (basic)	30	$4320
stable boy	10	1440	first footman	30	4320
scullery / kitchen	13	1870	gamekeeper	40	5760
& laundry maids			housekeeper	40	5760
head groom	15	2160	butler	50	7200

nurse	15	2160	house steward	74	10800
chamber maid	20	2880	head gardener	120	17280
governess	25	3600	land steward	200	28800
head nurse	25	3600	cook (super-star)	300	43200
lady's maid	25	3600			

So what happened to the servants? The very rich still have them, but they are more apt to be best-selling authors and rock stars than **middle-class** land-owners. For starters, both wars took a lot of people out of the workforce. Some didn't return for very unpleasant reasons, but many didn't go back into service because they found better jobs after the war. Next there came various labor saving devices like washing-machines, vacuum cleaners, and such that made it faster & easier for people (women) to do their work. Certainly social fashions played a part. It simply came to be seen as tacky to have a house full of servants. With more women working, other women could earn good livings working as a char-woman or *dailies* without the employer providing room and board. But the biggest reasons were economic. Various tax reforms beginning in 1909 and continuing on to pretty much on to this day made owning large estates increasingly expensive. Adding to this problem was a decline in the cost of food during the 20's, followed by a long general depression during the 30's, and then finally another long downward trend in the cost of food starting in the 50's and continuing on to this day. This also made owning land less profitable, if not actually an expensive money pit.
* British English for American Readers, A Dictionary of the Language, Customs, and Places of British Life, Life, and Literature, Grote, David, Greenwood Press, Westport Connecticut London. An excellent resource for serious study.

Severn, River   At a whole 220 miles, the Severn is England's longest river. (The Mississippi River is 2320 miles long) The Severn empties into the Bristol Channel on the southern border of Wales.

service lift   -what American call a dumb waiter, This is the elevator thing that appears in English mysteries for hiding dead bodies and other nefarious purposes. The British *dumbwaiter* is what Yanks would call a *Lazy Susan.*

serviette   -a napkin, usually a paper one.

set up   -the opposite of America's setting up someone for a downfall or to be a target, in England to *set up* someone is to give them a good start.

sexton   -an officer of a church, congregation, or synagogue charged with the maintenance of its buildings and/or the surrounding graveyard. In smaller places of worship, this office is often combined with that of **verger**. The sexton is the head usher in The Church of England

shandy   -a mix of beer and ginger ail or lemonade. A polite and not-quite-serious drink for women and children.

Shakespeare, William   -born in 1564, died 1616, wrote a lot of stuff in between. Your literature teacher undoubtedly mentioned he wrote 38 plays, 154 sonnets, two long narrative poems, and a few things for which he wasn't get credit. Your teacher might have mentioned that he was a friend of Queen Elizabeth I and should have stressed that much of the way both the Brits and the Yanks speak and write can be laid at the Bard's feet. But what your teacher may have missed is that when he was 18 he married a 26 year old woman who had a baby six months later. Furthermore, no one knows for sure what he looked like; he never sat for a portrait. The image we have of him today with what is called the Shakespearean brow comes from an

engraving on the cover of a book published seven years after his death, but people who knew him said it was a pretty good likeness. BTW, *bardolatry* is excessive idolatry of the Bard of Avon.

sheep   Today England's sheep industry ranks behind Nigeria, but ahead of New Zealand. Nonetheless, sheep play an important role in England's economic history. In 1265 the crown enacted an export tax on wool and a century later it was so important that the speaker of the ***House of Lords*** sits on a ceremonial sack of sheep's hair -the *Wool Sack*. The American colonists were forbidden to trade wool anywhere but with the mother country in 1699. (Things did not improve till 1776, but this is another story.) It was the industrial revolution and the perfection of power looms in England that really kicked wool into high gear using a lot of wool imported from another English colony–Australia. Aside from the wool, the English eat more lamb and mutton than Americans do, and a lot of it is in ***curry***.

sheriff   Not unlike American sheriffs, or American sheriffs of the 18th century anyway. They were local police but in England they were far more involved in protecting the king's deer from poachers and making sure everyone paid their taxes than they were involved in protecting the local peasants from the bad guys. 'Sheriff' is the contraction of *shire reeve* or local royal representative in the shire. By the 18th century, the sheriff's job came to be more of an expert in farm and estate management. In Scotland, sheriffs are judges.

Sherlock Holmes   -a consulting detective who was the product of the imagination of Sir Arthur Conan Doyle. Doyle's character was the very embodiment of cold logical reasoning, but Doyle himself was a bit out there.

Besides writing detective stories, he researched and wrote The <u>History of Spiritualism</u> and tried to contact his dead wife thru seances. To his credit, however, he was also a fervent advocate for justice and his efforts lead to two innocent men being exonerated.

His first success was in 1887 -*A Study in Scarlet*- and he wrapped up his career in 1927. The total was four novels, and 56 short stories. As for Sherlock himself, he holds the world record for being in more movies than any other character in all of the world's literature. BTW -he never said "Elementary my dear Watson," but he *was* keen on saying "Come Watson, the game's afoot!"

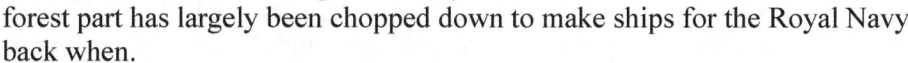

Sherwood Forrest   Yes, it's a real place where the probably fictional character Robin Hood hung out. Sadly the forest part has largely been chopped down to make ships for the Royal Navy back when.

shillings   -a coin worth twelve pence -12p- or one twentieth of a pound. 20s = £1. The first shilling was issued by Henry VIII and up until 1971 the shilling was a basic coin in the country, but when England went metric, it was discontinued. The sChilling is the Australian spelling.)

shinglers   -were roofers in oak, elm, and later, red cedar from America. see *tylers* and *thatchers*

Ship Master   -the technology superstars of the day who were rated in various competencies like inland or offshore waters, oceans, types of ships, navigation, sail / steam etc. Think of them as the airline pilots of the day.

ship of the line   The largest battle ships of the Royal Navy from the 17th thru 19th century. They were all about fire-power; whichever side could get the most and biggest cannons in the right place usually won. Three decks and 60 to 90 guns were common, but here were some small number of four deckers with upwards of 100 cannons. Compared to smaller ships, *frigates* for example, ships of the line were slow, lumbering, and of questionable sea-keeping ability. (One such Swedish ship, the *Vasa*, sank on its maiden voyage.) The most famous and perhaps the most important ship of the line is Lord Admiral *Nelson*'s flag ship the *HMS Victory*. It still exists as a museum ship in *Portsmouth*.

shipshape and Bristol fashion   The expression 'shipshape' meaning the right way to do things, it goes back to about the 1600's. 'Bristol fashion' (first appeared in 1840) is more than merely *shipshape*. The harbor of Bristol has some huge tides -as much as 40 feet. So ships at anchor there regularly were completely out of water laying on their sides because of their keel. Things needed to be tied down much more carefully in Bristol than they did in other harbors.

shire   A handy word that means what ever the author wants it to mean but it is pastoral and probably either sheep or hobbits wandering about. It used to mean a *county*, but this is also a nebulous thing in England.

shooting   -obviously hunting with a shotgun, but the *hunt* is riding a horse after a fox and does not involve a gun. (Only the Scots hunt deer now and they use rifles. *Henry VIII* used a lance to hunt boar. One nearly killed him.) To throw a *shooting* meant you owned enough land to be out hunting your own private birds and would invite your friends. A *shooting box* is the comfortable little house out in the county where the shooter lived while hunting and a *shooting brake* was the carriage used to carry the hunting party and all their equipment out there. Today it's what Americans would call a station wagon.

Shooting in England comes it two varieties. The sort American hunter would recognize comes in two sub-categories. The first is called *rough shooting* -a single hunter and his dog tromping around the countryside on the lookout for the right sort of bird. The related *wild fowling* is hiding next to a cold body of water before first light and waiting for the ducks or geese to come flying over.

The second variety is iconic of Victorian English rich people having weird fun. This is where a line of peasantry (the people -not the bird) go out and beat the bushes to drive the grouse, ptarmigan, or pheasants (the birds, not the people) toward a line of people with shotguns who blast away with varying degrees of skill as fast as their servants could load their several guns. After all the excitement and noise, they pile back into the hunting brake and head back to the manor house where they would change their hunting togs to luncheon togs for a big meal and nice nap before dressing for dinner. As this was happening, the servants—including the beaters who had the good fortune not to get shot by their betters—went around and picked up all the dead birds.

The English are generally not as keen on guns as are Yanks, and so hunting and shooting is now a very expensive status thing. Today there are shooting clubs where—for astonishing amounts of money people can participate in a proper (Victorian) shoot.

shop   An English shop may be either a small neighborhood convenience store, or a store specializing in a certain line of merchandise. In this case, the store was referred to by what it sold, i.e. the grocers, the stationers etc. Shopkeepers still sometimes live above the shop, but England is slowly coming to follow America's example with mega or *big-box* stores. S*hop assistants* are American sales clerks, and s*hop-gazing* is window shopping.

Americans must remember that refrigeration and cars came to England later than they did in America, so readers will find English women seem to spend an inordinate amount of time shopping for small purchases. A final historic note, Napoleon is said to have insulted England as "a nation of shopkeepers" but there is no record of his ever having done so.

Shrove Tuesday -the day before Ash Wednesday and the first day of lent. It has also been called *Pancake Tuesday* because people wanted to get rid of all the good perishable stuff they were giving up for lent. To s*hrive (or shrove),* is to go to confession which is required at the beginning of lent.

silly season -August & September. Parliament in in recess and people are on vacation resulting in so little real news that the media is reduced to telling silly stories.

singing hinnies -currants (raisins) fried in (pan-)cakes. The singing refers to the sizzling sound they make and the *hinny* is a term of endearment.

singlet —a man's wool undershirt or -more currently, a vest-like athletic top. A *doublet is* a man's padded jacket from about 1300 to 1600 and a jerkin is about the same thing, but made of leather.

Sir -the proper way to address a knight or for that matter, any other armored chap carrying a sword.

sitting room In a lower middle class home, the sitting room just for sitting. This is to say a room -often behind the kitchen where the family might just sort of slouch around, sometimes with a friend of the family. An important guest was to be entertained in the parlor in the front. The modern English sitting or drawing room would be a modern American family room and separate from the front room of today, or the parlor of 100 years ago. The word 'drawing' is a shortening of the word 'withdrawing' or where you could withdraw from more formal doings and let your hair down and enjoy a little privacy. The 'living room' is a fairly recent thing, even in America. see ***house, the English***

six, hit for -in cricket, a hit out of bounds is good for six runs, so hitting for six is like hitting a home run in baseball with the bases loaded. It's a very good thing.

Six Counties -the six counties that make up Northern Ireland.

six of the best -six strokes with a cane administered to a misbehaving boy. It's synonyms with punishment in general.

six over six -perfect vision or what Americans call *20-20.*

sixpence -half a shilling. see ***money***

sixth form -in school it is the optional grade level for college prep

skinners -processed the skins of ermine, lambs and rabbits. Their work differed from tanners in that skinners preserved the hide with the hair still on. Now they would be called furriers.

skittles -a lawn bowling game in Europe, but a miniaturized version is played in English pubs. It's a little like American shuffleboard, but harder.

slate miners / slaters   -dig up slate in various places place in England from Roman times. Wales had the biggest and best slate quarry in the world and still has. Because slate can be cleaved into thin pieces, it is an excellent roofing material, but it also has many uses such as chalk boards, kitchen sinks, mantles, millstones, and tombstones.

sleeping partner   -in business, a silent partner.
sleeping policeman   -a speed bump.
slimming / slimming cure   -an old fashioned term for a diet.

slipper   -both a bedroom slipper, and a man's slip-on or loafer. It may also be a formal leather shoe suitable for dancing.

Sloan Rangers / Sloanies   Sloan Square is a very expensive corner in south-east London. Young women who live and shop there have been called Sloanies. From the 70's, they are seen as coming from old money, entitled, arrogant, rude, and often clueless.

slot machine   -a vending machine

small beer   -low alcohol beer or anything week.
small holding   -a farm that is not profitable but is operated for fun. It's likely to be bigger than an American vegetable garden.
smalls, the   -personal adds.
smalls / small clothes
              -men or women's underwear.
Smalls   -a first year placement test given at Oxford on Latin and Ancient Greek. It was set aside in 1960.

smelters   -melted and cast various kinds of metal for various purposes like cannons (bronze), cannonballs (iron), and comparatively high tech things for the day made from steel. The Celts were an iron age crowd, but it would have to wait for the industrial revolution for smelting and iron or steel to be more that a rare, exotic, and expensive material in England.

smocks / smock makers   -made smocks, but the words smock / slop / frock are all related and have a confusing history. A smock might have been everyday outerwear, or a woman's linen undergarment, or a long-skirted coat worn only by men or an elaborately embroidered Sunday-best worn by country folk.

smoking jacket   -a jacket a man would wear while slouching about the house and smoking. It served to keep ashes off his shirt. It also serves to illustrate what to American would view as crazy British formality. A man would still be fully dressed with shirt and tie, and wearing his smoking jacket, but if an important guest arrived, he would take off his smoking jacket and put on a more formal and proper coat.

snooker -not quite like pool or billiards. The army brought it home from India about 1884. It's played with a white cue ball and 21 other balls to be knocked into the standard 6 pockets of a pool table, but the snooker table is much larger -70 by 140 inches vs. a pool table of 52 by 84 inches. Snooker players look down on mere pool players.

snug / snuggery -a cozy back room in a pub, or a private room in a men's club.

Social Democrats -splintered off from the Liberal Party in 1981 because some *MP*s thought the party had become a little too liberal. see *political parties*

social security -not retirement, but public assistance and what Yanks would think of as welfare.

sod -a general purpose expletive. It's used in things like *Sod it!, sod-off, sodding mess,* etc. An *old sod* may be a good guy.

Solent the channel between the *Isle of Wright* and *Portsmouth*. It shows up in sea stories a lot. see *Southampton*

solicitor -the public side of the law profession. These are the chaps you go to when you need a contract sorted out, or to sue your landlord, or–heaven forbid–need to be defended in a criminal trial. In this last case, the solicitor will hire a *barrister* who will put on a wig and stand up before the justices on your behalf. see *barrister*

Barristers	Solicitors
Advocate (in the courtroom)	Legal advice
Hired and instructed by solicitors	The client's point-man
Wear the silly wig and gown, and work in the higher levels of courts.	Business law, children / family law, divorce, criminal, wills & probate, and general ambulance chasers. In general -the same specialties we see in America
Education: After undergraduate work, both do a year of Common Professional Exam or Post Graduate Diploma, then...	
1 year Bar Professional Training course	1 year Legal Practice Course
1 year 'pupillage'	2 year training contract

Somerset House -a magnificent neo-classic palace in London started in 1776. A variety of important institutions have been at home there over the years, but it is currently houses Inland Revenue–England's IRS.   In literature, it shows up as either the home of the *Admiralty* or the *Registry* where the records of all wills etc. must be recorded. It also shows up in movies when they need a magnificent English-looking government building.

Southeby's   -an important auction house for art and other very expensive things. It was founded in London in 1744, but is now a multinational business with headquarters in New York and 90 locations worldwide.

sovereign   -a gold coin worth one pound (of silver) until 1971 when they changed it to a coin worth Ł (a *pound*) and not at all the same thing as 16 ounces of silver. The word 'sovereign' comes from the Latin *super* by way of the Frengh *soverian* (meaing 'above') -as in *soverign nation*. see *money.*

Special Branch   -a crack team in Scotland Yard (The London Metropolitan Police) set up to deal with terrorism and political criminals. But it may not be what you think; it was started in 1887 to deal with the Irish.

spotted dick   -dessert *pudding* with raisins.

sportsman   -a hunter or fisherman, as well as an athlete.

squadron   In the navy, a squadron is a variable number of ships sent off on a specific task and usually commanded by a Rear Admiral, In the RAF, it is 10 to 20 aircraft also with a specific mission, and in the cavalry, 100 to 200 men. From the Italian *squadra* -a square. see *military*

squire   One of those useful flexible words that has changed so much as to have no specific meaning anymore. Originally it meant a knight's personal servant and / or young knight in training. A knight might be given non-inheritable land that he could not ordinarily pass on to his heirs, but gradually a squire came to mean a land owner and by the middle of the 1600's, a country gentleman -one who both came from a good family and owned enough land. Even then, it was a flexible word, but he was probably the richest guy in the neighborhood who lived in a *manor* and didn't seem to do any work. Squires, or their wives, were the source of second sons who went off to the army, clergy, colonies, or into Her Majesties Service in various places. Such sons were very useful to period writers. After about 1800, the squire evolved into a literary character who was a generally well-meaning but none-to-bright gentleman more interested in hunting, his dogs, and whatnot than in running the farm. He had an estate steward to do this.   see *gentry, manor, kinghts*

starters -appetizers

steeplechase   -a long distance **horse** race going back as far as 1752 from a wager in Ireland. They involve jumps, hedges, and water filled ditches. The word comes from a combination of the fox hunt which was similarly long and cross-country, and the tradition of running from one church steeple to another.

stationers   -made pens (dressed quills), pencils, ink & ink stands, seal wafers, and in short, everything *but* paper. Stationers were also involved in much of the book making & selling process, but *not* the actual printing. The first *Stationers Company* was formed in 1556 under the rule of the church because the church more or less had a monopoly on literacy. see *religion*

steward   -originally a butler-like servant, and later an employee of a nobleman to supervise household matters and perhaps the finances. Only in the 20th century, did stewards become waiters on ships and even later, on airplanes etc.

sticky wicket   -a difficult situation. In cricket, something like baseball's home plate is actually three wickets –sticks about 30 inches high and three inches apart. Two bails (little wooden do-hickeys) are set to span the top of the wickets. When the bowler (the English equivalent of the American pitcher) hits the wicket and knocks off a bail, the batsman is retired -he's out. If a bail does not fall when the wicket is hit by the ball, it's said to be a "sticky wicket."

stocks   -bonds in America. American stocks are *shares* in England, so while an American stock broker handles stocks and bonds, the English chap handles shares and stocks.
     Stocks were also the punishment device from the medieval to the early 1700's wherein the feet were fastened between two timbers. The pillory was the one with the head, wrists, and sometimes feet being immobilized. Humiliation was part of the punishment, but depending on the time of year and the length of the punishment, either could be fatal. It must be said that such punishments were practiced in the colonies longer than in England.

stock jobber   -the initial underwriter of a stock offering. A *stock broker* in England is much the same person as in America.

stone   -14 pounds or 6.35 kg. The use of stone as a measure of weight goes back to biblical times and varied both from place to place throughout Europe and varied based upon the commodity it was to measure. It's very confusing, so it was standardized in 1814. It is only ever used in the singular -i.e. *twenty stone*.

Stonehenge -a prehistoric monument and a primitive observatory carefully laid out to mark the solstices. It is the most popular monument among hundreds of other trilithons* and burial mounds in the area. Each stone is 13 feet high, 7 feet wide and weighs about 25 tons. Construction began about 3000 BC and was finished a thousand years later. This would put late it in bronze age or early iron age, but there is no evidence they used iron tools. Its builders left no written records, so other than archaeological evidence, very little is known about Stonehenge or its builders. A 12th century legend claims the wizard Merlin and a cooperative giant built Stonehenge. *Two vertical stones, topped by a third horizontal stone.

stoppage -a labor union strike.

Strand More often *the Strand. F*rom old English *stroud* -the river's edge. Basically, it's a road from ***Trafalgar Square*** to the east where it becomes ***Fleet Street***. In the medieval era, it was a trading street from that ran from the City of London to the Palace of ***Westminster***. It was also where rich courtiers put their houses. Later, from about the 1600's to the 1750s', is became a very fashionable shopping neighborhood. In the 1800's it was theaters and restaurants, and today they have added expensive hotels and offices. It shows up in the writing of Virginia Wolf, T. S. Eliot, and of perhaps greater renown, in the English version of the game Monopoly.

Stratford (Stratford-on-Avon) -an ordinary little bridge town (to cross or *ford* the River Avon) and farming community with lots of potatoes -until Shakespeare came along. There are actually about four Stratfords in England so it's necessary to add the *at Avon* to make it Shakespearean.

subaltern -an obsolete and generic word for junior officers like lieutenants (army) and ensigns (navy).

subjects England has no citizens, only subjects.

subway -a passageway for pedestrians. America's subway is England's *underground.*

succession The question of who will be the monarch next is endlessly fascinating to the English; it's also complicated. As late as 2013 and 2015, Parliament amended a 1701 law, the *Act of Settlement,* to codify the idea that queens were every bit as good as kings, but Catholics simply would not do.

(But a monarch marrying one is permissible.) Today next in line is Charles, who has two sons, Elizabetg's grand-kids, and now a male great-grandson, so who's next is nailed down, at least for the next few generations.

Otherwise, and thru most of English history and literature, the order of succession runs as follows: eldest male son, next oldest etc., grandsons etc., and then if there are no male sons or grandsons, the daughters are in line. Failing this, brothers of the monarch are next and then sisters. Then it moves on to cousins. There are examples of all of these succession in England's history.

This is only for royalty. The nobles are far more chauvinistic; only men could inherit titles. This makes sense, if only a little. All the land that nobles historically *'owned',* the king had technically lent to them in order to extract value from the countryside. Even more than this, the nobility (and to a lesser degree, the knights) were all about their ability and willingness to raise armies for the monarch should he need some. Such are tasks best left to men.

Suez Canal   -a shortcut from the southeast corner of the Mediterranean Sea to the Red Sea and from there, on to the Indian Ocean. It was built by the French, and the English bought a partial interest in it in 1875 because of the importance of England's trade with India. The Brits took care of it up until 1956 when the Egyptian government nationalized it. There followed a very complicated scene involving diplomats & paratroopers. France, Israel, Egypt, and even the US all got involved. The final result was England being labeled "imperialist" and withdrawing. To the English, the whole thing is distasteful and a little like America's Vietnam.

Sun, The   This newspaper started as a serious unbiased paper and lost money. Ownership changed in 1969 and it became a tabloid with celebrity gossip, UFO stories, and pictures of (mostly) naked young women. It quickly came to have the largest circulation of any paper in England.

Sunday   The English take Sundays pretty seriously indeed. Everything is closed. They don't go to church necessarily, but they do do the big family mid-afternoon dinner thing. With the coming of big-box stores and multi-screen theaters, this may be changing. see *weekend*

Sunday performance / Sunday show   -because the theaters are closed on Sundays, this is when and where amateur theater clubs give their performances.

Sunday School -late in the 1700's, as the industrial revolution was unfolding, the local parish taught reading and writing to worker's children. Other than reading the Bible, such schools were not strictly religious, but by the early 20th century, they had come to be primarily for religious instruction -on Sunday- as other schools did the academic stuff during the week.

Sunday Trading Act   It was only in 1994 did Parliament gave shops the option of opening on Sunday if they wanted.

Sunday tripper -someone out on a cluttering up the roads like an American *Sunday driver.*

superannuated -an old fashioned word for old-fashioned. A superannuation scheme wold be a retirement plan in America.

supper -usually a late light meal. see ***meals***

Supreme Court of the United Kingdom -12 justices appointed from and by the ***House of Lords*** who act as the last court of appeals for all of the United Kingdom except for criminal matters in Scotland. They have been around since 2005 when they took over from the ***Law Lords.*** It's impotent to remember that the separation of powers of which the Yanks are so proud, doesn't entirely attain in England. All England's courts are under Parliament, and for that matter, the ***Prime Minister***, is also technically, a member of Parliament.

Surgeon Up until late in the 19th century, surgeons were sort of the laborers of the profession who were instructed by the doctor. They were addressed as Mr., not Dr. This follows a long history beginning with the medieval barbers who extracted teeth, incised boils, applied leeches etc. The red and white stripes on the barber pole are symbolic of bandages and blood. In 1163 the Catholic church forbade clergy from performing surgery and so medicine and surgery were separate practices until science began sorting out anatomy, anesthesia, germs & infection, etc. A s*urgery* is a doctor's office even if no surgery is ever performed there.

surplice -the ceremonial loose white vestment worn by clergy over the ***cassock*** -the usually black work-a-day garment with the odd collar. The word comes from the Latin super -*over.*

surveyors -someone who does surveys or appraisals. A *chartered surveyor* measured land with transit and chain in the past but now uses computers and lasers. A surveyor may also be something like America's building contractors.

suss -slang for suspicion or more recently, to ***suss out*** something is to consider it carefully before deciding about it.

sweater Yes, it's a knitted top, but Brits wear sweaters only when sporting. Otherwise, a knitted top may be a pull-over, a jumper, or a jersey. see ***clothing***

sweet -candy.
sweets -as a part of a meal or dessert of any type. see ***pudding***
sweetmeats -candied fruit often in fruitcake.
sweet shop -candy store, a *sweet kiosk* is smaller and temporary.
boiled sweets -hard candy like lemon drops etc.
sweetbreads -the pancreas and thymus.

swell / swells   From old English, the contraction of 'tis well' -later, 'the swells' refers sarcastically to the posh. Later it came to mean something that is so yesterday as to be completely-over-with.

Swiss-roll   -jelly roll

swings & roundabouts   What you loose here, you gain there. Literally, a swing is a child's swing-set and roundabouts are the little merry-go-rounds you also find in kid's playgrounds. What the children lose when the swing-set tipped over, they gained on the marry-go-round.

Everybody likes *T*. In English, it's the most popular consonant and second only to **e** in the whole alphabet. In some of the oldest languages, it is the last letter; too bad for *U* thru *Z*. It has also been left pretty much alone from the Greek *tau* on to today. BTW -the rules as to when to use one *t* or two *tt*'s? Forget it; they don't work.

table   In English meetings, to table an issue is to pull it out and talk about it. This is the opposite of the American meaning; which is to set it aside for another time –if at all.

take away   -take out food like curry or fish and chips etc.

tartan   -the woven wool pattern Yanks call it *plaid*, but plaid is actually the tartan cloth thrown over the shoulder as part of a **kilt**. Many Scot clans have one or more of their own family tartans.

TD   Territorial Decoration -an award for long service in the Territorial Army which is the all volunteer reserve looking after things at home

tea   To understand England's fascination with tea, begin by boiling some tap water. Let it cool and slurp it down. Tastes filthy doesn't it? Having boiled it, it will not give you cholera so that's a good thing. Now imagine it's not tap water you start with, but pond water, or perhaps worse, water from a well in the wrong part of a crowded city surrounded by a sketchy sanitation system. The boiling part is to kill the wee bugs, and steeping some leaves in it just to make it palatable. Add to this understanding the fact that tea comes from places England colonized. It's not clear they colonized these places to get tea, but it is clear that once they colonized them, they discovered tea to be a very good and profitable thing.

These days, Americans can make tea out of anything that grows: mint, chamomile, seeds, roots, rose petals, and many other varieties of flowers for that matter. Agaths Christi's Hercule Poirot was keen on *tesane* -essentially herbal tea. The Brits insist proper tea can only be made from an evergreen bush that grows best on hillsides. It comes from China from before the time of Christ.

Tea was sold in London coffee houses as early as 1657. Coffee and tea were neck-in-neck till the next century. This had to do with the price of sugar having come down. The restorative effects of tea were essentially from a generous sugar jolt. To put some dates on it, the various Townsend Acts began in 1767 to raise money for the crown. The Tea Act of 1773 was to raise more money as well as an attempt to monopolize the colonist's supply of tea.* The Yanks threw their famous Boston Tea Party later that same year.

Yet more political and financial difficulties arose in 1841 when the English tried to break China's monopoly on tea by bringing it to India. The plants they smuggled out of China died, but they shortly discovered a local variety that worked very well. The price of tea continued to drop thru the 1800's and its popularity increased apace. An advertising campaign in India in 1950 made hundreds of millions of Indians as mad for tea as were the Chinese, the English, and most of the rest of the world. Today it is second in popularity only to water as a beverage.

*The British East India Company had attempted to corner the market for tea, failed, and wound up with way too much tea in its warehouses. Prices were taking a beating so they lobbied for, and got a tea monopoly in the colonies. In a very real way, the American Revolution started in part because some businessmen drastically over estimated the demand for some dried leaves.

teacake   -yeast raised bread with dried fruit, usually served toasted and buttered.

technical school / college   -a secondary school analogous to America's vocational-technical school.

Teddy-boy   -a fashion fad in the 50's involving young men wearing Edwardian era clothing and rock-and-roll hair styles like Elvis Presley.

telegram   Distances in America are so great that a telegram was the fastest way to communicate between cities back in the day, but in England, they were often used for quick communication across town. Faster than even England's excellent mail until the telephone came along.

Telegraph, the   -technically, the *Daily Telegraph*, but it is only ever called the *Telegraph*. It goes back to 1855 and is now considered the paper of record for the conservative middle-class.

telephone   Alexander G. Bell brought the phone to England in 1878. It was something of an expensive novelty at the time, but would become pretty widespread by the time of WW II. The post office ran things till the phone company was privatized in stages from 1969 to 1981.

term   Like in America, sessions at university come in terms, but unlike America's fall, winter, spring, summer etc., various schools in England have very old traditional names like Michaelmas, Hilary, Lent, Eastern, and Trinity terms. It depends on the school and the length of a term like American school's quarters or semesters.

terrace -these would be *row houses* in America with common walls, along an entire block. They are typically two or more stories tall, and comparatively narrow. In certain parts of London they are on elegant streets but by the 1900's they were being built for the working class. They may or may not have *terraces* (balconies in America) nor level or raised terraces in the back yard (patios in America), but they are called terrace houses nonetheless.

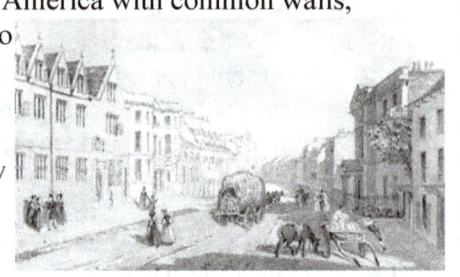

Territorials Like America's National Guard. They stay at home (unlike the expeditionary forces) and help out with emergencies.

test -a cricket match

Thames, River The most important river in England. It flows thru London, and is navigable all the way there. It's 215 miles long and drops 115 feet. It empties into the North Sea where tides run 20 feet from high to low and tidal effects extend 55 miles upstream. Thames is Celtic for river so it's really the River River. BTW -it's pronounced to rhyme with *gems*.

thatchers -roofers who used straw, reed, heather etc, to cover and waterproof a roof. Thatch is very picturesque, but also very flammable, so it outlawed in various places in the 17th and 18th century. Today it can still be seen either in rural areas, or trendy little cottages built for eccentrics or for historic preservation. BTW -Mark Twain's Tom Sawyer descended from a *sawyer* and his girlfriend, Becky Thatcher descended from a thatcher.

Threadneedle Street In London this is the address of the Bank of England which is called the *Old Lady of Threadneedle Street* for its conservative practices.

tie An Englishman might choose between his school tie, regimental tie, or club tie. It depended on whom he expected he might encounter that day.

Times, the A London daily paper going back to 1788. It is considered the most authoritative paper in England and also the dullest. It's primary market is the upper class and government bureaucracy.

tithe The word derives from the same Germanic root that gives us *ten*. Historically, one tenth of agricultural product paid to the church and stored in *tithe barns,* but it is a moving target thru out history. Tithing goes back to the old testament and later was expected of European Christians from the late 400's, and codified in England in 855. The English crown got involved in

1188, and in 1285 wrote various laws involving tithes, transfers of property, inheritance, etc. The crown got even more involved, with **Henry VIII**'s help, when the Catholic monasteries fell apart and some tithes came to be payable directly to the crown. After 1836 tithes –rents actually– were payable in cash rather than agricultural products. They were still adjusting the laws as late as 1936, and only in 1970 were tithe-like rents abolished. For the reader, it's all a part of the historic movement of power from the nobility and church, to an increasingly 'democratic' monarchy, and finally, to a secular government.

toad in a hole   -sausage baked in batter like an American *pig-in-a-blanket*.

toff   -a derogatory term for an upper class git or a ***swell***.

toilet   -from the French *toilette*, meaning to get dressed, so a woman at her toilet was doing her hair, makeup, and getting dressed. The porcelain plumbing fixture is a *lavatory* in England.

Tommy   -an army private soldier. It derived from *Thomas Adkins* in about 1815. It was England's equivalent to America's *John Doe*. By WW I it was shorthand to just *Tommy* for the British enlisted man.

Tommy-rot   -originally army rations but it came to mean worthless junk from the low quality food and tobacco etc. used to pay laborers instead of money.

Ton   -in England it's 2240 pounds and a tonne is 1000 kilograms or 2204 pounds. A ton may also be a whole lot, often 100 of something i.e., *going a ton* is going 100 miles per hour.

toolmakers   -made relatively simple–usually agricultural–tools with wood handles and black-smithed metal at the business ends. As the industrial revolution got underway, the more complicated tool-making work was done by **machinists**.

torch -a flashlight

Tory / Tories   This political proto-party goes back to about the 1670's. The Tories were largely Catholic and entirely landed-gentry who supported the Stuart kings as absolute monarchs. They fell apart in about 1832 when Parliament was reformed (to give more voice to the little guy) and resurfaced as Conservatives. see ***political parties***

The etymology of the word *Torie* is interesting and telling. When the English came to 'colonize' Ireland, the Irish farmers who were kicked off their land took up crime. The Irish word for robber or highwayman is *toraidhe*. The aristocratic English who dispossessed (stole) the Irish land came to be called *Tories,* and the title stuck to the conservative or rich-guy side of the political divide.

tosser   -idiot

toss-pot -an old expression (before Shakespeare) for a drunk. It may also refer to someone with other bad and/or self-destructive habits.

Tower of London At various times, the Tower was a palace, residence, fortified castle, armory, torture / execution chamber, administration building, and prison. It is actually a set of four rather squat towers surrounded by a castle. This is to say, a big tallish building surrounded by shorter fortified walls surrounded by other fortified walls with smaller buildings scattered around. They started building it in 1078, expanded it in 1190, and rebuilt it in 1285.

It's most nefarious use was as a prison but generally a smallish prison for important people who lived in comparative comfort while the king decided what to do with them. Perhaps the most famous person sent to the Tower was ***Anne Boleyn***. She stayed there for about two weeks before the king decided how to solve his problem with the pope. It ended very badly for Anne. Today the Tower is one of England's most popular tourist attractions.

Tower Bridge -just east of the Tower and with a draw bridge. It was built in 1896. It is not the old ***London Bridge*** which is now in Lake Havasu City, Arizona.

Toy-makers Toys give us a better picture of what was important to people than might appear to be the case at first glance. While dolls in burial practices show up in any number of ancient civilizations, so do dolls as toys. Dolls that survive till today say a lot about fashion. Doll houses, toy carriages, and model ships add to the picture. Toy soldiers go back as far as 1133; consider toy drums & trumpets, pop-guns, rocking horses, etc. (While stuffed animals show up throughout, Teddy Bears started in America.)

The Enlightenment was about the view that people were important and alongside this view, came the notion that children might also be important and their childhood deserved some enjoyment. Stir in the industrial revolution and we see a huge flowering of toys for children including intricate mechanized or *clock-work* toys, magic-lanterns, and toy trains etc., even if they were more for the rich than the working-class. As early as the late 1700's, toys were often educational. Board games and jig-saw puzzles were designed to teach children geography. Victorian rectitude of a hundred years later faced the quandary of children having toys and fun on Sunday. In some homes the solution was to only allow children to play with th eir Noah's Ark and animal figurines after church.

Trafalgar Square   A public square in the city of Westminster to the west of the ***City of London*** in the area of what used to be the ***Charing Cross*** neighborhood. It commemorates ***Neslon***'s victory in the ***Battle of Trafalgar*** off the coast of Trafalgar Spain in 1805. He had 33 ships against combined 41 ships of the Spanish and French. This battle was pretty much the end of any plans Napoleon had to invade England. Sadly, it was also the end of Admiral Nelson. It is the site the 169 foot tall ***Nelson's Column*** erected in his honor.

transported / transportation   The idea of rehabilitating criminals didn't occur to the English until well into the 1800's. Up until then, the best thing to do with bad people was to hang them. For minor crimes, and to the modern mind, these were very minor indeed, about 50,000 people were shipped off to Georgia. The American Revolution put an end to using America as a dumping ground so they shipped them off to Botany Bay in Australia. About 160,000 men, women, and children were shipped off to down-under before the practice ended in 1868.

traveler   -or *commercial traveler.* In America this would be a traveling salesman. When a sign in the pub says 'No Travelers', it means no gypsies / Romani / Roma. Salesmen were presumably still welcomed.

treacle   -a by-product of sugar making somewhat like corn syrup. It might be golden or dark syrup which is almost molasses. American *Shoo-Fly Pie* is a like an English treacle tart.

trench / trencher   -before the common man had plates, food was served on a flattish loaf of bread that was eaten once it soaked up the good gravy and fat. Today's expression for someone who is a good and copious eater, a *trencherman,* derives from this old practice.

Troubles, the   Beginning in about 1968, the Irish Catholics in Northern Ireland (part of the UK), wanted the six counties to rejoin the 26 Catholic counties of the ***Republic of Ireland*** to the south. The Protestants wanted to stay English subjects. The following guerrilla or 'low-level' war killed about 3500 people–slightly more that half of whom were civilians–by the time it ended with the *Good Friday Belfast Agreement* in 1998.

troop   In the cavalry, a troop was roughly equivalent to an infantry company, but with fancier uniforms. Individual troopers were more glamorous so *swearing like a trouper* was to do so more expressively and skillfully than the mere infantry. see ***military*** & ***commissions***

truncheon   -a constable's billy-club.
trunk *call*   -long distance phone call.

try   -in rugby, running across the goal-line didn't count till the ball carrier touches the ball to the ground. This is a *try* and worth four points, or three in professional games. What would be the *extra point* in America is worth two points in rugby and is called the *kick after a try*. It must be attempted by the scorer. Curiously, an American *touchdown* does NOT require the ball carrier to literally touch the ball down to the ground.

tube / underground   -London's subway. It actually got started in 1863 and ran on electricity. It sill runs on electricity, but has been improved and expanded repeatedly. In 2014 it carried 1.305 billion passengers; that's about five times the population of the US and almost 20 times the population of Great Britain. Even so, it's only the world's 11th busiest.

Tudor, House of   *Henry VIII*'s family–half English and half Welsh. It started with Henry II in 1485 and ended when Elizabeth I died in 1603 without an heir and the Stuart family took over.

Turk   -someone rude and bad tempered. In the 1800's it meant juvenile delinquents.

Turkish   An expensive cigarette made from tobacco grown and sun-cured in countries that had been part of the Ottoman Empire but not necessary Turkey.

Turkish Delight   After sugar got cheap enough for the commoners, England had something of a candy craze. This candy was the first popular brand of candy to hit England. It's made from sugar, starch, and flavorings and actually came from Arabia thru Turkey and the Ottomans.

turning   -a side street
turn off   -to fire an employee
turn out   -a thorough cleaning -often of a room
turn over   -to search so completely that everything is turned over.
              -or to start a car's engine
turn up   -a surprise
turn-ups   -trouser's cuffs. (TurnIps are the root vegetable.)

turnpike   -a toll road with barred entrances with a heavy spear-like *pike* crossing the road that would be *turned* out of the way when the toll was paid. They go back to the medieval, but became a major growth industry before the industrial revolution and trains came along. There is only one toll road in England today, but there are still a few toll bridges.

Tussauds, Madam (1761–1850)   Marie Tussaud was a skillful wax sculptor from France. She moved to London and opened her museum in 1835. It has been a major tourist attraction ever since. Its exhibits involving murder and torture show up most often in the movies, but are only a part of it all. Today there are about 25 Madam Tussaud's all over the world.

turners   -made wooden kitchen things. Originally they used primitive lathes to make platters. Today, the verb for using a lathe is to *turn* in England & America both.

tweeny -a servant of all-help working any and all of the floors as necessary.

Twelfth Night -the last of the twelve days of Christmas ending January 5. It was sort of a mid-winter's Mardi Graw until the Protestants re-invented Christmas as a stern and somber occasion and *Twelfth Night* came to be just one of Shakespeare's romantic comedies. The Christmas carol *The Twelve Days of Christmas* first appears in print in 1780 as a memory game in a little book for children. BTW -the meme that occasionally goes around explaining that the partridges, doves, hens, maids, lords etc are symbolic of Christianity is very nice, but without historic basis.

twit -an exceedingly stupid person.

two-fisted -not manly like in America, but clumsy and inept or *ham-fisted*.

U has a confusing ancestry. In Phoenician, it comes from *Y*, but by the late Middle Ages, it descended from *V*. Old buildings with what seems to be a *V* where you would expect a *U* to be, are actually following spelling rules as old as King Author. The *V* shape of *U* was to be used at the beginning of a word and the *U* went anywhere else. What is more, the English like to stick a *u* in words like *colour* and *labour*.

Ulster   -an ancient kingdom in Northern Ireland and the first place to be conquered by the Protestant English in 1690. In theory, it is the six counties of Northern Ireland, but the borders and meanings have shifted throughout. see *Ireland* and the ***Troubles.***

up the wooden hill to Bedfordshire   -going to bed

university   Technically, students study at colleges but sit for exams at university from where they are granted degrees. Up until the Victoria era, there were only Oxford and Cambridge in England, Trinity in Dublin, and Edinburgh in Scotland. It was during the Victorian, and in no small part because of the need for people educated in science and engineering (rather than Latin and Greek) that a number of other universities started and often did so in red brick buildings that were the architectural fashion of the day. These *Red-Brick-Universities* had less status, but taught more modern subjects and, after 1960, even did it for comparatively less wealthy students. Now they do so more along the lines the way America's universities do things.

up and up   -not honest and forthright like in America, but moving up and up in one's career or society.

upper class
-an impossibly subjective term and furthermore, one that changes with time. When it is encountered in English writing, it may have many implications, but almost universally, it at least suggests more than one generation of people with a good education.

up-sticks
-to move domiciles and sometimes in the middle of the night to avoid uncomfortable situation with the landlord involving overdue rent.

U. S. / US
-abbreviation for *unserviceable* from the RAF.

V is hugely important if only to the alphabet archaeologists. It's the father of *F, U, V,* and *Y. V* comes to Latin by way of *Y* but without *Y*'s stem. Consider the word for *W–double-ue–*or two *ues*. But W looks like a double *V.* The first written use of a pointy *U–*a *V–*in England was in 1386. But despite it's name, W isn't even part of the whole *F, U, V,* and *Y* thing. It's not the fault of the French, but in this case, it has more to do with Old German.

V for Victory   Winston Churchill's invention during WW II, with the palm outward, but turned around it is an insult possibly going back as far as the ***Battle of Agincourt*** wherein English longbow archers used the first and second finger to shoot arrows at the enemy.

valet   -a gentleman's personal servant sometimes refereed to as a *Gentleman's gentleman* who was largely responsible for the wardrobe, but he may have covered other duties as well. The excellent BBC comedy <u>Jeeves and Wooster</u> show how it worked more or less after WW I. see ***servants***

van   -any truck of a size up to what Yanks call a *semi*. Also the luggage car on a train, or a ***caravan.***

V & A   -short for the Victorian and Albert Museum. It goes back to 1853 and covers 12.5 acres with 145 galleries, It is technically a museum of decorative arts, but not an art museum per se. What ever it is, it has at least one of everything. EVERYTHING!

VAT   -Value Added Tax and essentially a high sales tax. Depending on the economy, it runs between 15% and 17% and is good for about 30% of the inland revenue.

vassals   -a large part of the glue that held feudalism together. A vassal was obligated to a lord or monarch usually in exchange for farmland.

vestry   -a little room off the side of a church where the priest vested or got dressed. Given that it not part of the church proper, it is also where the lay *vestrymen* met to deal with non-religious issues effecting the parish.

Someone who was born to parents who hadn't had a church wedding, was said to be *born in the vestry* or outside the church.

vet   -either to do as background check, or veterinarian. A veteran is an *ex-serviceman* in England and America both.

verger   -an official caretaker or attendant to a church. In the past, he was a layperson who assists in religious ceremonies by carrying a ceremonial rod, the *verge*. The Catholic Church as no vergers, but rather ushers who do not carry rods, but collection baskets on long handles

vicar   It depends on the religion; a Catholic vicar is the representative or deputy of a bishop and an Episcopal vicar is a clergyman in charge of a chapel. In the Church of England, he would be a parish priest supported by local tithes.
    In the various Protestant or 'English' sects (NOT the Catholics) the parish parson, rector etc, might enjoy the income of the parish without the bother of living in the neighborhood or doing much of anything at all, other than receiving the money, but he did need to appoint a substitute who lived in the *vicarage* and looked after things -and we hope- the parishioner's souls. This was the role of a vicar. In much of English writing, a Vicar is poor, but devout, and often has a wife who was the very model of common sense and community involvement.
    By the way, viceroy, vicar, and vice-president all come from the Latin *vicariou* meaning deputy or representative. see **clergy**

viceroy   -a local representative of the monarch or vice-royal. In 1858 the English Crown decided the sub-continent of India was too valuable to leave in the hands of the private ***East India Company***, so they took over and installed a Governor General or Viceroy. (A Vicereine can be either a female viceroy or the viceroy's wife.) Louis Mountbatten was the last viceroy of ***India*** when Indian gained its independence in 1947.

Vickers   -a steel and engineering company that goes back to 1828, but is most famous as the manufacturer of the Vickers machine gun used in WW I.

Victoria, Queen (1819-1901)   -crowned in 1837 at age 18. She was the last of the house of Hanover. Her mother was a German Princess. She had nine children who married into royal families all over Europe. Her oldest daughter, Victoria, would marry Kaiser Wilhelm of Germany and of WWI fame. Most Americans picture her a sour dumpy old women, but in her youth, she was considered beautiful, if in a Betty Davis sort of way.
    England was on top of the world during her reign, but it was also

firmly a constitutional monarchy. None the less, she tried to influence Parliament from time to time, but usually unsuccessfully. Her popularity with the public varied. But after the death of her husband -consort Albert and her long widowhood, her popularity increased. The Victorian Morality may not be entirely a consequence of Victoria, but she certainly exemplified these values. It has been suggested that it was equally a reaction to previous ribald excess of the previous king.

Victoria Station   -actually the London Victoria Station, but everyone calls it simply Victoria. It started in 1860 and while it's not the biggest in London (London's Waterloo is a bit bigger) 80+ million people pass thru it every year on their way to the southern end of the country and often on holiday. Sherlock Holmes, several Oscar Wilde characters, and many movies deal with Victoria with some regularity.

Vikings   The Vikings were Norwegians and Danes or actually seafaring tribesmen from what would come to be Norway and Denmark. They raided all over northern Europe and well into the Mediterranean. None the less, England was the favorite target of the Danish Vikings. A particularly nasty raid of the monks of Lindisfarne in 793 was recorded in the chronicles and Christian prayer, "Deliver us from the Northmen, oh Lord." This lead to the somewhat undeserved reputation of the Vikings in Christendom. Norwegian Vikings actually settled Cork and Dublin in Ireland. The Vikings were big on raiding monasteries not because they were particularly anti-religious bullies, but because this was where portable gold was. In the end, the Vikings were responsible for fortified cities on the coast of England. The Norman Conquest pretty much put an end to the Vikings.

village   -the smallest division of England's political entities usually with a church, but with no more than 1000 residents. In the earliest history, the village was pretty standard for anyplace smaller than a market town. People living there walked off to work in the commons, or the fields surrounding the village. As the ***Enclosure Act***s unfolded along with industrialization, people left the villages for the city, and the village became little more that a bedroom community for the manor's workers who lived in marginal poverty. (The squire's servants lived in the manor house, or surrounding out-buildings and were better paid and of higher status.)

     During the Victorian era, the urban middle-class came to idealized the village as a pastoral escape from the bustle and pollution of London and other industrializes cities. Early in the 20th century, there were a number of experiments at building utopian villages. (Most were failures and none survive today as planned.) The notion of a village -utopian or otherwise– proved to have had more in common with Disneyland than reality. First the trains, and then the automobile flooded villages with developers and built-communities with all the charm of America's sub-divisions like Levitt Towns.

Viscount   -the fourth level of the peerage. There are very few pure Viscounts, but about 250 who for whom Viscount is a secondary titles. Lord

Mountbatten (1900 - 1979), the last Viceroy of India was a Viscount *and* a Lord.

vole   -a rodent a little bigger that a mouse and smaller that a rat.

Volunteers   -originally a volunteer local militia presumably for defense of the homeland, like the Yeomanry, but more attractive to weekend warrior types of the 18th and 19th century. Shortly before WW I, it was subsumed into the army as a reserve force. When encountered in writing, and depending on the period, it is likely that it refers to something quite different from the pretty uniform wearing regular regiments, and later, even more different from the disciplined and highly professional 20th century army.

vote   The right to vote evolved gradually in England as follows:

1432	Only men who owned a *40 shilling freehold.* They were pretty rich.
1832	Men who rented valuable land, about 1 in 7.
1867	Men who owned valuable property in the city.
1884	Legislation to balance city and town voters, but still covered only 60% of men. see ***Reform Bill of 1832***
1895 - 1918	The woman's suffrage movement was active at this time, but more or less set aside during WW I.
1918	All men who fought in the war, all men over 21 and women over 30 who worked in the war effort.
1928	Universal suffrage for all citizens over 21 years of age.
1967	Suffrage for everyone over 18.

vote of no confidence   Given that the majority party in Parliament IS the government, the ***Prime Minister*** must have the confidence of Parliament to function. To put it in different words, the various secretaries, ministries, and departments are led –at least politically led– by members of Parliament, and when the greater part of Parliament has doubts about the prime minister, his appointees must also be suspect. This has happened only twice in the 20th century. The rules now are that after a vote of no confidence, the government has 14 days to get it together, or a general election is held. On several occasions, the issue was resolved by combining two parties into a ***coalition government.*** Ordinarily, elections are held every five years.

W is the only letter in English that does not come form people living thousands of years ago around the southeast corner of the Mediterranean, *W* is Germanic. This does not, however, make it a simple matter. It's all tangled up with *V, U,* and *Y*. Being as there is no Latin *W* and Latin was about the extent of literacy in England up until after the Protestant Reformation, *W* was considered barbaric, or at least Germanic, which amounted to about the same thing. In the 16th century, a German grammarian by the name of Valentin Ickelshamer wrote, "Poor *w* is so infamous and unknown that many barely know either its name or its shape, not those who aspire to being Latinists, as they have no need of it, nor do the Germans, not even the schoolmasters, know what to do with it or how to call it; some call it *we*, others call it *uu*, and the Swabians call it *auwawau.*"

WAAC -*Women's Auxiliary Army Corps* during WW I, It was changed to *ATS -Auxiliary Territorial Service* during WW II
WAAF -*Women's Auxiliary Air Force* during WW II and *WRAF, Women's Royal Air Force* after the war. see *voting*

wainwrights -made wagons with four wheels and steering mechanisms. They were considerably larger and more complicated than a carts with a single axle and two wheels that were made by *cartwrights*.

waistcoat -a vest.

Wales Wales is a wee country tucked into the western belly of the England. It is mountainous and has a long rugged coastline. The important thing to remember about Wales is that they resisted the Romans more successfully than the English (Anglo Saxons actually), and today the Welsh speak a derivation of the original Celtic language, which has the distinction of having the most unpronounceable words and some of the longest words of any know language living or dead. The Welsh were also successful at resisting the Franks and even resisting the English up until about 1485 when the Tudor family with Welsh roots, took over the crown. After that, the Welsh and English started getting along. This accelerated with the Industrial Revolution when England needed Welsh coal, iron, and copper.

Today Wales has both agriculture and metals but sadly, no oil. It's population is just north of three million people and where you will find the village of…

Llanfairpwillgwynglyllgoogerychwyrndrobwyllllartysiliogogogoch. This translates roughly as *The Church of Mary in the hollow of the white hazel near a rapid whirlpool and the Church of St. Tysillo near the red cave.*

walk   The English love to hike about, but they are not as keen on camping like the Americans. An English walking holiday probably involves a meal at pub after the day's walk and a nice comfy bed upstairs.

wallet   -a briefcase or note case.

wall safe   -kitchen cupboard. (An old-fashioned American *pie-safe* is a cupboard for pies.)

War of the Roses   -a series of smallish wars (1455 - 1487) fought between the Houses of Lancaster & York on one side and the House of Plantagenet on the other. It's complicated, but the House of Tudor came out on top and the Tudors weren't even in it.

War Office   -the ministry supervising the army till 1964 when it was combined with the *Admiralty* to look after the *Royal Navy* as well.

washing powder   -laundry soap
washing up   -doing the dishes
washing up liquid / powder   -dish soap

Waterloo   In 1815 a coalition of English, German (Prussian actually) and forces from pretty much all of Europe, defeated Napoleon in Waterloo. It had been a long time coming and the English were so enthused by Wellington's Victory that they named a bunch of things like bridges, streets, and railroad stations after this otherwise unimportant small Belgian town.

An interesting aside arises; Beethoven was a fan of Napoleon until Beethoven recognized Napoleon's imperial ambitions. He was composing his Third Symphony at the time, and had named this work after Napoleon. When Napoleon invaded Beethoven's hometown, the composer renamed his work the *Sinfonia Eroica* -the *heroic symphony*. In 1813 Napoleon's brother Joseph was defeated in Spain by the same Wellington who would defeat Napoleon himself at Waterloo two years later. Beethoven was so pleased with this first victory, that he wrote *Wellington's Victory,* a great rousing composition performed with actual cannon and musket fire.

If this were not enough, in 1880 Ilyich Tchaikovsky wrote the *1812 Overture* to celebrate Napoleon's frozen retreat from Russia in 1812. This is an even more rousing bit of music that has nothing to do with America and their *War of 1812* against Britain.

watermen   -sailors but not necessarily with sails. They moved boats and barges around inland rivers, lakes, and canals. *Wherrymen* rowed passengers around in *wherrys or* water taxis.

wattle and daub   For a good bit of England's history, this was how the common man built things like houses, barns, shops etc. A timber frame was put up, wattle sticks were woven between the timbers and daubed with lime and mud. A stone fireplace and chimney were built, and the roof was thatched. The floor was packed dirt possibly glued together with cow blood. Windows made of oiled paper or linen were put in, but there were not many of them and they were small. see *houses* and *architecture*

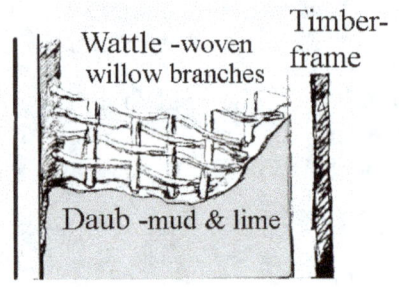

weddings   Marriage was hugely important to the nobility, and even more so to royalty. This had to do with carefully negotiated unification of estates and property for the nobility and unification of entire kingdoms for royalty. In no small way, it also had to do with whose son would be the next king. But for the common man without property, it was somewhat optional because weddings were often heavily taxed. From 1753 to 1827 all weddings had to be performed by the *Church of England*. Thereafter, what Americans would call a civil wedding could be done in the local registrar's office. Most of England's wedding ceremonies and traditions are faithfully copied in America with the exception of the multi-layer wedding cake. England's wedding cakes are fruitcake while Yanks go with white or sponge cake. This is one of the rare areas where the Yanks are more faithful to the medieval tradition of serving wheaten cakes at wedding feasts. Such cakes were made with white flour rather than other less expensive grains. see *marriage, women,* and *bhans*

weekend   -a comparatively modern notion, at least for working people. For the *middle class* and nobility, the week was *six Saturdays and a Sunday.* Working professionals enjoyed something like a weekend after 1870 when economic conditions lead at least some of them to have a place in the city usually for Dad, and another one in the country where he kept his wife and kids. This involved commuting and to make the trip worthwhile, they simply had themselves an entire weekend. The working class, on the other hand, had only a single home close to their jobs and had to soldier on until Sunday. Even then, they were not supposed to have any fun. see *Saturday*

webster   -a female weaver. In fact, jobs ending in *.ster* indicate a woman practitioner. Consider names like *Brewster* and *Dempster,* or for that matter, *spinster* who was a female spinner of thread.

Welsh rarebit / rabbit   A gourmet version of cheese on toast. The name is something of an English joke, coined in the 18th century when many Welsh were so poor they could not even afford a cheap meat like rabbit.

Given that it's often made with cheese, toast, and beer. The English beers are not to be trifled with, so rarebit could be a substantial meal with or without the rabbit.

West End   -the largest central business district in all of the UK and the most expensive. It might be thought of as England's Midtown Manhattan. As far back as Roman times, it was a wealthy neighborhood and remains so to this day. (Back in Medieval days, it was up-wind from the smokey smelly London proper.)

Abby

Westminster   The English get as lot of mileage out of the word "Westminster" and it gets confusing. There is the City of Westminster, as well as Westminster Abby, Westminster Cathedral, and Westminster Palace.

Westminster Abby   -a very old (1080) church west of The City that has long been <u>the</u> church for royal weddings, coronations, and burials etc. While it's a huge grand building, it's not a cathedral because it has no bishop, only a poor abbot, but it did have a bishop for about 15 years in the middle of the 1500's. Now it actually has neither an abbot nor a bishop, so it is technically a "Royal Peculiarity."

Westminster Cathedral   -a Catholic cathedral and home of the Catholic Archbishop of Westminster. By the standards of other big churches in England and Europe, the Cathedral is a baby, its construction began only in 1884. What is more, its architecture is Byzantine with domes and mosaics rather than the usual Gothic with pointed windows, stained glass windows, and all. In 1977 Queen Elizabeth came to a flower show at the cathedral. This was the first time since the Restoration that a reigning monarch had officially set foot in a Catholic Church.

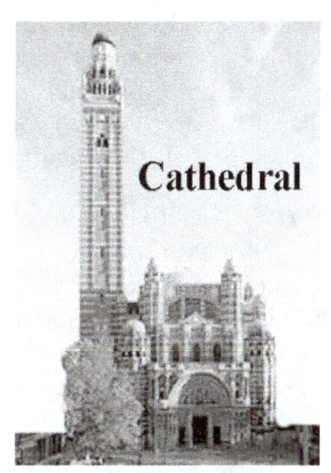
Cathedral

Westminster, City of   Technically, Westminster and London are two separate and equal cities, Westminster being the center of royalty and was therefore content with assorted palacIt didn;t grow. es that were converted to government offices after the middle of the 1800's. On the other hand, London grew commercially and geographically. Westminster has maintained its independence with its own government and traditions.

Westminster Palace / Palace of Westminster   -a Gothic Revival palace in London and the home of both Houses of ***Parliament***. It was started in 1016, burnt down in 1512 and again in 1834. From 1332 onward, some form of Parliament has gathered there. It is also the location of ***Big Ben.***

wheelwrights   -made wheels after the blacksmith made the iron rim, but also repaired wheels. This was necessary more often back in the day than fixing flat tires is now.

Whigs   -a political party popular between the 1680's and the 1850's. They were originally constitutional monarchists–as apposed to an absolute monarchy–and therefore concerned with aristocratic families and Protestantism. By the 19th century they supported the Parliament over the king, free trade, tolerance of Catholics, women's suffrage, and the abolition of slavery. They were comparatively progressive by the standards of the time. They would in fact morph into the Liberal party by 1870. After that, they would variously merge and split with the aristocratic Conservatives, and Unions. It's very confusing to Americans. see ***political parties***
      As far as word-origins goes, the word *whig* has two possibilities. First, it is old-fashion slang for moving forward in a slow steady pace like that of walking horse, and the *Whigs* were in favor of reform and change, but presumably done gradually. Or the word could be a shortened insult from the word *wiggamore* (also having to do with draft horses) and refers to a bunch of Scottish Presbyterians who did a clownish job of opposing ***Charles I***, They came to be called w*higs* which meant something like country bumpkins.

whist   -a predecessor of the card game bridge. It was played in the 1700 & 1800's with some passion in the military and by the leisure class. Like bridge, it is played by two teams, with the goal of taking trumps, but without bidding. No talking; in fact *whist* is slang for hush. The scoring is, however, so complicated that it prompted Edmund Hoyle to write a book on the subject and this gives us the expression ***according to Hoyle***.

white tie   -more formal even than mere *black tie*. White tie involved tails, stiff shirt and boiled collar. *Black tie* means dinner jacket and cummerbund.

Whitehall   -England's Washington DC. It's a road in London running from ***Trafalgar Square*** to ***Chelsea,*** and considered the center of Her Majesty's Government as the street is lined with government departments, ministries, and memorials. It might be thought of as a like like America's Pennsylvania Ave., but with a lot more history.
      As far back as the Middle Ages, it was more or less a suburb to the city of

London which was around the bend of the River Themes to the north. Buildings—halls—were build with a locally available light colored stone -hence Whitehall. By 1650 it had the largest collection of non-religious buildings. At this time, it would be a little misleading to call them 'government buildings' in the sense Americans might think of them, but by 1800 at the very latest, Whitehall WAS England's seat of government. Today you will find 10 Downing St. (England's Whitehouse), the Cabinet Office, the Foreign and Commonwealth Office, the Ministry of Defense, the Treasury, the Department of Health, the Department of Work and Pensions and more, as well as more than a few monuments.

wigs -the silly things worn by **barristers.** Everyone who was anyone back in the 17th century wore wigs as a fashion statement. Judges and Barristers (the English lawyers who appear in court) still wear wigs and robes because it lends solemnity to the proceedings, disguises an impoverished poorly dressed advocate so as not to influence jurors, and further disguises the various players so criminals would have a harder time finding them and taking revenge.

wilderness, in the -of politicians, it is the time spent out of office.

William the Conqueror William the Bastard was born in France in 1028, but after the Norman Conquest in 1066 he was promoted to William the Conqueror, at least in England. First he had to fight to keep control of Normandy on the continent after his father died, and then he fought equally hard to keep things under control in England.

William was forced to build castles all over England to stay in control. England's feudal government–and by now, the conquered government–was arguably more sophisticated than the government back home in Normandy at the time, and therefore a greater threat, so William replaced all the Anglo Saxon aristocracy with more tractable Norman families. The knights employed by these rich Norman families would later evolve into the backbone of the English Feudal system.

Castles and warfare being expensive -then as now- so William had to sort out whom he could tax and how much he could tax them. To this end, be sent assessors out to assemble what would come to be called the **Doomsday Book** because there was no appeal to its records and reckoning. The Saxon rich-guys (we can call them the 'nobility' but 'thugs' might be more accurate) were the big losers when William took over. For the little guy, slavery went away. It was replaced with serfdom, which was only marginally better, but it was progress.

Wimbledon -a wealthy town on the south-east edge of London there they have been playing tennis since at least 1877 when they did their first championship.

Winchester -the capital of Saxon England before the Franks came along. Its cathedral is one of the oldest and largest in England, and was the center of education until Cambridge opened for business. In literature, Winchester is the center of the Arthurian Legends like Camelot and all, and in the 1800's, it was the source of various educated and enlightened characters like Sherlock Holmes. Perhaps the best book set in Winchester is Ken Follett's <u>Pillars of the Earth</u> which traces history from 1123 to 1174 with a good deal of accuracy and a great deal of vivid storytelling.

Winchester Cathedral -a huge ***Church of England*** cathedral about 70 miles southeast of London. It was begun in 1079 and various sorts of construction has continued more or less ever since.

Windsor Castle

-one of six ***royal residences***. William the Conqueror first built a fortress a little ways west of London during the 1200's. It actually served a military function; it withstood a siege or two back then and more recently, it sheltered the royal family during the German bombing. It has three

concentric walls with actual crenelations (note the fiddly bits on the roof in the picture) and had a ***mote and bailey***. The showy *palace* part of the castle was started by Henry II and has been added to, plumbed, wired, remodeled and just generally improved regularly ever since. Today it is the Queen's favorite weekend home; but she usually spends weekdays in London. see ***castle***, ***royal residences***, and ***architecture***.

Windsor, House of -the last and current family of the monarchy. It had been the House of Saxe-Coburg & Gotha until about half way thru the First World War when German things were not popular. It started in 1901 with Edward VII followed by George V, then Edward VIII who hung it up to marry an American divorcee, then another George -this one the 6th, and finally the current Queen Elizabeth.

Wolsey, Thomas (1473 – 1530) The Archbishop of Canterbury was a hugely powerful politician and friend of ***Henry VIII***. He was sometimes referred to as 'alter rex,' or the *other king*, at least until he failed to get the Pope in Rome to let Henry set aside ***Catherine of Aragon*** and marry ***Anne Boleyn***. He fell out of favor and in 1529 went home to York to tend to ecclesiastical matters he had been neglecting while in London. The next year he was summoned back to London to face charges of treason, and in all likelihood, be beheaded, but he died along the way.

women in England   American women and
English women were much the same, at least for as long
as there have been American women. It is therefore
reasonable to speak to the subject of women in England
before the English (and the other Europeans) came to
America and in due course, fetched along European
women to become colonists. After 1776 or so, they
become *American* women.

　　For the reader, a brief study of the history of
women and their place in society might as well begin with the Roman
occupation up until 410 or so. The Celts, whom the Romans overran, left no
written records, so discussing the role of women during the Roman
Occupation, reading about the intrigues by the wives of various Roman
Emperors, senators, and generals might be useful at least for the rich people;
for the common man, particularly in Britannia, not so much.

　　When the Roman left, the Angels, Saxons and Jutes came. Consider
Anglo-Saxon women. Think of then as great tall blonds as tough as their
husbands. They had it better in many ways than the women who came later.
An Anglo Saxon woman could own land in her own name. (This right would
be denied *modern* English women until 1882 with passage of the Married
Woman's Property Act.) Make no mistake, Anglo-Saxon women ran the
household and raised children but men cooked or at least roasted game and
they evidently ate a lot of game being as they were more inclined to hunting
than farming, The proper role of a wife and hostess in those days was to
make and serve mead. Even before they were married, the man had to give a
gift to her father as opposed to later dowries when dad had to give the
potential husband some value to get him to take her off Dad's hands. Divorce
was even a possibility among the Anglo Saxons.

　　Marriage may or may not have been for love, but it was at least a matter
of individual choice with one exception. An Anglo-Saxon *peace-weaver* was
a woman who was married off to the son or brother of the next king down the
road to keep the peace between the two tribes. Per one contemporary
chronicler, "It is believed that, through birth, a woman wove peace by mixing
her blood with the blood of another tribe." While this is an admirable end, it
also hints at future dynastic marriages arranged to gain or maintain political
power. It is also the beginning of two ways of doing things—one way for the
rich and another for the poor.

　　With the Norman invasion, William the Conqueror took property from
the Anglo Saxon rich-guys and gave it to Norman rich-guys. The good news
was that slavery was much reduced under Norman law, not eliminated, but
reduced, and the Catholic Church was becoming a bigger and bigger thing.
This last would come to be a mixed blessing. As for women, they didn't have
it quite as good as their Anglo-Saxon ancestors. For starters, they couldn't
own property unless they were widows. Their children technically and
legally belonged to their husbands. They couldn't marry without their
parents consent, nor own a business without various guild and church
permissions. They could not inherit from their parents if there was a

surviving brother. They couldn't divorce, but in fairness, nor could men. This is about time we begin to see 'damsels' showing up in literature, but damsels –in distress or otherwise– were rich men's wives and daughters. Otherwise, life was "nasty, brutish, and short[2]." The common man -or women- didn't see much change with the arrival and subsequent exit of the Normans.

We might call this period the Anglo-Norman period to sound all academic, or just call it the *medieval* or even the *dark ages*. The time from the Norman Conquest in 1066, until the Protestant Reformation in 1517, is a big chunk of history with lots of war and world exploration and having a Renaissance, but a conveniently homogeneous period for women. It is necessary first to slice and dice the domestic history into smaller chunks. First and most obvious division is between men & women, then the aristocracy & commoners, and finally, between city and countryside. It turns out that this last one is by no means trivial. It must be stressed that the few records that survive on these matters concern the rich towns-people to a far greater degree than poor country folk.

Let's deal with rich town women first because they are easy. Their job was to bear male heirs and that's about all. They didn't even have to bother with raising them. There were wet-nurses, governesses (for girls), or boarding schools (for boys but a bit later in the chronology) to deal with these bothersome details. The only bad news was they often had to marry the fat ugly old guys whom their fathers picked out for them, and had to do so at appallingly young ages;14 and 15 years of age was about average.[3] Much literature about women in this era shows them with nothing much else to do but relentlessly scheme to get someone off the throne and their son onto the throne or otherwise in power. This was accomplished by hook or by crook, by assignation, seduction, betrayal, murder (often with poison) and all manner of nefarious deeds that make for great stories. This brings us back to Roman women, but the Roman intrigues are pretty well nailed down in history. It is not clear that the medieval women were quite so handy with intrigue, murder, and such, but even so, such plots show up in a lot of Shakespeare's work.

In one real-life example, Elizabeth Countess of Shrewsbury (1518 - 1608) married three times explicitly to consolidate her holdings. She buried three husbands and fought with two of the surviving families over inheritance. She finally married her fourth husband only after negotiating for one of her daughters to marry one of his sons, as well as one of her sons to marry one of his daughters. (Today's much divorced and blended family is simple by comparison.) Perhaps some of these women deserve just a little sympathy given the rules they had to follow particularly when viewed by the

---

2. The political philosopher Thomas Hobbes wrote this to describe things back in 1651 during and about the English civil war. It has, however, often been used to describe the dark ages. The quote runs... 'continual fear, danger of violent death; and the life of man, solitary, nasty, brutish, and short."

3. There are records of marriage for girls as young as twelve. In one case, they 'were seen abed' together, as was tradition after the wedding feast, but no one expected them to do the deed till they were at least little older.

modern liberal reader.

Among the ordinary folk, things were quite a little different. Everyone worked. Often from the age of eight or nine. Eleven and twelve year-olds were considered adults. BUT, and this is surprising, the average age for marriage among the common folk was twenty five and this is among people who were apt to be dead at forty. Women were paid less, and getting paid at all was likely only to happen during harvest season. A day spent reaping would pay a man eight pence, but a woman would earn only five.

Aside from farm work, the guilds controlled who did what we might think of as skilled middle-class work and women who did such work, did so only under the supervision of their husbands. There are rare court records of cases wherein the husband died and his wife was accepted into the guild and was able to continue doing the work, but the fact that these records are from court proceedings suggests that it only happened as a consequence of what probably was a pretty contentious litigation. What we would think of factory work would come along much later and manufacturing of the day was done in the home or in a workshop in the back yard.

The picture of Sleeping Beauty pricking her finger while spinning wool is accurate. Women were active in the fabric industry, but only under their husband's supervision and she wasn't paid.[4] The *Grimm's Fairy Tale*[5] Rumplestiltskin is perhaps more revealing. The heroin didn't know how to spin straw into gold for the king, but Rumplestiltskin–a man–did and saved her if only to blackmail her later.

Much is made of the fact that women had no role in politics or society at large, but nor did men. The medieval household was a considerably larger more complicated thing than the 20th century family with its 2.3 children. If it was a freeman guild-member's home it was also a factory with servants, apprentices, workers, and step children.[6] (It's harder to draw comparisons between the village guild household and the farm because farms were usually large and owned and managed by rich people but the farm had many workers and the manor house had many servants as well.) So a woman who played a large role in the household, arguably played a larger role in medieval life as a whole; far more than did the aristocratic wife and mother.

Here are some revealing statistics from the period and once again, it must be stressed that they are sketchy given the level of literacy and record keeping of the day. In 1520 only 25% of men (and probably their wives, but these numbers are even harder to pin down) were wage laborers, and 75%

4. Lace-making was an important exception. This was ever a woman's specialty from 1600 to about 1750. It is interesting to note that the average age for these comparatively well paid independent contractors was older than among women in general.

5. The Grimm brothers were German and published Grimm's Fairy Tales in 1812 -considerably later than the period in question, but the analogy is apt.

6. Given the mortality rates –particularly in childbirth– remarriage with step-children was far more common then than today, at least until the high rate of modern divorce and blended families is considered. As anecdotal illustration, consider all the evil step-mothers and step-fathers that figure in fairy tales -*Cinderella* and her evil stepmother being but one.

were employers, guilds-men, or otherwise self-employed. By 1650, money was necessary even in the most self-supporting farm; even more so in the village among the guild shops making things. This is to say that serfs were increasingly paid in money rather than turnips. By 1850, the ratio of self-employed to employees had been more than reversed and nearly everyone received a monetary wage. This was chiefly because of the industrial revolution and the factory. But we are ahead of ourselves.

In the early middle ages, a woman's' status was almost entirely a function of her husband. At the top were wives and daughters of the nobility like dukes and earls and such. A bit lower were *gentle-women*, who were the wives of non-hereditary aristocrats like knights. Some small number of women held these titles independent of husbands and there was a degree of blurring between a noblewoman and a gentlewoman.

A *lady* was a married woman who was the head of a large household that had servants. She was probably the wife of a successful merchant or master guilds-man. A bit lower were *citizen's wives* whose husband was a freeman or master of his craft and who had some standing in the community, but without apprentices, employees, or servants. There seems to be more opportunity to improve one's status in society than there would be later, but for women, it was done by either advancing her husbands status, or becoming the mistress of a rich nobleman.

At the bottom were women who were widowed or had been abandoned, spinsters, and aged women. Atypically good records from 1570 in Norwich indicate that 62% of the citizens over 16 were women, and 68% of those on parish poor relief were women over 60 years of age. These numbers are probably low because women were less likely to attract the attention of courts in one way or another.

Women have always lived longer than men, but less than might be expected if warfare and violent death is factored in -or *out* as the case may be. This came down to childbirth. Between the age of 25 (marriage age for common folk) and 35, a woman was four times more likely to die than a man of the same age. She was twice as likely between age 35 and 45. To put it differently, if she survived the birth of her first child and subsequent childbirths up thru the age of 45, she was likely to live to 60 or more. Mortality apparently rose and fell equally for men and women with all the usual causes like famine, disease, and so forth. Turning one again to the good Norwich records of 1570, there were two men and five women aged between 95 and 100 in a community of 1,400, and about 15% of the poor were over 60. In general, mortality among both sexes, for all ages, and between the classes would not surprise the modern reader. Fewer car wrecks obviously, but more boys doing dumb things and getting killed. High infant mortality, horrible medical practices, and epidemic diseases killed people across the board. Diseases resulting from poor nutrition etc. killed more poor people. War killed more men. What's interesting during the middle ages is that excluding famine and war, wealth or poverty didn't have much of an effect on mortality. This was because medical treatments of the day were often worse than no treatment at all. Drowning was a popular way to die among women who fetched water from open wells and rocky creeks. Fire in wooden houses with fireplaces killed both sexes about equally. And so it went.

Marriage among the common folk is another area that might not hold many surprises for the modern reader -other than perhaps the fact that people worked and saved up in order to set up housekeeping till their mid-twenties. Economics explains much of the delay both because of the need to save up for a house and household as well as a marriage tax. Marriage among regular people was usually 'affective rather than dynastic' which is to say out of affection rather than to preserve or grow political or economic power. Husbands and wives were about the same age -usually no more than a few years apart. When there was a large difference, it was usually a (rich) old widower marrying a younger woman, or occasionally a rich widow marrying a younger man. A large portion of the population never married. One inclusive study of demographics finds that only 33% of the whole population was married,[7] about 6% widowed, and whopping 61% single. Very few women over 40 lived independently, most unmarried women of this age lived with her parents. Those women who did have their own household were almost always widows.

A medieval woman might expect six or more live births in her lifetime but it was not uncommon for only two to make it to adulthood. Nor was it uncommon for the first child to be born less than nine months after the marriage, but teenage pregnancy and illegitimate births were very rare. This is perhaps misleading because illegitimate babies were not baptized and therefore did not make it into the record books. On the other hand, there were–at various times and in various places–taxes on marriage, so these babies might have been born to a committed loving couple that simply hadn't gotten around to the paperwork, tax payment, and the church ceremony.

Given late marriages and life expectancy, it was unusual for more than two generation to live in a given household. Four or five was the usual size of a family (mom, dad, and the kids -not counting servants and apprentices) but because it was at twelve years of age when kids went out on their own, the youngest child might have many older brothers and sisters who he or she only saw on feast days–if at all. Add to this migration and from the 16th century onward and it is easy to see how an otherwise large blended family might only have two kids at home. Do not think of these people as cold hearted toward their children. While they sent their own kids off to learn a craft, they often took in other children as orphans (for which the parish paid them) or took in apprentices to the household craft.

Migration within England during the late Medieval was mostly about leaving the farm and coming to the city. London, for example was as much as 70% immigrants. Men tended to migrate in their teens, and women do so in their twenties. More domestic servants (women) migrated than farm

7. Except the Irish. They got married more often and at younger ages than the English, even the English Catholics.

workers (men) and so in a middling large market town the ratio of unmarried women to unmarried men might be as high as ten women to seven men.

In general, a thoughtful reading about life for the common woman would not surprise the modern reader. Less divorce, less opportunity, and earlier death not-with standing, women–then as now–act in their own best interest but with what must be called Christian Charity. They loved their children, and often even their husbands. Even then it was recognized that a woman's work was never done. A book of advice to women in 1580 said, "Some respite to husbands the weather sends, but housewives affairs have never an end." But it is also clear that they had time for gossip, shopping, and a little recreation & travel.

Before we finish up with the middle ages and bump along to the Protestant Reformation, we need to stir the Catholic Church into the mix. There were various religious communities for women. Hamlet's advice to Ophelia to 'get thee to a nunnery' was all well and good, but usually only useful to rich families who needed to store an inconvenient daughter or spinster aunt. They were refuges from the world as well as being centers for learning, one of the few places where women actually could learn something besides a craft, but the number of nuns and almost-nuns had been dropping from about 1500 onward.

So how did things shake out for women with the Protestant Revolution? Hard to say one way or the other. On one hand, people got to worship the way the wanted to, and some of these people were women. On the other hand, the flavor of Protestantism called Puritanism was virulently repressive and intolerant of sin of all sorts, particularly carnal sin. Oddly enough, women were seen as temptresses more than the victims, at least in the eyes of the old, the self-appointed, and the self-righteous. One of the things that the Pilgrims felt was contrary to their religion were new rules that forbade them to exact corporeal punishment on people the felt needed a little whipping or a good long spell in the *stocks*. This increasingly fell to the crown–or local secular authorities–so the Pilgrims set off to the colonies where they could torture people as they saw fit. (About forty years after they got there, the Puritans hanged fourteen women and six men between 1692 & 1693 in Salem Massachusetts.) On the other hand, this was a drop in the bucket compared to what the Catholic Church and assorted Inquisitions had done somewhat earlier all up and down Europe.

In general terms, Protestantism reduced the possible roles of women in church activities. A Catholic wife could go out and about, do things for the church, celebrate various Saint's Days, or even enter the convent if she were that devout. A good Protestant wife on the other hand, was expected to stay home, educate the children in religious matters, defer to her husband, and read her prayer-book.

From the Reformation forward, it's all about economics. The industrial revolution was still a little ways off, but as food became more plentiful, England turned to manufacturing. To say the same thing backwards, as England got better making things, they could afford to import more food that someone else grew somewhere else. This manufacturing was different from that done in the earlier times of the craftsmen and his workers and apprentices working in his home-shop producing finished products or local consumption. These products would also be sold by the craftsman, or his wife if he were busy out in the shop. As things got more industrialized the ***putting-out***[8.] system came along. It would be used for many forms of making, but fabric will serve as an example. Someone–typically a ***merchant*** of some sort–would bring a pile of wool to the home shop to be cleaned and come by later to pick it up and drop off another batch. At this time he would do some quality control and pay for the work done. He would then take the clean wool to another shop to be carded, and yet another shop to be spun, and on thru the other necessary specialized processes to achieve what ever end-product was sought. Specialization is more efficient, but it also reduces the need for craftsmanship and thereby reduced wages. What is more, this sort of arrangement required something approaching our modern notions of formal agreements and contracts. Such things were thought to be outside of the proper place for women. So the trend for women as the putting-out system grew was lower wages and they were removed further from participation in the economy. This also meant fewer employers and more employees.

There was some small good news for women about then. The tiny germ of the idea that maybe women had rights equal to those of men just barely begin appear. This idea would grow as the industrial revolution hit its stride toward the beginnings of the 1800's. Now at last, women were coming to have plenty of work opportunities outside the home. This work was in huge factories. The problem was that this work was done under pretty deplorable conditions, and some of the worst jobs–those needing the least skill and that paid the least–were being done by children.

It was these factories that WERE the industrial revolution. Both cause and effect attains. Factories had to be big because they were full of expensive machines. Expensive machines had to be run day and night if they were to be profitable, therefore people had to work around the clock. (Except Sunday. England was still a Christian nation.) If people did shift work, they had to live nearby. The machines first ran on running water, and water runs only where there are hills and hills are not good for farming nor for cities. It was easier to get workers to come to factories near hillsides that it was to move hills to cities, so they had to build better roads and railroads to get food to the workers and get the finished product to big city markets. Beyond water power, even bigger machines ran on steam which came from burning coal. Air-quality? Forget it. Various lung diseases were responsible for one quarter of all deaths in industrialized England during all of Queen Victoria's reign. These big expensive machines also needed to be paid for

8. The putting-out system continued to work in the manufacturing of small arms for the English military thru the 19th century. In fact, a modern form of the system was quickly set up to provided England with the bits and pieces to be assembled into fighter planes during the ***Battle of Britain*** during WWII.

and England's financial markets came to be the biggest most important in the world. (This might be a good thing or a bad thing depending on your views of capitalism.)

We have wondered a bit far afield from our topic of women. During the 1700's, a woman's choices came down to coming from a very rich family, marrying a moderately rich professional man, being a wage earner on the farm or in the factory, or going into domestic service. (Domestic *servants* are a hugely important issue in understanding the role of women -and men- during the 19th century.) In the later case, a woman had to hope to meet a husband by the time spinsterhood descended on her -about age 25 to 30. Not all of them succeeded.

Much beyond the Victorian era (Queen Victoria died in 1901) the differences between American women and English women is of trivial importance. They are pretty much the same in terms of all the things people with fancy degrees study, measure, and natter on about. But there were a couple of World Wars that changed the Brits far more than the Yanks. America arguably gave women more political power sooner than did the Brits. Wyoming, being a wild and woolly wilderness, gave women the vote in 1869 just to attract more of them. The rest of America got around to this only in 1920, but the Brits dawdled around till 1928 before they gave women full suffrage.

Worcester / Worcestershire   Worcester is the town in Worcestershire County. *Worcestershire / Worcester Sauce* was invented in the town of Worcester despite its spelling, but it is pronounced *woster sauce, Woster* being the shortened slang for Worcester. No one is entirely sure why this is so, but it may have had to do with 19th century trademark law.

What is rather better known is that a couple of chemists, John Lea and Bill Perrins were trying to come up with a curry sauce. One batch was a failure so they set a barrel of it aside, but happened to taste it again about a year and a half later. Lea and Perrins was born in 1830. The Japanese of all people have began to substitute Worcester Sauce for soy sauce on some foods.

work   In your reading, you will come across job titles, most of which are obvious to the American reader -farmer and teacher, for example, but some will be confusing or utterly impenetrable -consider *loriner* (made bridles and saddles for horses) or *costermonger* (sold fruit and vegetables from a handcar). Furthermore, some of these occupations will sound like common last names: Fletcher, Sawyer, Cartwright, etc. but were in fact occupations, occupations that no longer exist, but the surnames live on. From the middle ages, people had the first names their parents gave them, and the family name which was often the family's occupation. Some occupation names sound familiar, but describe jobs that have changed considerably over the years; *engineers, milliners* and *mechanics* for example do not mean now what they meant back in the day.

Up until the repeal of the *Articles of Artificers* in 1653, the *guild* and *apprentice* systems very strictly prescribed who could do what, a little like labor unions times ten. In the bustling economies of the 16th and 17th century London for example, shoe makers, bootmakers, and clog makers were permitted to make only shoes, boots, or clogs, and even clogs had both the guy who made the wooden sole -the *clogger*, and the *clogmaker* who made the upper leather part. This explains all the X-makers, Y-makers, and Z-workers that would all seem to be doing much the same thing in literature.

Occupations that are still last names today include Archer, Barber, Bowman, Brewer, Butler, Carpenter, Carver, Cook, Draper, Farmer, Fisher, Forester, Fowler, Gardener, Hunter, Mason, Miller, Piper, Potter, Sadler, Sheppard, Shoemaker, Skinner, Tanner, Taylor, Weaver and Wheeler.

England was not unique in this. For example, a German baker's last name would be *Becker* and the same guy in France would be *Boulanger*

working class   When the peasantry left the farm for the factory as the industrial revolution unfolded, they became the working class, but the term is from rather later in the game, actually, the late 1800's.

For the reader to understand what an English writer means when he used the term, he must remember two things: first, the **middle class** was very rich, but they were just not nobility, and the working class had the very un-American view that being in the working class was just fine thank you. There was no burning desire to work one's way up. In general terms, the working-class had their own religion -Methodist, entertainment -music halls, social places -pubs, and eventually, even their own **political party -Labor**.

Towards the end of the 20th century the term became synonymous with unemployment, but only because manufacturing jobs were becoming increasingly scarce.

Not much to be said about **X**. It's Greek in origin and pronounced in various ways. The Yanks and the Brits use **X** pretty much the same way. There are some minor fussy spelling differences though: the Brits favor ending certain words *-xion* and the Yanks use *-ction*.

X-factor   -a union contract stipulation regarding special circumstances and usually extra pay. Also a contemporary reality TV show involving singing.

Y goes back to the Semitic, but the Romans only used it for foreign words. The English Great Vowel Shift made it a vowel. Sometimes. It's also part of the whole **U, V, W** controversy. When printing first came to England, there was no way to do a **Þ** (called a thorn and meant *th)* so they used a **Y** to get to *ye* in place of *the*. This gives us silly things like *Ye Olde Shoppe* trying to be clever and archaic.

yellow lines   Yellow lines are painted on the side of the road to indicate parking restrictions.

Yeoman / Yeomanry   Originally the word meant small land-owning farmers. During the French Revolution and later Napoleonic Wars, there was fear England would be invaded. Yeoman officers were recruited from the nobility and they in turn recruited soldiers from among their tenants and other locals. These soldiers could not be sent offshore to fight; they were strictly for home defense.

Yoeman of the Guard   The bodyguard of the monarch and the oldest military corps in continuous existence in the realm. They were created by Henry Seven way back in 1485. They still dress that way, all red and gold, and carry a *partizan** which was a long ornamental

spear. They are nicknamed the *Beefeaters* and are not to be confused with
the **Queen's Guard** .

* The word *partizan* in this case refers to the spear from the Old French
pertuiser "make full of holes"!?!!. Partizan in the political sense comes from
Italian *partigiano*, which means "defender of a party".

York   Founded by the Romans at the confluence of the Rivers Ouse
and Foss. It is in the far north east of England with a population of a little
over 200,000. In the Middle ages, it was the wool trading center and capitol
of the Church of England. In the 19th century it was a railroad hub and
manufacturing center.

Yorkshire   The largest county in England -so large that it has been
subdivided into confusing boroughs, districts, regions, and authorities. It is
to the northeast corner of the country and is flat, green, and has lots of sheep.
It was about as far north as the Romans got. It's also where the Romans first
brought Christianity to England. The Celts re-emerged when the Romans
left, and while they weren't exactly Christian, nor were they entirely opposed
to Christianity. Then an early Viking, Eric the Bloodaxe showed up and
things went downhill fast. They didn't get much better when the Normans
came, followed by the Black Death, followed by the War of the Roses
-between the House of York and the House of Lancaster, followed by the
English Civil War. The 19th century was fairly calm and Yorkshire went
about mining coal, making steel, and weaving wool. Today the heavy dirty
industries have gone down and service & tourism have taken their places.

Your Grace   -proper form of address for a duke, duchess, or
archbishop.

Your Ladyship   -considerably more complicated than *Your Grace*.
Before the early 1700's, Your Ladyship was for wives of mere barons and
bishops and *My Lady was* for wives of **vicounts, earls, marques,** and **dukes**.
After that, *My Lady* became more common, and by the 20th century it didn't
make much difference one way or the other.

Your Lordship   -proper address for a lord (a barron), judge, or woman
sheriff, but like *Your Ladyship / My Lady*, the distinction between *My Lord*
and *Your Lordship* blurred after about 1750.

Your Worship   -a magistrate or mayor. It's a little like *Your Honor* in
America.

Z's history is pretty normal among the letters. First it was the Semitic letter-picture for sword or weapon, then Phoenician, and then Greek, but Z is unique in that it came from Etruscan before it got to Latin. It has been a part of the European alphabets for a comparatively long time. Except in England. They used *G* or *J* until the French came along. *Jealous* and *zealous* actually used to be the same word. The letter is the least used on both sides of the Atlantic, but more used in America with words like *extemporize and eulogize* that end in *ize*. In England, the same words end in *ise*. Finally, it's called *zed* in England. BTW *Z* has not always been the last letter in the alphabet; up until the 19th century, English school children finished the alphabet …*x y z &*.

zebra crossing   -crosswalk

zero-longitude   The English were the first to develop a clock accurate enough for navigation, so they took it upon themselves to nail down the prime meridian in London's back yard at the Greenwich Observatory. As the location of this imaginary line, they also got to claim that this is where today becomes tomorrow for the very first time for the whole world. see *CANOE*, **Greenwich,** and the ***Royal Navy.***

Z-car / Zulu car   -police car from the radio call sign for Z -*Zulu*

zimmer   -a walker

zip   -a zipper for clothing

www.ingramcontent.com/pod-product-compliance
Lightning Source LLC
Chambersburg PA
CBHW060913120626
46553CB00001B/310